Faction detected by the evidence of facts : containing an impartial view of parties at home, and affairs abroad.

Egmont, John Perceval, Earl of

Faction Detected,

BY THE

EVIDENCE

OF

FACTS.

CONTAINING

An Impartial View of PARTIES at Home,
and AFFAIRS Abroad.

Quo quò scelesti ruitis? Aut cur dexteris
   Aptantur enses conditi?
Non ut super hos meæ dæ Carthaginis
   Romanus arces ureret
Sed ut, secundum vota Parthorum, sua
   Urbs hæc periret dexterâ.
Neque hic lupis mos, nec fuit leonibus
   Unquam nisi in dispar feris.
Furorne cæcus, an rapit vis acrior
   An culpa? Responsum date.
Tacent, & ora pallor albus inficit,
   Mentesque percussæ stupent.

Hor. Epod. Od. VII.

The SECOND EDITION.

LONDON:

Printed for J. ROBERTS, in *Warwick-Lane*. M.DCC.XLIII.

E R R A T A.

PAge 147. line 35. inftead of *Influence upon the Legiflature* read *Influence upon the other Members of the Legiflature* ; p. 171. l. 42. inftead of *by* read *thro'* ; p. 173. l. 6. dele *late* ; p. 174. l. 43. inftead of *fomented* read *inflamed.*

LONDON.

To the E. of B——,

Occasion'd by a late Pamphlet, entitled, Faction detected.

YOUR Sheets I've perus'd,
    Where the Whigs you've abus'd,
And on Tories have falsely reflected;
    But, my Lord, I'm afraid,
    From all that's there said,
'Tis you, and not they, that's detected.

    Both Parties, I hear,
    Most freely declare,
That 'tis not approv'd of by either:
    If it's damn'd then by both,
    It must be the Growth
Of *somebody* who is of neither.

    'Tis easy to name
    From what Quarter it came,
And the Thing of itself stands confess'd;
    'Tis that pitiful Crew,
    Of your Creatures and you,
That both Parties scorn and detest.

    But stay——let me see——
    Which Tool could it be
That such a huge Book cou'd indite?
    For of all those you made,
    If there's one that can read,
I'm sure there's not one that can write.

    'Tis above poor Sir *John*,
    Nor by S——s could be done,
And B——e's too stupid and dark;
    O——d hardly reads well,
    Jeff. never cou'd spell,
And you know H—— V——e sets his Mark.

    Then since all your Tools
    Are such ignorant F—ls,
It must be your L——p's own doing:
    You have taken your *Plte*,
    But you'll soon own with me,
That you've settl'd yourself in your Ruin.

    As diff'rent Winds blew,
    Like the Weather-Cock you,
Long waver'd both Parties betwixt;
    But did not you know,
    That Weather-Cocks grow
Quite useless the Moment they're

sign'd for the Garrisons on the Coast, consisting of twelve 36 Pounders, twelve of 24, and thirty-six of 12, with the Arms of England neatly engrav'd on them, were landed at the Tower from Woolwich their Carriages are already made, and in a few Day they will be sent to the Places where they are mol wanted.

The same Day the Commissioners of the Victual ling-Office contracted for 500 Oxen, for fresh Mea for the Ports of London and Chatham; at the fam Time they order'd a large Quantity of fresh and dr Provisions to be cask'd up and shipp'd with all Expe dition to Jamaica.

On Thursday Thomas Watson, Esq; Muster Master-General of the allied Forces in the Britis Pay, arriv'd in Town from the Army.

From Shrewsbury we hear, that at the Election for Mayor of that Corporation, Mr. Edward Elisha Son to Mr. Samuel Elisha, one of the Aldermen of that Town, was chosen.

Yesterday Mr. William Palmer, one of the At torneys in the Mayor's Court, was chosen Clerk the Ironmongers Company, in the room of M Samuel Morris, deceas'd.

The Lords of the Treasury have appointed M James Lownds Inspector of the Customs in the Po of Dover, in the room of Mitchel Jackson, Es deceas'd.

Last Thursday Mr. Whitebread, an eminent an wealthy Hardwareman in Cannon-Street, was ma ried, at St. Paul's, to Miss Hinde, Daughter of Pe Hinde, Esq; an eminent Brewer in Leather-Lane; young Lady of great Beauty and Merit, with a Fo tune of 15,000 l. The new married Couple imm diately set out for her Father's Seat at Cheshunt Hertfordshire, there to celebrate their Nuptials.

Thursday was married, at St. Mary Rotherhith James Wilson, Esq; a Gentleman of a large Estate that Neighbourhood, to Miss Amelia Gibson, of Borough of Southwark; a fine young Lady with Fortune of 10,000 l.

Last Sunday Mr. George Gord, a Farmer, at G stone in Surrey, aged 83, was married at the Chur there to Mrs. Susannah Waters, a Widow Gentle man of that Town, aged 95; several of their Gr Grandchildren attended at the Ceremony, the young of whom was 15 Years of Age.

We hear from Hanover, that the Beginning of t Month died there the Countess of Piginbourg, fo merly Governess to the Princesses Anne, Amel and Caroline, for several Years, at St. James's.

Faction Detected,

BY THE

EVIDENCE of FACTS.

OPPOSITION to the Meafures of Government, whether good or bad, is no new thing in this or any other Country, where the People have any Share in the Legiflature. For wherever that Circumftance is found, the Materials for the Advancement of private Views abundantly occur: And in proportion to the Importance of fuch a Country, Subjects ambitious of Preferment have more Incentives to urge them on to Purfuits of this Nature, more Inftruments to affift them in their Undertaking, and more Pretexts to delude and to impofe upon the Multitude. The Employments in fuch a Country muft of Neceffity be numerous and lucrative, the Engagements of the Publick frequent and expenfive, the Dangers from its Neighbours greater, their Jealoufy and Ill-will more to be apprehended, and confequently with more Privacy and Caution counteracted. This enables artful Men to raife Murmurs againft the moft neceffary Charges of the State, and to quarrel with the beft Means of Publick Security with a manifeft Advantage, becaufe it is eafy to difpute the Wifdom of Meafures, which can never be intirely difclofed, till they are fully executed; and the Poifon infufed into the People has performed its Operation before the Nature of the thing can poffibly admit a Detection of the Falfities and Mifreprefentations employed againft them; while the Publick, already prejudiced, never give themfelves the Trouble to examine what is paft; either taking more Delight in the Difcovery of Error, than in the Purfuit of Truth; or not having the Means furnifhed with equal Induftry, or being diverted by fome frefh Objection, ftarted to fome new Conduct.

In proportion to the Riches of any Country, Poverty becomes more preffing upon many by a natural Contraft. In all fuch Countries the Wretched are certainly more wretched than in others which flourifh lefs; becaufe the Neceffaries of Life are dear, and not to be had without that Induftry, which

Numbers

Numbers will be found to want, in all Places, however opportune the Means of Employment may be ; and Men of this kind may be induftrious in a Faction, which is carried on by Noife, Drunkennefs and Riot, when they can be fo in nothing elfe. In all trading Countries the Profpect of Gain allures many to adventurous Undertakings above their Abilities, by which fome muft be undone, and thefe never fail to attribute to Mifmanagements of Government, thofe Evils which arife from their own Sloth, Incapacity or Avarice.——Again, in fuch Countries, the Luxury of fome induces others to follow them in the fame Expence, to the Ruin of themfelves and of their Families, and the Generality of thefe unite in Views of a like Nature.——As in all populous Countries, from a Variety of Diftrefs, fuch Objects muft be very numerous ; fo from the very Numbers of a People alone, Faction always derives a great Advantage, fince from the Difference of Difpofitions, with which Men are born into the World, fome will infallibly arife from time to time, framed by Nature itfelf of a reftlefs and difcontented Temper, form'd, whether they have Caufe for it or not, to be as well a Torment to themfelves, as a Plague to the Society in which they live.——Nor can Oppofition, right or wrong, want even Property to gild it over and to grace it ; for Men arifing from the loweft Level of the People, and advancing into confiderable and eafy Fortunes, are by a natural Confequence, too often led to confpire againft that very Felicity, Peace, Quiet and Profperity, to which alone they have owed their Exiftence.——Arrogance and Pride, without a more than common Share of Underftanding, are the univerfal Product of all hafty Advancement. Thefe Men repine at what they never before had Leifure to confider ; that there is ftill a certain Difference between their Condition and that of another Rank, which they cannot remedy by all their Efforts to exceed them in Expence.——This fomething, which they find ftill wanting, fours them with their own State, and inclines them to fall in with any popular Difcontent, partly, to gratify their Vanity in infulting thofe above them ; and partly, to create a Chaos, out of which they hope to emerge upon a Level with thofe they envy.—From whence the Obfervation holds moft true, That all Nations, in proportion to their Increafe, grow turbulent and factious, and from this Quarter arife thofe levelling Schemes, in the Contention for which, fooner or later, Anarchy enfues ; and in procefs of time, the Lofs of that real Liberty, whofe facred Name is fo often fpecioufly prophaned by Malice and Ambition. Even Liberty itfelf, the more perfect it is, produces thefe Effects more ftrongly ;

for

for Wantonnefs and Licentioufnefs, which are its evil Genii, tempt all depraved Tempers to abufe it, and expofe many to the Lafh of the Laws, and to the juft Indignation of Power; which none, who feel, forgive, however they deferve it. At the fame time, the natural Tendancy in all Mankind to expect more Favour than they merit, provokes unjuft Refentments againft Government, and a certain Infirmity (of which we all in fome Degree partake) to be uneafy with what we have, and to endeavour after more, inclines Multitudes, either out of Views of private Benefit to themfelves, or general Views of Encreafe of Privilege to the Order in which they ftand, to follow any Set of Men, who take the Lead in Oppofition of any kind.——— All thefe move by a fecret Principle to that Quarter where it erects its Standard, be it juft or unjuft, be it to fave or to deftroy their Country.

It is obvious from hence, and it is a Truth that cannot be difputed, however it may affect the Credit of many pretended Patriots, that the *difcontented Party* of all Denominations confift *in general* of Men of no Principle, and of very unworthy Character. Its Root is always the fame;——but indeed its Effects are very different. It becomes in fome Conjunctures of very beneficial Confequence, when it is led by Men of honeft Views; and equally pernicious in others, when conducted by Men of a different Character.—In the firft Cafe, it is an *Oppofition*; in the fecond it is a *Faction*.

Faction is of two kinds in this Country.——*Oppofition led by Republicans*; and *Oppofition led by Jacobites*;——Of the two great Parties into which this Nation has been long divided--- the *Whigs* (though not *Republicans*) have formerly joined the firft——the *Tories* (though not *Jacobites*) do conftantly abet the laft.——They who know the Nature of this Country, who are acquainted with our Hiftory, need no Definition or Defcription of thefe two Parties, and all who are capable of Obfervation and Reflection can eafily trace the Reafons of their refpective Conduct. It is therefore fufficient for us in this Place, that this is a Fact, which cannot be denied; and without a zealous Attachment of one or other of thefe two Parties, Faction is incapable of doing much Prejudice to *Britain*.

A Faction of the former kind once deftroyed the Liberties and Conftitution of this Nation. It grew up unobferved with the great Improvement of its Commerce, and was nourifhed in the uncommon Meafure of Profperity, which arofe from a long Tranquillity, and a wonderful Encreafe of Wealth after the Difcovery of the *Weft-Indies*, which diffufed itfel through the *Commons*, and gave them Ability to contend with a *Prince*, who, ignorant of this new acquired Vigour of the People, and vainly fond of Power, provoked it by avowed Attempts to introduce an absolute Authority.

This Faction, by the Imprudence of that Prince, appeared at first no more than an honest Opposition. But abetted at length by the Majority of the Nation, (who neither perceived how dangerous it was, nor could have well avoided joining with it, if they had, to preserve themselves against the violent Attack then made upon their Freedom,) grew too strong both for the Prince and for the Laws. The miserable Consequences that it brought upon us are related at large in the Histories of *England* from 1642 to 1660.

These Evils of Faction in a Republican Form, prevented its Revival again in the same Shape.—The People of *England* had (since the Union of the two Houses of *York* and *Lancaster*) never seen it in another.—They therefore feared it in no other. This gave it Opportunity to shew itself in a new Form, and Opposition became again a Faction in the Reign of the late King *William*, and a Faction of a much more dangerous Nature than the first.

For whereas the Republicans, who are the Leaders of the first Faction, are in this Country little more than Whigs overheated by Oppression, and an extravagant Abuse of Power; as in reality there is very little of that Principle existing among Men of Property and Fortune, and as it is chiefly confined to Men of an inferior Class; they may be easily brought to moderate their Views by what it is in the Power of every honest Government to apply : But the Leaders of the second Faction set out with Expectations, that no Government, without being *felo de se*, can gratify. For they set out upon the View of changing the Prince upon the Throne, and in necessary Consequence to transform the Constitution and Religion of the Kingdom.

In a word, a Jacobite Faction assumed the Shape of Opposition in that Reign, that is, the People under the Circumstances I have mentioned, and the Discontented of all Denominations acted in a Party, directed either secretly or openly by Leaders, whose Views intended the Restoration of King *James* II. or of his Family.

Now that this Faction was more dangerous than that which had appeared before, is farther manifest from hence. That the *Republicans professed a Principle*, and of a kind, which led them to do very great and glorious things. Their Zeal was indeed mistaken, but it clashed in its Pursuit, neither with the Honour nor the Independency of their Country, and the Strength of

this

this Party lay in the Accession of those who had the greatest Share of Sense and Honesty. — They were therefore steady in every Conjuncture to defend the Nation against its Enemies a-broad, and particularly against its most dangerous Enemy of all the *French*; and unless in Times of extream and rare Necessity, were deserted constantly by their *Auxiliaries the Whigs*, before they could bring their Scheme to any mature Effect.

But the *Jacobite Faction professed no Principle at all*, or such as deserves the Name of none. They had indeed a View, but it was private Title, the Interest of one Man, and of one Family. An Object in itself unworthy any Party, and criminal too in the highest Degree, in this Instance, because it was the private Title, and the Interest of a Man and Family, who by their Education and Religion were nourished in a fatal Enmity to their Country. — These Men therefore, from the indispensible Nature of this their first View, could be animated with no good Sentiment for the Publick, and from the Circumstances of their Case, were obliged to assist the Ambition, support the Power, and abet the Views of *France*, by whose Force alone they could hope to bring their Point to bear. Their Opposition therefore tended in every Step to destroy the Honour and Independency of their own Country. The Strength of their Party lay in the Accession of those who were the weakest and most dishonest Men; for who else could join in such a View as this, and therefore as all who furnished them Assistance must be either tainted in their Principles. to their Country, or wrong in their Heads before they could engage with them, their Conduct was constant, or wilful Error; and thus their *Auxiliaries the Tories*, if ever they separated from their Faction, never did it till it was almost too late, and never saw that they were deceived, or that they blindly concurred to the Ruin of their Country, till that Ruin was at the very Gate.

It is visible from hence, that there is much less Danger from a *Republican* than from a *Jacobite*; or in softer Terms, from a *Whig* than from a *Tory Opposition*. A Whig Opposition is therefore that alone with which the People for many Years have ventured to concur, and the only one with which they can *for a Moment* concur safely.

But even when they follow this, they are not *always* without Danger. For when Opposition under any Title rises high, and becomes formidable, demanding such Terms, as Government is honestly under equal and real Difficulty either to grant or to refuse, the Symptoms are strong, and the Suspicion generally just, that such an *Opposition* is converted into *Faction*. — Nor can the Generality of Men distinguish easily of what Species it may be; for both the *Republican Principles*, and

the

the *Jacobite Faction*, being long since sufficiently detected, and being therefore both become detestable to all honest Men ; both the one and the other are extreamly careful not to avow their respective Pursuits.---When they take off the Mask with greatest Freedom, the *Republicans* denominate their Faction by no harsher Name than that of a *Whig*, nor the *Jacobites* than that of a *Tory Opposition* - Nor would the *Whigs* be brought to support the one, nor the *Tories* to abet the other without this Artifice; and yet by this Delusion of Names, both Parties have been at different Times led on till they have very near destroyed the Constitution. In fact, every Faction will, without Scruple, assume any Appellation to impose upon Mankind ; and the most inveterate Jacobite Faction, to carry its View, will profess to act upon a Whig Principle, when that becomes the favourite Principle, as it is at this Time. An Opposition therefore may become *Republican* or *Jacobite*, when the Vulgar little conceive it to be either. The Judgment must be formed not upon what Men call themselves, but upon what they do, upon what they act, upon what is the visible Tendency of their Measures and Pursuits.--- Whether they are a Faction or not, or of what Species their Faction is, can be determined only by their Conduct, and may be infallibly determined by that means. Now the Criterion of a Whig Conduct, *is* (as may be collected from what we have already observed) *to resist and reduce the Power*, and the Criterion of a Jacobite or Tory Faction, *directly or indirectly, to assist, encourage, and support the Interests of* France.

This I have premised to give a general Idea of the Nature of Opposition, and of Faction in this Country, that I may with more Facility lay open to the Publick what I have to offer as to the Opposition of this Time---and which I think it my Duty to offer, because I will be bold to affirm, that they are grosly deceived in it, and that instead of pursuing a Whig Opposition, which they conceive it to be, they now abet and support *a Tory Opposition, and a Jacobite Faction, which from the Circumstances of this Time, and the Impudence of its proceeding, is become more dangerous than ever that Faction yet has been in this Nation.*

Had this been asserted two Years ago, it would have met with nothing but Ridicule, and it would have been impossible to have induced the Majority of the People of *England* to have believed that the Jacobites could have ever given this Country any Uneasiness again. --- The Reason is very evident.

All the ill Humours of the Nation collected together had, for several Years last past, combined a very strong Opposition; but this Opposition was led by Whigs, by Men known to be of this Principle, and they had the Ascendant

both

both by their superior Abilities and Experience, and by the Turn of the Nation, to such a Degree, that they kept down all Efforts of the *Jacobites.* They directed the Means of Opposition; and the Tendency was therefore to Points wholly free from any Symptoms of that kind. The *Tories* and *Jacobites* sullenly worked on under these Leaders, and could never attain any Degree of Influence over Men of better Parts, and better Principles; they knew not directly whither they were going, but they hoped towards Confusion, and that they might have a Chance to work out something if that Confusion should arise.—The People at the Beginning of that Opposition, which lasted near twenty Years, were living in great Numbers, who remembered the Conduct of this Faction in the Reign of King *William* and Queen *Anne.*—They remembered how, after King *William* was seated upon the Throne, and after being grown detestable by various Attempts of Plots and Assassinations, they had been obliged to soften their true Name into that of *Tory*; how under that Title they had disclaimed their secret Tenet, and professed only to maintain certain Opinions as to *Church and State,* which had been plausibly introduced among the People in the great Rebellion by the Clergy, and inculcated from the Pulpit, to make a Party against the violent Doctrines of the Republicans of that Time.—The wrong Opinions of the one begot those wrong Opinions of the other: And though the *Passion of the first* had been disgraced by the Issue of that Rebellion, the *Nonsense of the other* had not yet disgraced itself so far — The *Presbyterians* had ruined both the Church and Monarchy; but the *High Churchmen* had not brought in Popery and arbitrary Power, they had even assisted (at last) in some Degree at the Revolution to keep it out—The Publick in general were not able to judge but of what they saw; and they did not see how near they were to have done both before they had the Sense to stop, nor how they were puzzled to reconcile their Nonsense with that Conduct These therefore were the favourite Party of that Time.---Of these the *Jacobites* laid hold :- -All this the People, during the late Opposition, saw very clearly; (for many, as I have observed, were at the Commencement of it living, when the *Jacobites,* thus under the Name of *Tories,* led the Opposition of that Time,) how the People were deluded by it; whither they were carried, and what Pretences they had used

They remembered that this Faction set out with a furious pretended Zeal for *Monarchy, Non-Resistance,* and *Hereditary Right*; they remembered how they stirred up the People

with

with *imaginary Degrees about the Church*; they remembered
above all the infamous Endeavours ufed to diftrefs the Government in its Attempt *to reduce the Power of* France, and to prevent the Exertion of our own Weight to maintain the Ballance
of *Europe*.--- The various Means exercifed by different Perfons
at the fame time according to their different Capacities to effect
this End, and according to the different Capacities of thofe upon
whom they practifed--fometimes pretending that we had nothing
to do with Affairs upon the Continent---fometimes that the
View of reducing *France* was impracticable, that the Expence
was not poffible to be borne, that our Trade was ruined--fome-
times that *France* was really not dangerous--- equally magnify-
ing every Succefs of that Power to terrify, equally mifreprefent-
ing every Defeat to betray their Countrymen into a falfe Secu-
rity---ridiculing every Meafure that was taken for that End---
infinuating, that the King was a *Dutchman*, and had only the
Intereft of *Holland* at Heart---that every Alliance was made for
the Intereft of the *Dutch* alone --- that the Nation was beggared
for a Foreign View---that the King delighted in War, becaufe
it afforded a Pretext to maintain great Armies--- that *Holland*
was not yet attacked, and the *French* King, whatever he propofed, could never be rafh enough to attempt that---at leaft that
till he did attempt it, this Nation had no Reafon to ftir, nor
any thing to fear.

They remembered this Conduct, and they remembered how
by poifoning the People by thefe and an Infinity of other falfe
Infinuations, and by Mifreprefentations of the Expence which
they themfelves rendered infinitely more grievous, by the Obftruction given to the Supplies, and the Neceffity, which proceeded from thence, of borrowing large Sums at high Intereft,
they laid the firft Foundation for the Debt under which the Nation yet labours---That by thefe Means they at length reduced
the King to the Neceffity of confenting to the Partition Treaty,
for which they reviled and abufed him, and raifed the Ferment
of the People upon him, though it was the Infant of their own
Faction---That by this means they preferved *France* in the Zenith of her Power, at leifure to prepare againft the Death of the
King of *Spain*, an Event which was expected every Day---That
though the Profpect of a new War was fo immediate and fo certain, they forced the Reduction of the Army to feven thoufand
Men; fo that when the War of 1702 broke out, before the
Grand Alliance could take place, by the Management of thefe
faithful and fteady Friends of *France*, that Prince was enabled
to make an entire Seizure of the *Spanifh* Monarchy, and to
ftrengthen himfelf to fuch a Point, as to carry on a War againft

moft

moſt of the Powers of *Europe* for twelve ſucceſſive Years, to which *England* alone contributed above Seventy Millions.

They remembered farther, (though this pernicious Conduct had eſtranged the Nation from them for a time, and had caſt the Adminiſtration of Affairs into the Hands of the Whigs; during which whole Period, this Nation was attended with the moſt amazing Series of Succeſſes ever read of in Hiſtory;) that the ſame Men continued the ſame Practices, till by low Arts, they had frightned, and by infamous Inſinuations gained both upon her and upon the People, ſtill concealing their grand View till they had got into the Adminiſtration.

They remembered farther (though it ſeems to be forgotten now) what they did when they came there.——That they betrayed the *Faith* of this *Nation* and deſerted their *Allies.*—— That they did it with Circumſtances, which clearly proved their Intention to yield them up a Sacrifice to *France.*—— That they made a ſeparate and an infamous Peace, by which they ſaved *France* from inevitable and immediate Ruin, and caſt away that immenſe Treaſure, which had been expended in the War, entailing a future Expence ſtill greater even than that they had thus iniquitouſly thrown away; expoſing us to greater Danger than we had even then eſcaped, laying a Foundation for her Advancement to a much higher Point of Power, and preventing at the ſame time, by their Perfidy to the Confederates, as far as in them lay, all Probability of the ſame Union to obſtruct her Views again.

They remembered how clearly and how ſteadily this Plan of ſerving *France,* had been purſued, and how it was brought to its full Effect.——And they remembered how near their Grand View, to which this was ſecondary, was brought to an Iſſue too.——In what manner before the Death of the Queen, they had deeply laid the Plot of abuſing her Authority to bring the Pretender to the Throne.——How notwithſtanding their affected Loyalty to their Royal Miſtreſs, by which they had not only duped her, but deceived the Nation; they baſely meditated her Ruin, to whoſe Weakneſs they owed their Advancement. ——How by their dark Intrigues they broke her declining Conſtitution and cauſed her Death.——The only Service they ever did her; ſending that unhappy Princeſs, by this Precipitation of her Fate, to a better World, before ſhe had experienced in this, far worſe Calamities, which they were preparing for her; the Loſs of her Crown and Dignity, perhaps a violent End, at leaſt Impriſonment for Life.

They remembered the Deliverance of this Nation by the Acceſſion of his late Majeſty in the moſt critical Conjuncture. ——They

—They remembered the Confidence of this Conspiracy, which had ripened so far in four Years Tory Administration, that they thought themselves able to effect that by Force, when they had lost all Power, which could not have been defeated had they continued a few Months longer in it.—They remembered the late Rebellion, which broke out immediately after, and which was suppressed, more by the Interposition of Divine Providence, than by human Means.

Remembring all this, the last Scene of which happened not eleven Years before the Commencement of the late Opposition, which may be properly dated from the *Hanover* Treaty in 1725.—The People could not entertain a Fear of a *Tory Faction*.—This Scene of Wickedness had so fully detected those, who set themselves in the Front of such a Faction, that even the *Tories* themselves blushed to see the Tools they had been made; and trembled equally with the *Whigs*, at the Hazards which their Folly had brought upon the Nation; such as, to do them equal Justice, their *Heads* had never comprehended, nor their *Hearts* ever intended to promote.—The shameless Conduct of that Administration, with regard to *France*, and the *Pretender*, caused an universal Aversion to the Tories; and many of them, sensible of the Errors of their former Conduct, retained nothing of what they were but the Name.---The whole Nation appeared united in a warm Attachment to the present Royal Family.---The *Faction* of which we speak, sensible of their wounded Interest, hardly shewed themselves in any Shape, for some Years.---Any new Opposition avowedly begun by them in that Conjuncture, would have ruined them for ever. —*Their Arts and their false Pretences were too recent to impose upon Mankind.—And their Conversion, had they pretended any, would have been too sudden and unnatural to have gained Belief.*

As Security rarely fails to be the Mother of Danger, so it was with us,—This seeming Security deceived both the *Minister*, and the *Publick*. I shall speak frankly and without Partiality to either.—It tempted him to act with too much Wantonness, and Negligence in Power.—It tempted *others* too much to indulge their Resentment and private Views.---The *Faction* was no longer dreaded but despised.---When that has been the Case, it has been always found, at length

---

Incedimus per Ignes
Suppositos cineri doloso.   Hor.

The Minister, void at first of all Apprehension of this latent Danger, gratified his ill Humour to, or took no Pains to manage
the

the ill Humours of, thofe he happened to diflike, neglected Popularity too much, and ftudied only how to avoid War, as the Means to procure the Continuance and the Eafe of his Adminiftration.—He knew that in War, if not fuccefsful, the ill Succefs is always attributed to the Minifter.—If fortutunate, that it was unavoidably attended with great Expence, at which, in the long run, the People murmur.—He likewife faw, that in War, military Men, and active Spirits muft, by degrees, obtain fome Share of Power; which he was determined to engrofs.—All *Europe* quickly faw this Foible, and the two Powers, from whom we have to fear the moft, the *French* and *Spaniards*, play'd him off unmercifully.—Their Methods were different, but both tending to the fame End.—The *French* flattered him with an infidious Friendfhip, and the Affectation of a pacifick Difpofition.—The *Spaniards* bullied him upon every Turn.—It muft be candidly confeffed that the Peace of *Utrecht* in 1713, and the Difficulties unadjufted then, had greatly embarraffed all the Affairs of *Europe*.—*France* and the Emperor had agreed by the Treaties of *Raftadt*, and *Baden* the following Year; but great Differences between the Emperor and *Spain* fubfifted till long after this Minifter was taken into that Employment.—His Predeceffors had been puzzled with thefe Differences.—And in endeavouring to appeafe them, had already, by the *Quadruple Alliance*, and feveral fubfequent Treaties and Proceedings, in a great Degree difgufted both thofe Powers. At the Time therefore, when the Reins of this Government were put into his Hands, it required greater Abilities for Foreign Affairs, and another Turn to extricate this Nation out of thefe difficult Circumftances.—Inftead of adhering firmly to the Emperor, this Minifter yielded to the Views of *Spain*, who infulted us till fhe had carried one Point, and then infulted us again, till fhe had obtained another.—The Minifter ftill vainly flattering himfelf with gaining that Power by conftant Obligations. — But the Queen, who governed there, knew neither any Sentiment of Gratitude, nor any Limits to her Ambition.—By this Conduct he ftill provoked the Emperor to a higher Degree, which *Spain* obferving, took that Opportunity to accommodate her own Affairs with the Imperial Court.

This fudden Friendfhip between the Courts of *Vienna* and *Madrid* alarmed the Minifter, who knew he had not the Friendfhip of *the one* Court, whatever he had done and fuffered for it; and that he had juftly incurred the Refentments of *the other*. He therefore grew jealous of this Union, and dreaded fome Effect from it, though he knew not what.—

He

He apprehended that the Peace of *Europe* was upon the Point of being diſturbed again ; and without conſidering the Nature of ſuch Diſturbance, that it could not prejudice this Country ; that it was, on the contrary, the moſt deſirable Event that could have happened, and that *France* could alone have Reaſon to conſider this Union with a jealous Eye:—He ſuffered himſelf to be impoſed upon by imaginary Fears, inſinuated by *France*, and immediately exerted himſelf to form a Confederacy againſt the *Emperor* and *Spain*; whoſe Union was effected by themſelves, for no other Reaſon but becauſe we had refuſed to mediate for them ; and that neither Decency nor Reſentment could permit *Spain* to accept the Mediation of *France*, from whom ſhe had received a recent Indignity of a very high Nature, by ſending back the *Infanta*, who had been betrothed to the King of *France*.

This Confederacy, which went by the Name of the *Hanover* Treaty, was concluded between *France*, *Pruſſia*, and *Great Britain*, the 23d of *September*, 1725, about four Months after the Treaty between the *Emperor* and *Spain*, concluded at *Vienna*.—The late King of *Pruſſia* was then living, and it is obvious by the Conduct of the *Son*, what Views the *Father* might have had to induce him, among other Diſcontents with the *Imperial Court*, to come into this Meaſure.—And it was ſtill much more obvious, why *France* ſhould have joined in a Project, which was of her own Invention, and the only Meaſure, that could have recovered her out of the moſt dangerous Situation that ſhe was ever in.—The Houſe of *Bourbon* was divided againſt itſelf, and ſhe was very ſenſible it could not have ſtood, if this Alliance between the *Emperor* and *Spain* had continued in Force.—The natural Antipathy of the Imperial Court, and the Reſentments of *Spain* to *France*, too plainly accounted for the Sums remitted from the *Spaniſh* Court to *Vienna*, and the vaſt Encreaſe of the Imperial Armies.——Theſe Armies could not have waded through the Ocean to have attacked *Great Britain*: The *Emperor* had not a ſingle Ship to bring them hither, and the Fleets of *Spain* had been deſtroyed in the *Mediterranean* in the Year 1718.—Had it therefore been as ſolemnly true, as it was undoubtedly falſe, that thoſe Stipulations had been made in the *Vienna* Treaty —to affect *Great-Britain*, which the Miniſter had been impoſed upon himſelf, or deſired to impoſe on others to believe, *Great Britain* muſt have been out of its Senſes to have been alarmed at them.—A Squadron of Ships of War ſent upon the Coaſts of *Spain*, and another of Obſervation on our own Coaſts, together with the Body of Forces conſtantly maintained at Home, would

have

have prevented all Poffibility of the fmalleft Danger of Invafion, which can never be juftly feared but from *France* alone, or *France* and *Spain* united, a Cafe vifibly not then exifting, and more remote than it ever was.--The *French* therefore well knew that thefe Preparations muft have been defigned againft themfelves ; and if the very diftant Sound of War had not terrified the Minifter to the Lofs of his Wits, we might probabl, have feen an Event at that Time, which we fhall probably never have in our Power to fee again---The Houfe of *Bourbon* ruined by itfelf, and *France* reduced, without the Expence of a fingle Shilling to this Country.

We have now feen *France* preferved, and the Houfe of *Auftria* confederated againft by its natural and old Ally *Great Britain* ; we have feen the fame effected by the Pufillanimity of a *Whig Minifter*, which was the conftant View of a *Tory Adminiftration*.---The fame honeft Zeal which animated the Whigs againft the Tories, moft juftly and indifpenfibly educed many of them to enter into an Oppofition to an Adminiftration, who with different Principles purfued the fame End.--This will warrant, before God and Man, the Oppofition that we have lately feen.--- It fhews, that it was carried on upon Whig Principles ; that it was the grand Principle of humbling *France*, and of affifting the Houfe of *Auftria*, to which they adhered, and which they intended to maintain by this Oppofition---It was not a Quarrel about particular Laws or Alterations of the Conftitution, as it is now falfely fuggefted to have been. Something of this kind is attempted in the Courfe of every Oppofition, and fomething of this kind is from time to time neceffary, within the Bounds of Moderation, to be done, to confine Government to its firft Principles, and proper to be attempted in fome Conjunctures, even in a further Degree than it is intended to be done, to keep Minifters of a certain Character in Awe, and to maintain the People in a Senfe of their Advantages, which fuch Minifters, without that lively Senfe in them, might have it otherwife in their Power to impair---But thefe were fecondary Views, the grand Point intended, and what thefe were employed only as Engines to attain, was *to remove the Minifter, and to bring back the Councils of this Country to its true Intereft.*

The Conjuncture was now come, which had been long impatiently expected by the Faction---Confufion was begun---and the Government attacked without the leaft Appearance that the Faction had been the Authors of it---The Whigs, who oppofed, did it with great Vigour, but were ftill known to be true in their Principles, both to the King and to the Conftitution---The Faction, who could not, as I have already obferved, *venture to*

C

have

have avowedly begun a new Opposition themselves, or practised their
former Arts, which were too recent to impose upon Mankind, or
pretended a Conversion, which would have been too sudden and un-
natural to have gained Belief, found the Occasion extreamly apt
to busy themselves again — They would have joined with the
Minister, who was now indiscreetly doing what they wished, if
they had believed he had wished it too; but as they knew he
did it by a kind of fatal Necessity, which a Series of Errors had
induced, they knew that neither he, nor that Part of the *Whigs,*
who continued to support him, some through the same Blind-
ness, some through Gratitude to *him,* some through the very
Apprehension of *them,* and some for other Reasons; yet none of
them did it upon *their* Views, or would ever concur to bring it to
their desired Conclusion.—They therefore knew that they would
sooner or later change this Conduct, and that besides they would
never join with them.—The only Game they therefore had to
play, was to act an under Part with this Whig Opposition—
By this Conduct they had a double Policy; *first,* to concur in
raising the Ferment of the Nation to the highest Point they
could (which by long Observation never was yet raised since
the Revolution, but that it took a Turn in favour of their great
View) and *secondly,* to efface the Suspicions that the Nation
entertained of them.

The grand Criterion of the Conduct of the two Parties being (as I have already observed,) of the *Whigs, to oppose the*
Growth of the Power of France, and of the *Tories, to advance*
the Interests of that Power—The Faction concurring in this Opposition, which so directly formed itself upon the *Whig Prin-*
ciple, exerting themselves with the utmost Rancour and seeming Sincerity against the Minister, for his Conduct with regard
to *France,* uniting in all the popular Bills, and Republican Propositions, (which were by this, and have commonly been by all
Whig Oppositions, more especially indulged,) and being silent
upon the Topicks of *Passive Obedience, Non-resistance,* and the
Danger of the Church, from all these Circumstances joined to a
Partiality to believe well of those who assist us, let the Motives
be what they will, and a Tendency to disbelieve the Minister,
who very constantly rung the Alarm against their secret Principles, all which was improved by the most solemn Assurances of
their good Intentions; they at length wrought upon the Publick
to believe, that their Views were intirely changed—Many were
by this Time dead, who remembered all those Arts and Practices which I have formerly mentioned, and a new Race were
by this Time sprung up in their Room, by their Age, and the
Nature of Youth, susceptible of light Impressions, actuated by
warm Passions, and ignorant of what had passed before their

Times.

Times.—To this were added such a Series of Mistakes, and such unfortunate Events, as brought the Interests of all our Allies, and consequently the Interests of *Britain*, into the utmost Danger, the Minister still unavoidably blundering on, not able to make a Peace, nor to carry on a War—Harrassing the Country by great and fruitless Expences, to provide Forces against Events, which were neither sufficient to answer the End, and which he never had Resolution to employ towards the End—bubbled by *France*, insulted by *Spain*, hated by the Publick. Thus the Resentments of the Nation rose at last so high, that they became incapable to consider any Danger, or to suspect any Treachery but from him.—In this Situation of Affairs, it is easy to account why the Faction still subsisted, and why it must have been a vain, perhaps not a wise Attempt at that Time, to have endeavoured to have convinced the Publick that they did.— The Whigs, in the Opposition, thought honestly, and they thought truly, that the Nation was inevitably ruined, if this Minister continued to govern in our Councils longer. The House of *Austria*, which is as much the Barrier to the Liberties of *Britain* as the strong Towns of *Flanders* are to the *Dutch* Republick, was reduced to the lowest Ebb, and upon the very Brink of utter Destruction —No effectual Means proposed, no Means in his Situation possible to give it any Assistance. In this Condition they were compelled to use the Aid of any Set of Men whatever, to procure the Removal of this Minister; and they thought they might depend safely upon the national Experience of the past Behaviour of the Faction, upon the Integrity and Well-meaning of the Generality of the People, upon the real Excellency and peculiar Blessings of this Constitution, never in any Event to be overborne by either a Jacobite or Tory Faction.—In fine, they trusted to their own Influence, which then governed and directed the whole Opposition without Controul, to settle and consolidate the Principles of the Nation, as soon as the Minister was removed, and his Measures rectified

These are the true, and they are sufficient Reasons to explain why the Nation gradually lessened in its Apprehension of this Faction, why the Tories thus combined were conceived to be no longer what they had been formerly. But the Whigs, who led the Opposition, and were most considerable in it, who now compose the Administration in Part, and who now oppose no longer, were not so easily deceived. ---- They could not but observe the Views of these Men in their pretended Coalition with them, ---- They could not avoid seeing (though they prevented, and discouraged them as much as they could, and kept them down in a very great Degree) the malevolent En-

deavours

deavours of thefe Men, to poifon the Minds of the People
againft the Royal Family, and to give the general Difcontent
a Tendency to a Difaffection againft the *Prince* upon the
Throne ; which they laboured wholly to confine to the Perfon of the *Minifter*. ---- They faw too evidently, to be duped
by any of their Pretences, that they maintained the fame Inveteracy to the Whigs. ----- They fupported no Whig in any
Election, where they could poffibly avoid it, without a Detection of themfelves, or the Ruin of an Oppofition fo convenient to their View. —The Whigs even faw much more, which
in that Circumftance it was not their Intereft to difcover to the
Publick, that they endeavoured, by refufing to concur in feveral
perfonal Propofitions againft the Minifter, to try whether they
could not induce him to ftrike a feparate Bargain with themfelves—and at the Clofe of the Oppofition, in the firft Seffions
of this Parliament, when they adhered more firmly to thefe perfonal Propofitions, they knew it was becaufe the Minifter had
not catched at the Bait they had thrown out for him, and was
not to be deluded by their Arts.

From all that we have here obferved, it is very notorious,
that the laft Oppofition was a *Whig Oppofition*, and not a *Tory
Faction.* — That the plain Origin, and avowed Views of this
Oppofition, were the Removal of the Minifter, and the Change
of his Meafures —That when this was done, they, from the
very Beginning of that Oppofition, intended no more, never
meant, nor were ever expected to maintain it longer. — That
it would have been inconfiftent with their avowed Profeffions,
and with their real Principles, if they had.

It is farther obvious, that the Tory Faction, though they
concurred with them, had done it without either *Principle* or
Affection, and never had the Influence to give this Oppofition
any Taint or Colour, nor were they fuffered to compafs one
publick Meafure of their own —That the Whigs, though they
could not refufe the Concurrence of their Votes, and their Affiftance to fwell the Number of Opponents, never pretended,
or had any real Friendfhip with them, nor ever had Reafon
from their Sincerity to have it, much lefs ever gave them any
Encouragement to hope that they would join with them any
longer, than till they had changed the *Minifter*, and changed
the *Meafures*.

If then it fhall appear, that the Minifter and the Meafures
are now changed—If it fhall appear, that thefe Men after this
commenced a new Oppofition, when the principal Whigs, who
before directed the Oppofition, had done with that Direction,---
What Man can deny, *that the Leaders of the late Oppofition have*
acted

acted consistently and honestly both in their first Beginnings to oppose---and then in desisting to oppose at the Time they did

And if it should appear, that the *Whig* Leaders of the late Opposition, though they had no further Connexion with these Men after that Change of the Minister, and the Measures, was effected, which was the only View they intended or professed, or concurred with these Men in, did yet endeavour, out of a Desire to destroy (as much as in them lay, and till they found it an *Utopian* Undertaking) the Evil of *Parties* in general, and the Distinction of *Tory* in particular, by using their Influence to advance many of these, (who seemed the least violent) into Employments, where they might be placed without the Danger of their influencing the publick Measures, and where they might have given Probation of their Sincerity. — If they had actually in a very few Days begun to do this, and if it will appear that for no other visible Reason but this, that the *Tories* and *Jacobites* were not permitted to take the Government by Storm, and that their Ambition could not be satisfied, or their Views answered, without those Employments were conferred upon them, which would inevitably give them the Power of influencing the publick Measures; and if the Terms were such as to force their whole Faction into the Administration, without allowing the Prince to except against a single Man, and their Impatience, such as to desert their Leaders, and to form a new Party before they had given them any reasonable Time—What Man can have the Confidence to deny, that they acted *not only with greater Friendship to these Men than they deserved, but with as much Honour as it was in human Power honestly to do?*

And thirdly, if it should appear, that by this new raised Opposition, it is the manifest View to do that, which, as we have already observed, is the Criterion of the Conduct of a *Jacobite* Faction, viz. *to advance the Interests of* France; and if this manifest View is now followed by the very same wicked Arts and Measures, which that Faction in all former Periods have pursued, I may be justified in that Assertion which it is my Point principally to prove — *That the Opposition of this Time is not an Opposition, but a Faction, and that of the most dangerous kind to this Nation.*

Now that this is true, and rather to illustrate than to prove this (for Things self-evident, and what arises from the Recollection of Facts, neither will admit, nor stands in need of Proof) I shall make it the Plan of my Discourse in the following Sheets·--First, *To shew the State of our Affairs, as they stood previous to the Change of the late Ministry, and to give a short Deduction of the Conduct of the Opposition till the Whigs and the present Faction*

separated

separated from each other.--- I shall then observe the Conduct of the Faction thus separated from the *Whigs* to the End of that Sessions of Parliament --- I shall in the third Place observe the Conduct of the new Administration, the Success of their Measures, and the Difference that appeared in the Situation of our Affairs upon the second Meeting of the Parliament.--I shall shew in the next place, the farther Measures of the Faction in their Attempts to delude the People, in their Methods of Opposition, and the Tendency of both.--- I shall then proceed to offer a few candid Reflections upon those popular Topicks, which are the Engines principally used to play upon the Passions of th' People, and to divert them from a cool Reflection of the true Condition of our Affairs in this Conjuncture, and conclude with some general Considerations, which will lead the Publick to a just Sense of those Dangers to which they are exposed, by a further Concurrence with what is now plausibly called by the tender Name of the present Opposition.

We have already mentioned the Conduct of the Minister, with regard to the *Emperor*, *Spain* and *France*, at the time of the *Hanover*-Treaty, which throwing this Nation into the Arms of *France*, and breaking off from our old and natural Connexion with the House of *Austria*, divided the Whig Interest, and was the Ground of the late Opposition.---We are now to see the Measures afterwards pursued by the same Minister, and the Consequence they had.—But before I quit this Subject of the *Hanover*-Treaty, which was the fatal Ground of all our present Confusion, to confirm what I have already said, with regard to the just Alarm the *Whigs* took at it, I must observe, that by a separate Article of this Treaty, *Great Britain* engaged, " in case War should be declared by the Empire against *France*, " that though she was not comprized in the Declaration of such " War, *Great Britain* should act in Concert with *France* till " such War should be determined ;" and by Virtue of the third Article of the same Treaty, " should, if Necessity required, " declare War upon the Empire." *And thus*, says a [a] Foreigner, who is quoted often upon Occasions of this Nature, and cannot be suspected of any Party Concern in the Affairs of this Country,---*By this Treaty, the Duke of* Bourbon, *then First Minister to the Most Christian King, brought to Maturity what his Predecessor had projected, and* France *at length attained what she had so long wished, and for which she had in vain expended such immense Sums in the preceding Reign*

The Consequence immediate upon the Conclusion of this Treaty, was a vast additional Expence. — And without all Doubt, the Rashness of this Measure had engaged us in a War, which

which would have ruined the Balance of Power in *Europe* —without Refource, (the Powers of the grand Alliance being now upon the Point of purfuing the Deftruction of each other, with the fame determined Rancour, which they had formerly exerted againft their common Enemy the *French*,) if the Emperor, notwithftanding the Pride and Infolence, of which he was accufed, and the fhameful Indignity with which he was treated, obferving the Danger in which we had, by *our unnatural Apprehenfions*, involved ourfelves, had not, with an happy Moderation, himfelf opened a Way, (in a very uncommon Manner, through the Channel of a Nuncio of the Pope at *Venice*,) to bring this Matter to an Accommodation, till at length, upon the Sufpenfion of the *Oftend* Company, which was one of the pretended Subjects of the Quarrel, a Preliminary Treaty was figned at *Vienna*, in *June* 1727, which eafed our Minifterial Fears of a general War for fome certain Time: During this Interval we fuftained an immenfe Expence in defending *Gibraltar*, raifing Troops at Home, and hiring Troops abroad, the ineftimable Lofs of many thoufands of our Seamen, and the Ruin of the never to-be forgotten Squadron fent with *Hofier*, to rot in Sight of the Treafures of *Peru* and *Mexico*, at *Porto-Bello*.

But there yet remained great Matter of Anxiety ; for *Spain*, under frivolous Pretences, which fhewed her manifeft Contempt for the *Britifh* Minifter, refufed to ratify this *Preliminary Treaty*, and continued her Hoftilities, till the *Emperor*, with great Candour, detefting this Chicane, took part with our Court againft her —And *Spain*, finding no Support, was at length obliged to accede by a new Act figned at the *Pardo*, the 4th of *March*, 1728.—By which it was agreed, that all Hoftilities fhould ceafe, and all the Differences between *Great Britain* and *Spain* be fubmitted to the Decifion of a future Congrefs.

The Minifter, fenfible of the Danger he had efcaped, was glad of the Opportunity, which offered itfelf in that Congrefs (which was held at *Soiffons*) to reunite with the Imperial Court.— Notwithftanding all the Indignities that had paffed, and all the Provocations he had received, the Emperor retained fo juft a Senfe both of his Obligations, and his Intereft to cultivate the antient Friendfhip of the Houfe of *Auftria* with *Great-Britain*, that he was willing to overlook all that was paffed ; and as his Union with *Spain* before, had given fo much Umbrage here, he thought by raifing Difficulties, and by delaying the Execution of fome Articles of the former Treaty with *Spain*, he fhould give us Proofs of his Sincerity.—But alas ! he had not yet experienced what he had to fuffer from the pacific Councils, or (as they are

termed

termed by the great Conductor of them himself,) the *preventive and defensive* Measures of the *British* Minister.— *Spain* was incensed at this Conduct, and at the Emperor's candid Behaviour with regard to the *Preliminary Articles*; we now began to be as much frightened at the *Variance*, as we had been terrified before with the *Union* of these two Powers; we had practised our *defensive* as we have seen; we must now try our Skill in *preventive* Measures, and with the like Success.

The Emperor's Conduct deserved the Gratitude of the whole Nation; and merited the best Returns that could have been made him.—On the other hand, during this whole time, even after the signing the Act at the *Pardo*, *Spain* had treated us with the utmost Insolence, taken and plundered all the Vessels of this Nation, that fell into her Hands, with as little Reserve as if we had been at open War. These Circumstances together should, in all human Wisdom, have induced the Minister, to have laid aside his old Way of alliancing with *France*, to have improved the Misunderstanding between the *Emperor* and *Spain*, and to have endeavoured, with the utmost Vigour, to crush that Insolence of *Spain* by force, which he saw visibly, was not to be reclaimed by generous Usage, by the Moderation of suffering her to declare War without any reciprocal Declaration on our Part, by our signal Abstinence from a Seizure of above four Millions Sterling in *America*, nor by the Patience we had exercised under so many Indignities, Insults and continued Depredations. But instead of doing this, in Conjunction with his good Ally the *French*, he concluded a new Treaty with *Spain*, which was signed at *Seville*, the 9th of *November*, 1729.

The Emperor, who had shewn himself so truly desirous of preserving the Peace of *Europe*,—who had acted with so much Moderation and Candour, to preserve the Friendship of this Nation, was not acquainted in the least with this Treaty, till it was concluded; ---- it was kept secret from him; and no Wonder,---for it contained an Article, which has since proved, as we have seen, and as he always foresaw it would, of the most fatal Consequence to his *Italian* Dominions ----This Article was the immediate Admission of 6,000 *Spanish* Troops into the Places of *Tuscany*, *Parma* and *Placentia*, to secure the Reversion of those States, after the Deaths of their respective Princes, to Don *Carlos*, which in the *Quadruple Alliance* the Emperor had consented to be done only by *Neutral* Forces, and even that very much against his Inclination.

It may be easily conceived what Effect such a Treatment as this must have had upon the Emperor. It justly gave him the greatest Alarm, as well as raised his Resentment to the highest degree.

gree.—Even in his Conjunction with *Spain* in 1725, intimate, as it had been reprefented to be, he was never brought by *Spain* to confent to this Alteration,—and what made the Matter ftill worfe, thefe Territories being Fiefs of the Empire, this arbitrary Settlement with relation to them juftly incenfed the Empire too.

Thefe *preventive Meafures* put us into worfe Plight than ever.—*France* had brought us about again, and we were now upon the Point of joining, not only *France*, but of uniting with the whole Houfe of *Bourbon*, not only againft the *Emperor*, but the whole *Germanick Body*.—*Spain* and *France* urged us openly and vehemently to compleat thefe new Engagements.—The *Emperor* in the mean time marched a powerful Army, and filled all *Italy* with his Troops, determined to refift the Execution of this Treaty, which he thus prevented for the whole Year 1730.—The *Minifter* was now in Defpair, his Fleets at *Spithead* had not terrified the Emperor's Armies in *Lombardy*.—But the Refentments of *France* and *Spain* at his Inactivity, and contradictory Proceedings, terrified the Minifter.—The Marquifs *de Caftellar*, the *Spanifh* Minifter at *Paris*, publifhed a Declaration there, by Order of his Mafter, upon the 28th of *January* 1731, with bitter Reproaches againft this Conduct, *renouncing all his Engagements with us, profeffing that he now looked upon himfelf as intirely at Liberty to act what Part foever he fhould find moft fuited to his Interefts.* Thus he had vifibly difobliged all Parties, he thought a War inevitable, and himfelf undone.—His new Treaty of *Seville*, upon which he had plumed himfelf fo proudly, now vanifhed into Smoak.—But the Emperor's good Senfe and Moderation faved our Minifter once more.—He confented to this ruinous Meafure, tho' with Tears in his Eyes.—He confented to admit a Prince of the Houfe of *Bourbon* into *Italy*, whom we were vifibly carrying thither to eftablifh in a great Monarchy at the Expence of his Dominions.—Willing not even yet to defpair that this Nation would fee its Errors at laft, he determined to try us once more, and fubmitted to make this Sacrifice, on condition that we fhould accede to the *Pragmatic Sanction*, and guaranty the reft of his Dominions to his eldeft Daughter.

This Treaty concerning the Admiffion of the *Spanifh* Troops into the *Italian* States, and the *Guaranty* of the *Pragmatic Sanction* was concluded at *Vienna* the 16th of *March* 1731.—between the Emperor and *Great Britain* alone. Its View was to enforce the Treaty of *Seville*.—Yet it was concluded without the Participation either of *France* or *Holland*, who had

a *Rouffet*, Vol. VI. fol. 11.

been

been the contracting Parties to that of *Seville*.—The *Dutch* were however at length prevailed upon to accede to it.

We now began to think again that we had done great Matters, for the present we had pacified the *Emperor*, and prevented a War. —We obtained a Declaration from the Court of *Spain*, dated at *Seville* the 6th of *June* following to revoke that of the Marquis *de Castellar*, of the 28th of *January* before mentioned · And as a Proof of our Reconciliation with the second Power, we were permitted to have the Honour, upon the 17th of *October* 1731, to escort the *Spanish* Troops into *Italy*, with a Squadron of sixteen *British* Men of War, at the Expence of 200,000 *l.*

But we are come at length to the final Period of the Success of these *preventive and defensive* Measures—they could no longer hold—the whole World clearly saw, to what the Politicks of the *British* Minister amounted—and that he was determined to be moved neither by Indignity or *Danger*.

France had carried her Point, she had heartily regained the *Spaniards* to her Interests, she had destroyed all Cordiality between the *Emperor* and *England*, she had detected the Weakness of this Nation so far, that she saw *she* had nothing *to fear*, and that *all other Powers* had nothing *to hope* from *Britain*.— She had been a contracting Party to the Treaty of *Seville*, and we had bound ourselves to enter into no new Engagements without her Concurrence. Yet the late Treaty with the Emperor, which was to enforce it, had been concluded without her Participation, nay without her Knowledge.—She highly and loudly resented this Treatment, as a manifest Neglect, an Instance of Contempt, and a publick Affront; and she had the better Handle to exclaim against us for it, because we had affected to think ourselves so ill used, by the like Conduct of the Emperor, with regard to the Treaty of *Vienna* in 1725.—From this Moment she thought of nothing but Revenge, and to avail herself of the Means we had so manifestly given her, to take it with Impunity.

The *Spanish* Troops had not been long landed in *Italy*, before an Alliance was formed between *France, Sardinia* and *Spain*, to attack the Emperor's Dominions in *Italy*.—The King of *Poland*'s Death was foreseen, and she took such Measures as she thought had effectually secured the Election of King *Stanislaus* to that Throne.—With the Assistance of that Prince she projected to have fallen upon the Emperor's Hereditary Countries, while she diverted his Forces upon the *Rhine*, and her Confederates employed him in the Defence of *Italy*.—Not many Months were pass'd, before the Minister had a more fatal Cause of Inquietude than ever.---War became inevitable---his Conduct had delayed it, only to make it fall with more ruinous and irresistible Effect.

The

The King of *Poland* died the 21st of *January* O.S 1732-3.
and in *March* following the King of *France* declared that he
would support the Election of his Father-in-law.---The Emperor was sensible of what was preparing for him.---He knew
that if this Election took Effect, it would be impossible to resist
the Confederacy formed against him.---He therefore took part
with the Elector of *Saxony*, now the present, and Son to the late
King of *Poland*.---Yet endeavouring as much as possible not to
give any Pretence to *France*, for attacking him upon this Score,
he left it to the *Russian* Arms to support that Prince.---But
France never wanted a Pretext, when she found herself in a Condition to prosecute her Views by Arms.---Confiding in her Engagements with *Sardinia* and *Spain*, she grounded this Pretext
upon the fierce Negociations the Imperial Court had carried on
with *Russia* against King *Stanislaus*, declared War, and marched
her Armies against the Emperor----while on the other side the
6000 *Spaniards* conveyed by the *British* Fleet into *Italy* not a
Year before, shewed the Use for which they were designed.---
They joined the *Sardinian* Troops, attacked the *Milanese*, and
in Conjunction with a Body of Auxiliaries from *France*, soon
made an entire Conquest of that Dutchy.

The Emperor confiding in the Engagements we had entered
into, so immediately before, to support the *Pragmatic Sanction*,
had withdrawn his Troops from *Italy*.---The *French* had attacked him in the Empire, and were endeavouring to bring the *Turk*
upon him.---It was impossible for him long to make Head alone
against the different Attacks made and meditated upon the Empire itself, and his Hereditary Countries, and to defend his *Italian* Possessions at the same time.---He found himself however
able with great Difficulty for that Campaign to maintain his
Kingdoms of *Naples* and *Sicily*, and to keep his Footing in the
Mantuan.---In that perilous Interval he called upon *Great Britain* to execute her late Treaty, he shewed that it was yet in her
Power to save *Naples* and *Sicily*, at a small Expence, and by
her Fleets alone; he reproached us with the Ruin we had
brought upon him by engaging his Consent to the Introduction
of the *Spanish* Troops, and urged the Points both of Honour
and National Interest, by which we were obliged so particularly to interfere in this Quarrel, as our Support and Guaranty
had been the only Condition upon which he had given that Consent.--He implored us, in the most moving Terms, not to desert
an old, a faithful, and a sincere Ally, so strictly united by all the
Bonds of mutual Affection and mutual Security, in a time of
this imminent Distress, a Distress, which our own Councils,
and his Acquiescence to them, had reduced him to.

D 2

But the Minister, totally confounded, knew not how to act at all.—He stood insensible to the Danger both of his Allies, and of his own Country, unmoved equally with the Complaints, Reproaches and Intreaties of the Imperial Court. He sought only to cover his own Shame, by retorting the Blame upon the Emperor.---He reproached him with having brought these Difficulties upon himself by Negociations with *Russia*, to prevent the Election of King *Stanislaus* to the Throne of *Poland*, and abused him for not submitting to that, which must have reduced him to a Condition incapable of Defence or Relief.---Thus adding the most galling Insults to the most irreparable Injuries, he endeavoured to quiet the Alarms of the People of *Great Britain* by his Emissaries, who were instructed to preach up a Dependance upon the *good Faith* of *France*, who in her Declaration of War (which she so religiously adhered to, as we have seen) had solemnly engaged to make no Acquisition by it, thus abetting the Cause, and proclaiming both the Justice and Moderation of that perfidious Power.---In the mean while no Alliances were formed to support the Emperor.---The *Dutch*, who had unwillingly been dragged by us into some of our former Treaties, would now treat with us no more; they had been taught by fatal Experience to dread any farther Connexion with us. We neither assisted the House of *Austria* with Troops nor Money.---Our Squadrons, so ready to be employed to aggrandize the Glory of a *Spanish* Triumph, were not to be hazarded in the Defence of our Allies.---We first permitted the *French* Fleets to sail into the *Baltic* unmolested, with Troops and Supplies to sustain the Cause of *Stanislaus* in the North,---In the next Year we suffered *Spain* to transport a Body of 20,000 Horse and Foot, (without any Attempt to interrupt them) to join their Troops in *Italy*, who before the End of that Year 1734, ravished the Kingdoms of *Sicily* and *Naples* from the Emperor, and added two powerful Kingdoms to the Possessions of the House of *Bourbon*.

Stunn'd with these rapid Successes, and almost inanimate with the Fear of Dangers, in which that very Fear had thus involved the World; the Minister seemed to have forgotten every thing,---during all this Time he did nothing.---But as violent Passions, from the very Cause of their Existence, which is the Weakness of human Nature, cannot be of long Duration, he began to revive a little, and could not refrain, as soon as he did, to attempt again to exercise his Talent of Negociation; to which the Self-opinion of his Brother, and his own Apprehension of Arms, had given him an obstinate, fatal, and incorrigible Turn.---He began to make Proposals, pofals, and to offer his Mediation to the Courts both of *Paris* and *Vienna* :---But the Court of *Vienna* feverely wounded by thefe repeated Cruelties, Indignities and Ill Ufage, in the midft of her deepeft Calamity, difdained and detefted to treat with him any more,---and *France*, though fhe had reaped fo much Advantage from his Conduct, equally contemned the Man, to whom fhe owed it all. For even they, who profit by Infidelity or Weaknefs, abhor the Authors of it.--- Nothing proves the wretched Condition to which we had reduced ourfelves, and the Opinion fhe entertained both of our Councils and our Arms, better than the Anfwer made to *thefe Propofals* by the King of *France*; which was con- cluded in thefe Words, --- *I will do my utmoft Endeavour in* Ger- *many to weaken my Enemies; I have already declared that I would not keep Poffeffion of any of the Places I fhould take.--- Let* England *reft fatisfied with this Promife.---She would have pleafed me in her Mediation, if fhe had not at the fame Time armed herfelf ---But I would have her to know, that no Power in* Europe *fhall give Law to me. And this you may tell your Mafter.*

Thus defpifed and treated as we juftly deferved by all the Pow- ers of *Europe*, *France* herfelf extended more Compaffion to her greateft Enemy than we had fhewn to our beft Ally.---She now thought herfelf fecure of laying the Foundation of fuch Debility in the Houfe of *Auftria*, as would at leaft enable her to reduce it lower when fhe pleafed, if fhe fhould find occafion for it.--- She thought it more prudent to lie by after fhe had done this, till fhe might by the Emperor's Death, have Opportunity to break the *Auftrian* Succeffion, and avail herfelf of the Affiftance of the *German* Princes to undertake that then, which fhe had no Pretence to attempt during his Life, and which muft have inevi- tably drawn thofe very *German* Powers againft her, till that Event happened, much more fhe could not have done, without their Affiftance. She had fown, in all Appearance, a lafting Difcon- tent between the Empire and the Maritime Powers; fhe had it in her Power to join *Lorrain* to her own (already vaft) Domi- nions, and to add two Kingdoms to another Branch of the Houfe of *Bourbon*: Both thefe Acquifitions required fome Time to be fettled in a Way to be ufefully employed hereafter.---By de- clining any farther Advantage for the prefent, fhe carried a Shew of Moderation and voluntary Abftinence, which fhe knew would effectually deceive the Fools, who abound and ftrengthen her Party, by their Credulity, in every State of *Eu- rope*.---All this induced her to conclude Peace with the Impe- rial Court (in which we were in no Degree confulted.) And fhe made her Confederates fubmit to it about *October*, 1736.

By

By this Peace, notwithstanding all her former Assurances to the contrary, she made no Scruple to secure *Lorrain* to herself: Which Country, with its Revenues, is able to furnish and maintain an Arm of 30,000 Men, and brought her Territories above 150 Miles more forward into *Germany*, than they had before extended on that Side; this enabled her at a much shorter Warning, and with a much superior Force, to attack the Empire, when she should afterwards see occasion to do it : Compleating at the same Time, an entire Influence over four Electors of the Empire, *Palatine*, *Mentz*, *Triers* and *Cologne*.—The Effects of which, we have visibly seen by the Election of the present Emperor.—The Dominion given to the Infant Don *Carlos*, reduced the Forces of the House of *Austria* by above 40,000 Men, and added an equal Number to the opposite Scale :—All this the Minister of *Britain* brought about by his *loudly self-applauded Preventive and Defensive Measures*, and this, hampered by the Consequences of his pacifick Conduct, became, at length, out of his Power to prevent.

During the whole Period of this War, *France* was so little apprehensive of our being able to exert ourselves in Defence either of our Honour or our Interest, that contrary to what, in such a Conjuncture, would have appeared a politick Part in her to act, she took every possible Means to insult, to disgrace, and to triumph over our Weakness.—*Dunkirk* had been gradually and privately restored, in Contravention to the most clear and positive Article of the Peace of *Utrecht*, that it should never be made a Port again, and the Minister had connived at this Violation of that Treaty; though its dangerous Situation, in case of a future War with *France*, is sufficiently known and understood.—But now *France* openly employed great Numbers of Men to cleanse the Harbour, and to raise Batteries upon the old Foundations of the former Works; insulted the Ships, not only of our Merchants, but of the Royal Navy of *England*, in very many Instances, affecting the same Superiority at *Sea*, as she had too visibly acquired, by our Conduct at *Land*; encouraged the *Spaniards* to continue their Depredations; debauched and invited publickly, both *them*, and the *Indian* Nations in *North America*, to attempt our Settlements there; and what is even yet beyond all this, issued an Arrêt, commanding all the *British* Subjects then in *France*, upon Pain of the Gallies, either immediately to *depart the Kingdom*, or to *inlist in her Troops*; and, in Consequence, imprisoned great Numbers, both of the *English*, *Scotch* and *Irish*, there.

Spain on her Part, had no sooner dismissed our Fleet, which had convoyed her Troops to *Italy* upon the Expedition before

men-

mentioned ; but she began to treat us even worse than she had
ever done before: her Depredations were excessive, and her Cap-
tures amounted to prodigious Sums ; she publickly laid Claim
to some of our Provinces in *America*, and interrupted not only
our general Commerce, but that of the *South-Sea* Company ;
which were both particularly confirmed by Treaty.—Our Navigation to the *West-Indies* was render'd almost impracticable ;
and by the Barbarities of the *Spaniards*, and the Insults of
France, the Spirit of our Seamen, nay their very Race, was
visibly running to Decay : Yet the Minister, *fearful of a War*,
submitted to all this.

At length, the Nation was exasperated to such a Point, and
the Complaints and Clamours of the Merchants ecchoed so
loudly through the whole Kingdom, that both Houses of Parliament in the latter End of the Year 1737 and the Beginning
of 1738, could no longer refrain from expressing a great Anxiety at this tame Conduct, with Respect to *Spain* ; declaring
their Opinion, that the Insolence of *Spain* ought no longer to
be endured, and that if immediate Satisfaction was not given,
and Security obtained to remedy what was *past*, and to prevent
what we saw was to be expected for *the Time to come*, this Nation
must seek Redress by Arms.

The Minister, still unable to resolve himself for War, still
infatuated with the Notion of his Brother's Abilities for Negotiation, depended upon his former Arts of Treaty-making.---
Spain knew him now so well, that she wantonly play'd with him ;
she kept him off till the very Time, that the Parliament was
to meet, without doing any thing at all ; by which she reduced
him to a terrible Distress.---He did not dare to meet the Parliament, after their Resolutions and Addresses, and the Temper
he had left them in the last Sessions, without having done any
Thing.---Yet the Time was come, and nothing at all was
done.---His only Expedient was to prorogue the Parliament ;
and to make use of this short Space to humble himself before
Spain; to shew them the Condition he was in, and beg their
Assistance, at any Rate, and upon any Terms, to give him
a Lift for the present---Whatever Form of Words he used, or
in what manner soever this Negotiation was carried on, this
was visibly the Nature of it ; for he could not conceal his Condition , and what immediately followed, evidently proves, that
it was fully understood by the Power with which he treated.

Spain having sufficiently gratified her Mirth, sported with,
and mortified the Man, began to think that she might carry the
Jest too far ; that a War, for which she was not yet effectually
prepared, might be the sudden Consequence ; and that it was

not

not her Interest to ruin a Minister, whose Pusillanimity had served her as effectually for many Years, as if her *own* had presided over the *British* Councils : She therefore consented to a Treaty, under the Name of *a Convention*, which was signed at the *Pardo*, not sooner than the 14th of *January* N.S. 1738-9. but then dispatched with the utmost Expedition

Scarce had the Courier cleaned his Boots, but the Parliament was called---they met the first of *February* 1738-9. and the Minister enlarged upon the great Advantages of this new Treaty, by which he bragged, [a] *That he had obtained more than ever on like Occasions was known to be obtained, more than the most successful Arms could have procured ; and that this Negotiation had been the best conducted, and the most happily finished, of any we meet with in History.---That he remembered he had the last Sessions undertaken to be answerable for the Measures of the Government, while he had the Honour to be a Minister, and that he was prepared to make good his Promise.*---He added, that if Gentlemen would persist to raise a Ferment without Doors against this *Convention*, they would thereby render *a War unavoidable*.

But the Publick were not so much terrified with this Argument of *an unavoidable War*. They on the contrary knew, that it was just and absolutely necessary, and had been already delayed too long ;---and when this *Convention* was laid before the House, which was done upon the 6th of *March* following, it did not lessen that Opinion.

And to shew how little Reason there was for that Opinion to be altered by it, I shall state in a few Words, what Points the Nation justly expected to be finally adjusted by this Treaty.

The first Point, *was the disclaiming all Right to search our Ships in the* American *Seas, under Pretences of their carrying on a contraband and illicit Trade.*---Now as there neither ever *was*, nor *is* any Treaty subsisting between the two Nations, which either specifies, intimates, or supposes any such things as *contraband Goods*, and as if the Pretence should be allowed of an *illicit Trade*, no Ships (from the Circumstances of that Navigation) could pass or repass to our own Settlements in the *West-Indies*, without being exposed to be rummaged and confiscated by the *Spanish Guarda Costa's*, it was absolutely a *Condition*, *(sine qua non)* without which, we could never end our Differences with that Nation.

2dly, *Spain* had, with intolerable Arrogance, and upon frivolous Pretences, claimed a Right to our Provinces upon the Coasts of *Florida*, which included *Georgia*, and a Part of *South-*

[a] See this Speech in the Debates of the House of Commons, Vol. X, fol. 335, by *Chandler*.

Carolina,

Carolina.—The Honour therefore and Interest of this Nation, absolutely *required an actual Disavowal of this pretended Right.*

3dly, The Depredations committed upon our Merchants, under the frivolous and unjust Pretences of this contraband and illicit Trade, amounted to 340,000 *l.*—That just Claim and Debt was therefore to be allowed or paid, and this was *another just Condition expected by the Nation.*

4thly, The King of *Spain*, during the former Differences, having seized the Effects of the *British* South-Sea Company, to the Amount of above a Million, and 68,000 *l.* and during the former Negotiations, this Sum having been allowed on his Part a just Debt, and the South-Sea Company having on the other hand acknowledged a Debt on their Part of 68,000 *l.*—there was a Ballance due to the South-Sea Company of above a Million Sterling, the Payment of which was *a fourth Condition expected by this Nation.*

Now if the Nation had not received Satisfaction in these four Particulars, (especially the two first) Justice was not had, nor any Security obtained.

Let us therefore see in what manner this Satisfaction and Security were provided for by this Treaty.

As to the *first Condition*, (our Right to free Navigation, and no Search, the grand Point of all our Difference,) nothing farther was provided than had been provided for twenty Years before—It was again referred to be discussed in future by Commissaries, of which we had sufficiently seen the Effects before, and already experienced all that we had to expect from it, which was indubitably nothing.

As to the *second Particular*, to the great Astonishment of the whole Nation, they found, that their Right to Provinces, from which we derived a prodigious Benefit, *Carolina*, (which by the Encrease of the Commodity of Rice, is become of late Years one of the most profitable Colonies belonging to the *British* Empire;) and *Georgia*, (to settle which the Nation had put itself to a great Expence, and which by its Situation in the Gulph of *Florida*, and by a proper Use of its Ports, might command the Return of the whole *Spanish* Treasure, and was of infinite Consequence to prevent the Conjunction of the *French* upon the *Mississipi*, and their *Sugar Islands*) were not only submitted to the like Discussion of Commissaries; but what was more amazing and unworthy, that we had bound ourselves, till the Decision of these Commissaries, not to erect any Forts, or to do any thing to strengthen or secure our Possessions there, which was, in other Words to leave them in the same weak and defenceless State they were then notoriously in, to be over-

E

run

run upon the firſt Attempt the *Spaniards* ſhould think fit to make upon them.

As to the third and fourth Particulars, it appeared, that the boaſted Satisfaction we had obtained for our injured Merchants, whoſe juſt Demand, (including that of the South-Sea Company,) amounted to 1,340,000 *l.* was provided for as follows.

Imprimis, The Million due to the South-Sea Company *from the King of Spain* was left to the Deciſion of Commiſſaries, whether it was due or not, which all Mankind underſtood to be the ſame thing in effect, as to have *intirely given it up.*

2dly, The 68,000 *l.* due *from the South-Sea Company,* was agreed to be due, and *to be paid immediately.*

3dly, As to the 340,000 *l.* due to our Merchants, on account of the Depredations committed upon them,—this Account was ſettled in the following Manner.

	l.
1ſt, From the ſaid Claim of the Merchants was arbitrarily deducted by the Daſh of a Pen, *without any Reaſon at all aſſigned* - -	140,000
2dly, The King of *Spain* was allowed to deduct for the Prompt Payment *of what was never intended to be paid* - - -	45,000
3dly, The *Britiſh* Nation were to allow *Spain* for the Ships taken and deſtroyed in the Year 1718, *in time of actual War* - - -	60,000
4thly, The South-Sea Company were to make immediate Payment of the 68,000 *l.* due from them to the King of *Spain* - - -	68,000
5thly, *Spain* was allowed to deduct the Value of a Ship called the *Thereſa,* taken in the Port of *Dublin* in 1735, as alſo the Amount of whatever ſhe had formerly given in Satisfaction to our Merchants for their Loſſes; which two Sums amounted to more, but we ſhall only ſtate at	27,000
	———
	340,000

Thus it is manifeſt that the Plan of this Treaty was laid upon this Ground, that the King of *Spain* was not to pay one ſingle Shilling ; ſo that, in fact, all the Pretenſions, both of our Merchants and the *South-Sea* Company, were intirely abandon'd by it.—But what was ſtill worſe, the Court of *Spain* refuſed to agree, even to this Treaty, till the Miniſter had conſented to an *Act,* whereby the King of *Spain* declared, That he entered his *Proteſt* againſt the Execution of it *proviſionally,*

in

in cafe the *South-Sea* Company did not pay, in a fhort time therein limited, the faid Sum of 68,000 *l.* and referved farther to himfelf, a Right of fufpending their *Affiento* Contract, in cafe of Failure on their Part.—Now as it was impoffible, that the *South-Sea* Company would ever be induced to pay 68,000 *l.* upon one Head of an Account, in which they had, (after the Deduction of that Sum,) a Balance of *a Million* due to them ; and as they did immediately after refolve not to pay this Sum, the Cafe of the Nation was directly this; that *Spain* was prevailed upon to do this temporary Job for the Minifter.

1*ft*, By a publick Connivance (if it may be fo called) at their Pretenfions to fearch our Ships, and to interrupt our Navigation.

2*dly*, By a publick Agreement, that our *Trade* fhould fet down unfatisfy'd with the Lofs of 1,340,000 *l.*

3*dly*, By a tacit Acknowledgment of the Pretenfions of *Spain* to a Part of our *American* Dominions.

4*thly*, By a pofitive Agreement to leave thofe Dominions in a defencelefs State, that *Spain* might feize them when fhe pleafed.

And 5*thly*, By the Sufpenfion of the *Affiento* Contract.

To this Condition had our *preventive and defenfive* Meafures now reduced us.

With this *Convention* the laft Thread of pacifick Policy was fpun; the Nation could endure it no longer; the Minifter was at length compelled to draw the Sword.—His Majefty's tender Regard, both to his *own* Honour, and to the Interefts and Honour of *the Nation*, induced him to declare War againft *Spain*, in the Summer 1739.

How that War was carried on upon the fame timid Principles, is but too evident. The Court of *Spain* had Time to ftrengthen herfelf to fuch a Degree, that fhe became at length invulnerable in the *Weft-Indies* ; and *the War continues ftill without a Poffibility of any material Succefs in our farther Attempts upon that Part of her Dominions.*

And now the Diftreffes brought upon us by this unparallelled Chain of pufillanimous Proceedings, burft like a Torrent on the Minifter, who had been the Occafion of them.—Upon the 9th of *October*, O.S. 1740. the Emperor died of a Cholic, attended with a Vomiting and Inflammation of the Bowels, in a Conjuncture fo apt for the Views of *France*, that there was little Room to doubt, either of the Caufe or Confequences of his Death .—His Territories had been guaranty'd, long before, under the Title of the *Pragmatick Sanction*, to his eldeft Daughter, (the prefent Queen of *Hungary*,) by a Majority of the *German* Princes, by *Great Britain, Denmark, Holland, Spain* and *France* ; and of the two latter held (the one) *Naples* and *Sicily*,

(the

(the other) *Lorrain*, by no other Tenure than that of the Obſervance of this Treaty. But though *France* made no Scruple to declare, that ſhe would ſtrictly fulfil her Engagements with Regard to the *Pragmatic Sanction*; and that ſhe would keep clear of every Thing, that ſhould reſtrain the free Choice of a new *Emperor*, and though the King of *Pruſſia* gave the ſtrongeſt Aſſurances, that he would ſupport it to the utmoſt of his Power; yet it was eaſy to ſee, that theſe Engagements would meet with no Regard, and that theſe Declarations were deſigned only to amuſe and deceive.

The Elector of *Bavaria* begun by refuſing to acknowledge the Rights of the Queen of *Hungary*, and aſſerting a Claim to her Dominions.—In *December* following, to the Amazement of all *Europe*, the King of *Pruſſia* fell into the Queens's hereditary Countries, and entered *Sileſia* with an Army of 40,000 Men.—In the ſucceeding Spring, the *French* marched a great Army into *Germany*, and joined the *Bavarians*; they alſo ſent another great Body of Forces into *Weſtphalia* upon the Confines of the Electorate of *Hanover* —The Elector of *Saxony* likewiſe marched an Army into *Bohemia*.— *Sweden*, by the Intrigues of *France*, declared War againſt the *Ruſſians*. By which, and by the treaſonable Practices, which ſhe fomented there, that Empire became incapable to aſſiſt the Houſe of *Auſtria* The King of *Naples*, with a great Body of his own Forces, in Conjunction with a formidable Army of *Spaniards*, both Horſe and Foot, which again were permitted by the Miniſter to embark, and land unmoleſted by our Squadrons, was prepared to attack her *Italian* Dominions :—And by the Influence of *France*, the Elector of *Bavaria* was choſen Emperor.— *Upper Auſtria* was already, before the End of that Year, overrun ; *Bohemia* and the greater Part of *Sileſia* loſt, another *Spaniſh* Army marching towards *Savoy*; the King of *Sardinia* (from his dangerous Situation, and other Circumſtances) much ſuſpected ; the Electorate of *Hanover* unavoidably compelled by ſuperior Force to a Neutrality ; the *Dutch* intimidated by the ſame Force ; *Denmark*, encouraged by *France*, and wholly occupied to make its Advantage of the Troubles in the North ; and *Great Britain* exaſperated to the utmoſt Verge of Patience, upon the very Brink of domeſtick Confuſion, ſtill directed by the *ſame Miniſter*, who from this Situation of Affairs, and from the Temper of the People, naturally reſulting from it, was wholly incapacited from affording any material Aſſiſtance to the Queen of *Hungary*, and ſtill perſevered to demonſtrate, even in this laſt Criſis, by his Conduct of the *Spaniſh* War, and by his Permiſſion of the *Spaniſh* Embarkations, that his Inclinations were as foreign as

his

his Abilities to a vigorous Exertion of the Power of this Nation, at a Time, when Councils, *even desperately violent*, seemed the only Possibility, under Heaven, to preserve *us* and *Europe* from Destruction.---Even yet, incorrigibly bent upon inconsistent Schemes of Negociation, he turned his Thoughts to a Project of more Temerity and Indiscretion than ever he had hitherto projected, and attempted to form an Alliance to dismember *Prussia*; which render'd it a Thing almost impossible to bring him afterwards into a moderate Temper, or to effect a sincere Reconciliation with him.---Thus overwhelmed on every Side; Great Armies of *French, Bavarians, Prussians* and *Saxons* within a few Days March of *Vienna*; and no Part of her Territories unmolested, but the remote Dominions of *Hungary*; and those States, that bordered on the *Turk*, in daily Expectation of being attacked likewise from that Quarter, the unhappy Queen of *Hungary* was thrown, for her only Resource, upon a People, who, till this Time, had never afforded any Assistance to their Sovereign; but had, on the contrary, taken all Occasions to rebel and join a foreign Power. Her veteran Troops all destroy'd in the late War against the *Turk*; the Fountains of Supply from her richest Countries, then in the Possession of her Enemies, wholly turned against her.---This was the Condition to which the only Power, that could maintain the Balance, and without which no rational Man can think, that this Nation can long subsist without becoming a Province to *France*, was brought by this determined Suite of the *preventive and defensive* Measures of the *British* Minister.

Such was the State of our Affairs, when the present Parliament begun its first Sessions upon the first of *December*, 1741. I might expatiate here, to aggravate the wretched Condition to which this Country was reduced; but I am far from meaning to represent this Conduct, in the worst Light that it might bear. My View is very different.----Exasperated as the People are already, he that attempts to encrease the Flame, deserves to perish in it.---Would to God it were forgiven, upon Condition that it could be forgot; but it cannot be forgot, nor will, for this Reason, ever be forgiven: My Meaning therefore neither is to attempt the one nor the other.—But my Endeavour is to divert the Publick from that mad Resentment, which must complete their Ruin.—I shall shortly come to shew, how far already this Resentment has misled them.—How, deviating from the only Principle, that can warrant Punishment, they wound their *Country* and *themselves* in the Extravagance of *Passion*.----The Pursuit of Punishment, when no good End can possibly be answered by it, is Revenge; *Revenge* with *Nations*, as well as with *private Men*, is in itself *deteſtable* ; and, in its Conſequences, *fatal*. Let *Sweden* be the Mirror to reflect the Face of this Nation. We have lately ſeen that brave, that free People, *puſhing violently towards their own Deſtruction with a ſtrange Similitude of Fate.—Firſt, by ruinous Meaſures brought into deplorable Circumſtances ; then purſuing ſanguinary Vengeance on their Miniſters, Miniſters, from the Paſſion of the Time, neither ſafe to be given up, nor to be ſaved ; tearing every Fence of Government and Conſtitution down, to reach the Object of their Hatred, artfully led on, under this Pretence, to abuſe their Liberty with a dangerous Licenſe, taught to think themſelves entitled, becauſe they met with Obſtruction in this View, to invade the Privileges of all the other Parts of their Legiſlature ; yet all this Time ſtupidly forfeitful of the very Cauſe, for which alone they ought in Juſtice to have condemn'd the Conduct of thoſe Miniſters, or to have been thus enraged, embarraſſing their Government, labouring to plunge it ſtill deeper into the ſame Evil, by endeavouring to perſevere in the ſame Foreign Meaſures, and to prevent their wiſeſt and moſt honeſt Men from availing themſelves of the moſt fortunate Opportunities to preſerve the Nation, and to retrieve paſt Errors ; till, at length, from the Exceſs of popular Power, the Weakneſs of their Government, the Want of Virtue in Particulars to reſiſt the Temptation of falſe Popularity, the Want of Courage to withſtand a factious Calumny, and the ſecret Intrigues of a Foreign Court, inviſible to themſelves, tho' glaring to the whole World beſides, they were encouraged to attempt direct Rebellion, in Favour of a Pretender, whoſe Advancement to the Throne was morally certain to have fixed the Chains of Arbitrary Power, for ever on their Country.*

After this, ſome may poſſibly demand, Why then have you recalled to publick View, theſe former Errors of the Miniſter ? As I am ſure I have done it with Integrity, ſo I am deceiv'd if I have not done it with ſolid Reaſon.---The Sore, that rankles, muſt be opened and deeply probed : The Man, who would, in this Diſorder of the Publick, ſerve his Country, cannot hope to do it by concealing Faults.---To deny notorious Truths, is an Attempt to impoſe upon Mankind, too groſs to be borne ; the Nation is honeſt, though it is deceived, and will liſten to no Arguments, that are obviouſly mean, ungenerous, diſhoneſt, or uncandid.---Not to acknowledge what I have done in the preceding Pages, would be to accuſe the People of unjuſt Reſentment during a Space of 20 Years :—And, as in the preſent Conjuncture, I think it my Duty to accuſe them of unjuſt Reſentments, and to convince them that they are juſtly accuſed ; by a contrary Conduct, I could not fail to provoke, inſtead of

healing

healing Animofities ; to lay a Foundation of Prejudice, which no Solidity of Reafon could be able to remove, and infallibly defeat the honeft Intention, which alone has led me to give the Publick and myfelf the Trouble of this Difcourfe.

It was likewife neceffary to do this for another very important End, to give the Clue to the true Source of our Miferies, and to the Origin of the late Oppofition ; which can be the only Means, either to moderate the Rage of the Publick, to remove their Prejudices, to diftinguifh their Friends, to direct them to the Knowledge of their Enemies, to preferve their juft Attachment to their Prince, or to maintain the Conftitution of their Country.

For when the People miftake the Caufe, their Conclufions muft be falfe and dangerous---their Opinion of thofe, who fee more clearly, and act the beft for their Interefts, eafily abufed---they are liable from falfe Caufes affigned by wicked and artful Men, to think defperately of Government, and to feek for Remedies not adapted to the Difeafe, and of fo violent a Nature, as to tear the Body Politick to Pieces.

And that this has been the Cafe, will become very manifeft upon a due Confideration of this Deduction of our Affairs during the late Adminiftration---the People not confidering well the Spring of this unhappy Train of Conduct, have been falfely and infamoufly taught, that it took its Rife from the Treachery of the Minifter, and from a low and private Prejudice in the Prince to his Foreign Dominions, abetted by a Band of corrupt Mercenaries, and fupported by the Defects of a Conftitution, which gives too much Power to the Crown—None of which is true.

It was the Embarraffment of our Affairs, firft, by the Peace of *Utrecht*, and fince, by a timid, obftinate and indeed felfifh Character in the Minifter.—It was the unavoidable Confequences of the Treaty of *Hanover*, which was made before his Majefty's Acceffion to the Throne, but for which he was therefore not anfwerable, and which it was afterwards infinitely difficult to redrefs. —It was a Chain of fatal Circumftances, neither derived from a greater Degree of Corruption than will be found in any opulent State upon Earth, nor from any Defects, but what (or worfe) are found in the pureft Conftitution under Heaven · All which will more fully appear by the following Deduction.

But to return---In this Crifis of Affairs, Ruin abroad appeared almoft impoffible, highly improbable to prevent,---the Nation at home in fuch a Ferment, that nothing but Confufion was by every rational Man expected.---To avert either, it was obvious that the Minifter muft be removed, the Publick neither

would

would, nor could have engaged in those expensive Undertakings which were our only Resource, under the Conduct of such a Man.—But how to effect this Change was the great Labour.—There is Reason to believe, that his Majesty was as much convinced of the Necessity of a Change, as the Minister was convinced that it was high time to prepare for it.—It was even certain, that the best Men in the Opposition began to fear greatly the Effects of the Spirit they had raised, however necessary, however just it had been to raise it; but the greatest Danger of all was to have desisted in that Conjuncture. Thus even they who were most sensible of the dangerous Ferment, were by Necessity compelled to raise it still higher to prevent its fatal Effect.---Opposition was redoubled with a Degree of Fury, which nothing but this Circumstance could warrant.---The Dilemma was great on all Sides—the more the Minister was pressed, the more difficult and dangerous it was both for him and for the Publick to give way—and had he been disinterested enough to have resigned his Power in the Manner some would have advised it, to speak honestly, there was Hazard not only to his own Person, but to the Interest of his Master, and the Constitution of his Country.—It was dangerous to depend upon the Moderation of a Party so combined as it now appeared to be, and heated with so unavoidable a Fury. On the other hand, it was impossible for the honest Men, embarked against him, to have desisted either.—Matters had been driven too far to rely upon the Prudence of their Antagonist, and they had too many Examples to venture to trust that even this Danger could have reclaimed his indomptable Spirit of Peace. It was equally unsafe, both for the *Publick* and *themselves* to have risqued the double Danger of their Enemies, and the Resentment of their Friends.—If by such an indiscreet Retreat, *they had much weakened their Party*, they could not have had sufficient Assurance, that the Minister would have made that just and wise Use of it, which could have been their only Inducement for so disinterested a Measure.—He might have employed this Accession of Strength, to have confirmed himself in his imprudent Politicks, to have ruined Liberty, under the Pretence of destroying Faction, and have taken this Opportunity to have wreaked his private Revenge.—Again, if this Conduct should have had a different Effect, *and not much weakened the Party they left*, it must have served only, to precipitate the Views of bad Men, and left the Nation distracted and mad under the Lead and Direction of the worst and most dangerous Persons in the Kingdom.—Upon the whole, it was neither in the Power of the one to *retire*, nor of the other to *desist*.

Most

Moſt certain it is, whatever the ignorant Vulgar may think, or wicked Men pretend, that the domeſtick Peace was at this Conjuncture in the utmoſt Hazard, and that at this Hour we had been involved in horrible Confuſion, if his Majeſty's Prudence had not dictated, and aſſiſted us in the middle Way of Moderation, in which all Safety conſiſts, by yielding to a Change of the Miniſter, and yet reſolving to defend (as far as in him conſtitutionally lay) the Perſon of the Man removed, from the Rage and Fury of the Time. By this Meaſure, that intire Victory of Party, which muſt have produced inſufferable Inſolence, and raiſed unforeſeen, extravagant and irreſiſtable Expectations, was awarded with its Conſequences, which, like a Torrent, would have broke in upon us, and in a mercileſs manner ſwept away both good and bad who had given Oppoſition to it, and probably carried before it, in its Tide of Reformation, all the Guards and Securities of this happy Conſtitution.—Had the Government been taken by Storm, had the People been once blooded, who can ſay where he would have ſtopt, or who could have had Authority to caſt down the Bar before them.—In ſuch Conjunctures, Reaſon and Experience ſhew us, that the private Soldier drives his Officer before him—all Order and Diſcipline are at an end—and whoever endeavours to reſtrain the Violence, is looked upon as an Enemy diveſted of his Command, and new Leaders choſen out of thoſe, who with moſt Fury and leaſt Remorſe will carry Devaſtation furtheſt.—By this Meaſure therefore, Time was given for many to reflect, who in the Heat of ſuch an Event, would have been hurried Lengths they never intended to have gone, and plunged into Precipices, which many, who have eſcaped already, conſider with Horror, that they lately ſtood ſo near, and which many more, as they conſider and cool, will every day look back upon with equal Terror.—This Conduct likewiſe afforded opportunity to make the proper Alterations by degrees, and with a deliberate Choice, to put the publick Affairs into the hands of Men, who were diſtinguiſhed, rather by their Abilities and Integrity, than by their Heat and Paſſion, or popular Accompliſhments.—It gave room to weaken Faction, by the Gratification of ſome warm Men, but to do it ſo as not to encourage its haſty Growth again.—It prepared a way for a laſting Change of Meaſures, and ſecured an Intereſt to ſupport them at the ſame time, as it enabled thoſe who had acted under the former Adminiſtration upon wrong Principles of Policy without Fear of Ruin, or Shame of Tergiverſation, tacitly to reclaim their Conduct, and prevented that fatal Evil, (which was otherwiſe inevitable, and muſt have brought our Affairs

F

into

into a worse Condition than ever,) the raising a new Opposition out of the defeated Party, whose Number, though defeated, were at this very Conjuncture equal to those by whom they had been compelled to yield —Thus this prudent Firmness on the one hand, and prudent Condescension on the other, manifestly saved this Nation from Perdition – the best, the most able, the most considerable Men, and those of the true Whig Principle, were separated from a wicked Party, with whom Necessity had obliged them formerly to unite, and who were upon the point of getting the Direction of the Publick into their hands, under the pretence of delivering it from another Danger, which, great as it was, could not be worse than that.—And thus the Government now stands upon the Foundation of a true Whig Interest, upon which alone it can safely stand, supported by Men, united by the manifest Revival of that Principle, which would bring them both to Ruin.

We are now come to that Period of Time, when the late Opposition ceased, and a Separation was made between the *Whigs* and the *Tories*, they had travelled on in the same Road to this Point of a Change of the Minister; and the Power to change the Measures was in their own hand.—This, as I have very sufficiently shewn, was the first and sole Intention of the *Whigs*, so that their Journey was at an end; but the others were to travel further, and we shall shortly see through what miry Paths they went.—It was almost a Miracle they had kept company so long. —The *Tories* had plainly shewn, upon the late Motion, how little they were to be depended upon, even in the Prosecution of their common View; and for the *Whigs*, they had never pretended, never given any encouragement to think, that they should continue Opposition longer than till they had carried these Points.—Nay, till this Event, the present Leaders of the *Faction* themselves affected to intend no more.—All Men of Sense, who knew them well, knew, that this was only Colour, to take away Suspicion of their dangerous Designs.—What happened was therefore no Surprize to them, and, to say the truth, their Principles and Views being thus widely different, they must *both* have been inconsistent with themselves, if they had not *both* done as they did.

A Change of the Administration being now become absolutely necessary, the Equality of Parties being such, that no Business could be carried on, this Change was resolved.—In order to effect it, it was necessary to adjourn the House.—It required some Time to deliberate upon the first Changes, and for those Members of the Opposition, who were to be first taken in, to be rechosen.

To

To this Adjournment (which was for 15 Days) all the House agreed, the Whigs knowing the Necessity of it, and that a Change could not be safely made without it, and with these concurring, all those who had private Views, and expected to reap a personal Benefit from this Change.—The Leaders of the *Tories*, who have since treated this Measure as iniquitous in the highest Degree, made no Objection to it then ; they had one or other of the two Reasons before-mentioned to induce them to it. The Reader may assign that which he thinks most probable, upon a Consideration of their subsequent Behaviour.

In this Conjuncture, these Gentlemen thought it highly necessary to make their appearance at the Court, to which some had never gone since the Accession of the present Royal Family upon the Throne ; and many had absented themselves so long, that they feared they might be forgotten, which was by no means convenient, when so many great Employments were to be conferred in a few days.—It was necessary to convince the Prince, that their only Reason for abstaining from this Demonstration of Respect before, was their ill Opinion of the late Minister, and that they were now ready to support his Majesty's Measures, as warmly as the best Friends he had But alas ! the Sincerity of their Reconciliation, and the secret Condition of it, unhappily for them, were both as well understood at that time, in the Place to which they went, as they have since been clearly manifested in the Nation.

Thus far all Things proceeded well and quietly —not a Word was utter'd of any farther Reformation. The People were then suffered to think as they were naturally disposed to do. *A Change of the Minister, and the Introduction of honest Men into the chief Employments, was thought the utmost Object of the People's Wish, and must in the end ensure whatever else was wanting.*

Tranquility continued till an *Honourable Gentleman*, who had been considerable in the *Opposition*, was made *Chancellor* of the *Exchequer*.—This began to clash with the Expectations of others ; but still, as there were many great Employments left, they were not yet transported far enough to declare a new Breach—so that they suffered this Gentleman to be re-elected without any Opposition.—The next Thing done, was the Appointment of the new *Treasury*, which when they found composed of that Set of Men called *Whigs*, and but one *Tory* admitted upon that Bench, they began to murmur openly.—It was however still too soon to take their final Resolution—the Boards of *Admiralty*, and *Trade*, were not yet actually settled, and they waited the Event of the Disposition there.—But when that of the Admiralty was taken into consideration, for which some of the leading *Tories* were designed (and

which

which all were willing to accept) His Majesty having refused
to admit one particular Person, and they thinking that the
Reason assigned for that Exception might be a dangerous Precedent, which must equally affect great Numbers of their Body,
it was resolved to exert themselves upon that Occasion.—They
accordingly insisted strongly for this Person, and for some o-
thers, and in fine, for such a Disposition there, as was impossible
to be complied with—which as soon as they found, and that
the other Offices were not yet proposed to be changed, they
resolved to keep no further Measures. Nothing was to be left
to the Disposal of the Sovereign, as soon as it appeared that he
would not wholly resign himself into the Hands of Tories, and
that he presumed to make Difficulties in admitting, even any
one of those, who had been ever marked, by their Friends as
well as Enemies, as the Leaders of a *Party*, entitled to a stronger Denomination.

Some few Men of a different Principle, who deserve a better Fate, by the Heat of Passion, the Effects of Ambition,
and the common Fear of not being provided for to their Wishes
upon this Occasion, unhappily fell at this Time into the Views
of these People; upon whose Shoulders they vainly imagined they might lift themselves to what they now began to
fear they should never reach; and among these, *a Man*, whose
Merits, Abilities and Weight entitled him to the highest
Esteem of all Parties, whose Error (of which he has been
since too late convinced) is repaired to his own Conscience, by
his retiring from them, but can never be repaired to his Country, by his having retired from its Service in Consequence of
it.—This Appearance of a few *Whigs* on their Side had a very
ill Effect. Under this Colour, they passed for what they have
since shewn they were not:—Many young and undistinguishing Men, and many of the People, having no Apprehensions to
engage with an Opposition, which they at first ignorantly think
directed by *Whig* Principles, because they see a few *Whigs* a-
mong them. And the Difficulty of breaking from such Engagements of Party, being so great, that few have Honesty or Spirit
to do it afterwards, when convinced of their Mistake.—But
as we have already observed in the Beginning of this Paper,
*All Oppositions are composed of Individuals of all Denominations:
And an Opposition is not less a* Whig *Opposition, because it is joined
by* Jacobites *and* Tories ; *nor a* Jacobite *or* Tory *Opposition less
a Faction, because it is joined by* Whigs : *But the Difference lies
in the Spirit, that predominates, and in the Men that direct.—
For, if the* Whigs *have the Ascendant and can force the Rest into
their Measures, Methods safe and honest are pursued.—But,*

if

if the Jacobites *or* Tories *have the Lead, or* Whigs *only bear the Name of Leaders, and are in Reality driven, by the Spirit of those with whom they are connected, the Measures of Opposition are then equally carried on upon the* Jacobite *or* Tory *Views, as we shall prove it to be the Case at this Time ; and such an Opposition is, to all Intents and Purposes, a* Jacobite *or* Tory *Faction.*

Thus hurried by Impatience, heated by Despair, the *Faction,* with those unnatural Allies, after a vain and tedious Expectation of eight Days (for so much of the fifteen Days of the Adjournment had already passed, and they were not yet provided for) upon the 11th of *February,* 1741-2, a Day, which perhaps this Nation may have Reason never to forget, they came to a final Breach. -- From this exact Period may be dated the Death of the late memorable Opposition, and the Birth of a fatal Faction, who have already laid the Foundation of Calamities, which will require much Wisdom and Virtue to avert; and which, only that Providence, that has so often remarkably interposed to save this Nation, can entirely preserve it from.

It was given out in dark Whispers, that the *Whig* Leaders of the Opposition, who, by their Abilities and Services had obtained the foremost Rank, in whose Hands the Settlement of this great Affair therefore naturally lay, and with whom, upon the Knowledge of their Principles, the Government could only treat, had betray'd their Party, that the Circumstances of this Treason were such as to require a Conjunction of all honest Men to resist and to defeat it ; that the Proof was undeniable, and that it was necessary the Matter should be laid open before the whole Opposition: The Members of the Opposition were all summoned, and the Expectation of Mankind raised to the highest Pitch : As well they, who understood the Nature of this Meeting, as they, who understood it not, out of equal Curiosity concurred to attend it : And among the rest, the Gentlemen, who conducted the new Settlement, and those, who had been already taken into Employment, were desired to be present to defend themselves against this formidable Accusation.

The Charge was introduced with great Solemnity, "Gen-
" tlemen were reminded of the dangerous Situation to which
" the Nation had been brought by the late Administration ;
" how gloriously and steadily they had persevered in the Op-
" position; how happily at length their honest Endeavours,
" and the just Spirit of the People, had brought them in sight
" of the long wish'd-for Port; that as every Set of Men had
" contributed to bring this important Point to bear, it was
" just all Denominations of Men should receive an equal Re-
" ward

" ward of their Virtue ; that if a proper Use were made of
" this happy Conjuncture, this Reward might be obtained ;
" that the total Rout of the Ministerial Party was what they
" had a Right to expect ; and that this would make Room for
" all.—But that there was too much Reason to fear, that
" this Use would not be made of the happy Opportunity ;
" that a few Men had presumed, without communicating their
" Proceedings to that Assembly, to take this Work upon them-
" selves ; that by their Manner of doing it, they had sufficient
" Cause to apprehend they did not mean the general Ad-
" vantage ; that they had been now eight Days in this Em-
" ployment, and by the few Offices they had as yet bestowed,
" they were justly to be accused of not acting with the Vigour
" that was expected of them by the whole People.—That
" among other things, what administered Matter of great
" Jealousy was the Choice of those already preferred ; that this
" Choice having fallen principally upon *Whigs*, it was an ill
" Omen for the *Tories*; and that if they were not to be
" provided for, the happy Effects of the Coalition of Parties
" must be destroyed, and Parties again revived to the great
" Prejudice of the Nation ; that it was therefore highly ne-
" cessary to unite closely, to keep firmly together, and to
" continue to oppose, with the same Vehemence as ever, till
" Justice was done the *Tories*, and till the Administration was
" founded upon the *broad Bottom* of both Parties."

A Right Honourable Gentleman, since advanced into another House of Parliament, with whom the Management of
this Change was chiefly entrusted, together with some of those,
who were lately taken into Employment, answered these Objections to their Conduct with great Temper.—" They first ob-
" served, how hard a Treatment they had met with in return
" for the long Services they had done their Country, and the
" Share they had confessedly had in bringing the Opposition to
" the Point at which it was arrived, now upon frivolous Pre-
" tences, and a Jealousy, in the Nature of Things, not yet
" possibly grounded upon any solid Foundation, to be brought
" before such a Tribunal, accused publickly in the Face of the
" whole World, of that, which no single Man dare in pri-
" vate, to their Faces, charge them with ; loaded with Suspi-
" cions, which once raised are hardly ever to be wiped off by any
" Conduct ; and branded with the Imputation of an ima-
" ginary Crime, so easily to be believed in the then Temper
" of the Nation ,—that they deserved a very different Usage,
" by the Integrity, with which they had hitherto proceeded,
" and with which they were determined to proceed :—That

" as

" as to the taking the Management of this Affair into their
" own Hands, the Overtures having been made to them, it
" was their Duty, and it would have been the Duty of
" any Man, to whom they had been made, to have used his
" best Abilities to have brought about a happy Settlement,
" after the Divisions, by which this Country had been so long
" torn; and which could not longer subsist without the utter
" Ruin of the Interests of this Nation abroad, and the Danger
" of fatal Disturbances at home :—That the superficial Vulgar
" might imagine it a more proper and equitable way to refer
" this Settlement to the Decision of the whole Party ; but
" that no Man of tolerable Understanding and Experience
" could cherish an Idea so impracticable and absurd , that Go-
" vernment was not yet reduced to such a Point, as to sur-
" render at Discretion, especially to an Enemy, who had de-
" clared so publickly they would give no Quarter; that Go-
" vernment neither *could, would* nor *ought* to be taken by
" *Storm* ; and that it behoved Gentlemen to consider what
" must inevitably be the Consequence of such an Attempt ;
" that the great Points were to change the Minister, and to
" change the Measures: That the one was visibly already done,
" and they would engage to perform the other. That, as to the
" Distribution of Employments, there was neither Justice,
" Decency, Duty or Moderation, in dictating to the King,
" how to dispose of every Preferment in the State ; that his
" Majesty had shewed a Disposition to comply with the De-
" sires of his People in the most effectual manner ; for he had
" already supplied the principal Ministerial Posts with Men,
" who had hitherto been most confided in by the People, and
" such as could not have given Occasion to the People to have
" changed their Opinion of them ; because, though nominated,
" they had none of them yet done any single Act of Office :
" That as to the Changes already made, they were as nume-
" rous as the Importance of the Matter, and the Nature of
" the Thing could possibly admit so soon, and that it might
" have been more to the Credit of their Party, if their Pa-
" tience had extended a little longer than the few Days, that
" had passed since the Time of their Adjournment.———As
" to the partial Distribution of Employments to the *Whigs,*
" that so far as their Interest should hereafter extend, they
" would use it faithfully to his Majesty, and their Country,
" by recommending such to serve him, whose Principles they
" knew had been misrepresented, and who were true to his
" Family, let their Appellations be what they would : But
" that it might be well supposed a Work of some Time, to
" remove

" remove Suspicions inculcated long, and long credited, with
" Regard to a Denomination of Men, who had formerly been
" thought not heartily attached to the Interest of the Prince
" upon the Throne; that some Instances, of this Intention,
" had been already given in the late Removals, and there
" would be many more, but that it must depend upon the
" prudent Conduct of the *Tories* themselves, wholly to abo-
" lish these unhappy Distinctions of Party. In fine, they
" begged of them to consider how false a Step they had already
" made,——and that this passionate and groundless Division
" would infallibly give new Courage to the Party they had
" just subdued; that it discovered a Weakness, of which Ad-
" vantage would be certainly taken; that it must inevitably
" lessen the Power of those who were employed, and, if per-
" sisted in, would in a great measure prevent the Success of
" their Views, both for the Publick, and their Friends."

It is not to be supposed, that any of these Reasons had much
weight on the different sides of the Question.—The Abuse and
Indecency, with which the Gentlemen newly taken into the
Administration were treated, upon this Occasion, plainly convinced them, and every intelligent Man, that the Design of
this Meeting was to throw them off, that the *Tories* might
now disengage themselves from the Direction of the *Whigs*,
under whose Conduct they had been restrained, and with whom
they could never expect to carry the Point they had in view.—
They could never have taken a better Opportunity, than that
of the National Ferment of the Time, nor have done it with
less Suspicion, or encreased their Numbers more than by doing
it, when the Suspicions of Men were, as they always are in
such Conjunctures, diverted another Way, and when the Fears,
Disappointments and Disgusts of many of different Principles,
naturally led them all to join with any Set of Men that still
continued to oppose.—We have already observed how far those
Passions had misled some *Whigs*, that, insensible of the foolish
Part they play'd, they lent their Names to colour the Designs
of the *Tories*, and became the Tools to press publickly for their
Admission into Employments, which they could not, with any
Decency, nor without disgracing themselves with the People,
have so glaringly insisted upon themselves.

The Publick quickly found the Effect of this wicked Conduct, for it deserves no better Name.—It was no small Astonishment to many, who had hitherto concurred in the Opposition, and gave no small Disgust to observe it.——No Man of
Sense and Honesty thought he could justify adhering longer to
a Set of Men, whose Party-View was now so openly avowed,

and

and who, like a Band of *Huffars*, had abandoned themfelves to the Plunder, even before the Battle was half done, they knew the Confequence muft be, at leaft, that their mercenary Conduct would fuffer the Minifter to efcape uncenfured.——— All therefore they could hope farther to do, was to put off his Return into his former Station, and to procure a Change in his Syftem of Politicks, to get the beft Laws they could, to prevent the like Abufe of Power, and at leaft to fecure it in the Hands of thofe, who they thought leaft likely to abufe it in their own Time.—It is true, they never intended to have given the *Tories* the Lead in the Government, or to have made a *Tory* Adminiftration, from the Nature of that Party which I have fufficiently explained already, they had been falfe both to their King and Country, if they had done it.——— But they honeftly did intend to have promoted the moft moderate of that Party, defirous of uniting, by this Experiment, as many as they could, in Affection to his Majefty, and his Royal Family; to which the Gratification of private Expectations is with fome a very neceffary Step.—But their Conduct was fuch, as difabled them from carrying their Views much farther for them, and had they preffed it after this, their own Principles muft have come into Sufpicion.—They had therefore juft Grounds to have made a total Separation from them; but from a Regard to their Country, they ftifled their Refentments; they advanced feveral *Tories* fhortly after, and fome into very great Pofts fince that Time.—They united to promote an Enquiry into the Conduct of the late Minifter, which they pufhed as far as the Strength of the oppofite Party, who were now rallied upon thefe Divifions, could poffibly admit, and far enough to fhew fuch Errors in his Adminiftration, as rendered it impoffible for him to be employ'd again.—They engaged the Government to purfue Meafures entirely oppofite to the pacific Plan fo long fatally purfued; they maintained their Principle of fupporting the Houfe of *Auftria*, and furnifhed her with effectual Supplies; and they carried a Place Bill to leffen the Minifterial Influence in Parliament.—In Foreign Affairs they did every thing that could be wifhed, and much more than could have been expected; in Domeftic, they went, if not quite as far, as perhaps they might have fafely gone, yet as far as they could go fafely in fuch a Ferment; or indeed, as they were able to go, when thus deferted and weakened by the Madnefs of thefe Men.

We have now fhewn the Commencement of the prefent Oppofition, which from its Origin may be eafily judged what it is.—Its Origin plainly was, not from any wrong Meafures,

in

in the Leaders of the late Oppofition, for (as they juftly obferved themfelves) they had as yet done nothing when they were
thus deferted ; no more than *eight Days* had paffed fince the
Retreat of the Minifter; and the *Parliament* had not yet met ;
fo that it was impoffible the *Faction* could have done it from
any Obfervation of their wrong Behaviour *there.*—Had the
Tories been as wholly profcribed, as it was falfely fuggefted
they were intended to be, was the late Oppofition began upon
the Principle of bringing them into Employment, or was it
the *Right,* or the *Concern* of the People to infift who fhould
have the moft beneficial Places ?—The Principle of the late
Oppofition was, as it has been fully fhewn, to bring back this
Nation to its true Politicks with Regard to the Houfe of *Auftria,* and the Balance of Power.—Was the Purfuit of Places
ever avowed to be the Grounds of Oppofition? it has been indeed fatirically imputed to be fo upon all Occafions, but it was
never fupported by the Publick upon that footing, nor ever
avowedly confeffed to be fo, by any Oppofition, before this
which now diftracts this Country ; and which I therefore juftly
and truly call by no other than its proper Name, and fhall farther prove, by its fubfequent Proceedings, to be a *Faction,* if
ever a *Faction* did or can exift in *Britain.*—And as the Tree is
beft known by its Fruits, we fhall be particular in tracing its
Conduct ever fince.

As it was too foon to ftile themfelves *a new Oppofition,* becaufe the Parliament had not yet met, and they knew not what
Meafures would be purfued ; they therefore formed themfelves,
for the prefent, under the Title of the *Broad-Bottom* ; a Cant
Word, which correfponding equally with the Perfonal Figure
of fome of their Leaders, and the Nature of their Pretenfions,
was underftood to imply, a Party united to force the Tories
into the Adminiftration.

Thus intitled, they laid their general Plan of Action, redu-
cible to the following Heads, which were the known Eftablifhment of their Predeceffors in the fame Faction.

1*ft,* To villify and abufe, without Meafure, Mercy, or Re-
ferve, all, who in any one fingle Vote fhould differ from
them.

2*dly,* To advance or infinuate any Falfhood, or mifreprefent
any Meafure, however grofsly, to the better fort of Men, if
they could propofe to delude or inflame the People by it.

3*dly,* To fpirit up the People againft the Re-election of any
Member into Parliament, who fhould accept of any Employment.

4*thly,*

4*thly*, To wean the People from their Affection to the House of *Auſtria*, to diminiſh their Apprehenſion, or to encreaſe their Fears of the *French* Power, *either*, juſt as Events ſhould make it moſt convenient to do.   To undermine the great and ſalutary Principle of ſupporting a Balance of Power upon the Continent, by Pretences of the Inability of the Nation, of the Folly of engaging in Wars, in which we propoſed to make no Acquiſition for ourſelves, and of the Security of this Nation in its maritime Force alone, let what would happen upon the Continent.

5*thly*, To bait the People by the Proſpect of an Encreaſe of Popular Power, by propoſing Alterations in the Conſtitution, the *Effects* of which, and conſequently the neceſſary *Meaſure* of which, the common ſort are by no means able to underſtand.

6*thly*, To poiſon the Affections of the People to the Prince upon the Throne, by endeavouring to convince them, that every publick Meaſure was influenced by his Ambition, Reſentments, Paſſions, or Attachment to ſome Foreign Territory.

[a] Mr. *Addiſon* obſerves in one of thoſe excellent Papers called the *Freeholder*, which he wrote expreſsly againſt the ſame Faction, then in its Zenith, ſoon after the End of the late Queen's Reign ; that even at that Time perſonal Abuſe had been remarked to be the prevailing Characteriſtick of that Party,—and he gives the Reaſon for it, which ſtill holds good at this Day, *That having nothing of Weight to offer againſt their Antagoniſts, if they ſpeak at all, it muſt be againſt their Perſons ; when they cannot refute an Adverſary, the ſhorteſt Way is to libel him, and to endeavour to make his Perſon odious, when they cannot repreſent his Notions as abſurd.*—It was the *Fort* of their Party, and practiſed at all Times ; it was by the infamous Obſervation of that Maxim, *Calumniari fortiter ut aliquod adhæreat,* and by their ſcandalous Perſonalities againſt the great Duke of *Marlborough,* the preſent Dutcheſs, the Treaſurer *Godolphin,* and all the Whigs who ſupported their glorious Meaſures, that they routed them at laſt. —They met with too much Encouragement then not to tread in the ſame Steps,—the *Examiner* had then the Impudence to accuſe that Miniſtry of carrying on that War *upon different Principles from thoſe upon which it was begun,* which could not have been, unleſs that War had been begun upon the Principle of preſerving inſtead of diſtreſſing *France.*—And the preſent Faction, with equal Aſſurance, ſcandalouſly inconſiſtent, as they are themſelves, accuſe the new Part of the Adminiſtration of *Inconſiſtency,* at the Time they are carrying on Meaſures for reducing *France* with the utmoſt Vigour ; when it is noto-

[a] *Freeholder,* N° 19.

G 2

rious,

rious, to have been the grand Principle and View upon which they engaged in Opposition. Yet glaringly absurd and shameless, as this Charge evidently appears to be, upon the least Reflection, they have actually and incredibly, by their Emissaries properly planted, and properly instructed, brought Numbers of the Vulgar to join in the chorus of this Song.—No Man could venture to vote on a different Side in the most indifferent Proposition, but he was treated with immeasurable Abuse.—By this Excess of Calumny and Malice, they had more than one Advantage in View.—It served to terrify weak Minds to return and be more steady.—And though some Men of true Spirit might be the more determined to desert them, they found the Loss of these outbalanced by the Number of those, who were awed and intimidated by it.

In this manner the whole World must be sensible how far they have proceeded, sparing neither Age nor Sex, Rank nor Character,—which Abuse has been swallowed with as much Disgrace to those who have received it, as to those who have delivered it. But Envy and Malice are two great Ingredients in the Tempers of Men, and the Commonalty look upon the Indulgence of this crooked Disposition to be a Mark of an independant Spirit, according to that old Observation of the great Historian *Tacitus, Obtrectatio livor pronis auribus accipiuntur, quippe adulationi foedum crimen servitutis, Malignitati falsa species libertatis inest.*

The second Part of their Plan was pursued with equal Industry, the same [a] Author, in another of his Papers, observes, how steadily this Set of Men have constantly distinguished themselves by their little Regard to Truth, their little Solicitude for what the thinking Part of Mankind would consider of their Conduct, or how long the Lye of the Day would last.—He enumerates a Multitude of their delusive Inventions, in the Reign of King *William*, and in his own Time, adding a just and melancholy Observation, *that their self-interested and designing Leaders cannot desire a more ductile and easy People to work upon.*—Trusting to this Ductility, and the undistinguishing Nature of the common Race of Men, they made no Scruple to charge those, who support the present Measures, with a Change of Principles—Confounding thus the *Opposition* with the *thing intended by it,* and making *Opposition itself* a Principle, which no honest Man will ever make it. The People are told, *that it was the Principle of the new Administration to oppose the Government, that they do not oppose the Government now, therefore the new Administration have deserted their former Principle.* This passes for sound Logick, upon the simple Herd they lead. It is vain to shew the

[a] *Freeholder, N.°* 7.

bare-faced

bare-faced Falacy, *that it was their Principle to oppose the Measures, only when they thought them bad, and that it was the Measures and not the Government they opposed; that the Measures are now changed, and they think them no longer bad, that therefore they are no Deserters of their Principle, if they now desist from Opposition.*—Confiding farther in the Ignorance of their Creatures, they make no scruple to throw into their general Charge against those who support the present Measures, many of those past Occurrences and Errors, which happened before their Time, which they formerly condemned, and which are now, (if not equally exploded) at least equally counter-acted both by the new and old Part of the Administration, and the Consequences of which they are now every Hour labouring to remedy and avert.—Thus wilfully misrepresenting every Measure, jumbling and confounding Facts and Dates, Names and Things, so crude and so irrational, that none but the lowest of the Vulgar could be able to digest them.

They proceeded with the same Diligence in the Execution of the third Article of this Plan,—for no sooner was any Gentleman, who had been engaged in the late Opposition, admitted into Employment, than Heaven and Earth were moved to prevent his Re-election. When they had once given over the Thoughts of being employed themselves, the Note was immediately changed; and it is a Matter never to be sufficiently admired, how stupidly the People, in many places, fell into their Views, without considering the Absurdity of what they were put upon to do. When the House adjourned, the Doctrine then was, as I have before observed, that a *Change of the Minister, and the Introduction of honest Men into Employments, were the utmost Objects of the People's Wish, and must in the end ensure whatever else was wanting.* But it seems, since the *Tories* were not to be admitted, no other Men were to be deemed honest. Nay, after a little time, when it was found, that those of more obnoxious Principles were abandoned to Despair, even a *Tory*, under these Circumstances, found it difficult to be permitted quietly to be rechosen—so silly were the *little Tools* of this *Faction*, as to delight in, and admire at the Wisdom and Integrity of a Maxim now established, that none of the *Party* should *have a Place*, till the Views of their *Great ones* were complied with first—They still went on calumniating the new Administration for not making Changes fast enough, when they themselves had shut the door against it, and when no Man, who was not willing to sacrifice his Fortune, by the vast Expence of a certain Opposition, or expose his Person to the dangerous Insults of the Mobs they raised upon every such occasion, could

accept.

accept.—Thus the People were brought to infift upon a Point, which, like Ideots, they were led at the fame time palpably to prevent themfelves.—I have not mifreprefented this Matter; it is well known, that this was the Method of their Proceeding to all Perfons without Diftinction, and they begun it, before any Man could have given poffibly any Reafon to be diftrufted by his Country, becaufe it was begun before the Parliament met again, after the famous Adjournment. *An honourable Gentleman*, (who by the greateft Number of Voices, that ever any Man had upon fuch an occafion, was elected *Chairman of the Committee of Elections* but a few Weeks before, who in that nice Conjuncture, for his unexceptionable Character, with regard to all Parties, was pitched upon for that Office by the whole Oppofition, who neither had, nor could have had, at that time, given a fingle Vote to diminifh that Reputation,) being advanced to be a Commiffioner of the *Admiralty* by his Majefty, (for no other reafon, but that he was thought agreeable to the People,) was immediately marked out, as an Object of Deteftation to his Country, and not fuffered to be chofen into Parliament again.—Another *Right Honourable Member* advanced to the fame Office, was perfecuted, if poffible, with more fcandalous Circumftances, the Mob of the whole County, for which he ferved, were hired to infult him.—Subfcriptions raifed out of the Pockets of the *whole Faction*, nay preffed publickly in the very *Houfe of Commons* to make a Purfe to carry on an Oppofition to him : Though at the fame time, this *Noble Perfon* was a Servant to the *firft Subject* of this Kingdom, preferred at his Requeft and Recommendation, and advanced as a kind of Pledge of Union between the Royal Family itfelf; and though *his Mafter* was confeffedly the Perfon by whofe Influence and Concurrence in the Caufe of his Country, the late Oppofition was principally brought to its Iffue, who had fuffered infinitely more in the Courfe of it, than the meaneft private Gentleman in the Kingdom, and who had done that for the Publick, which no Man in his Station ever did before him, which could not have been expected of *him*, and after this Treatment, muft never be expected of *any other* in the fame Situation.—Thus they gave fair Warning to the *Father*, by their Conduct to the *Son*, what he had to expect from this Set of Men, who, hardened by Difappointments of their own creating, infenfibly loft all regard, either to Prudence, Decency, or Gratitude.

I fhall not in this Place proceed to obferve minutely, upon the manner of executing all the other Particulars of their Plan, becaufe it required a confiderable time before they could ripen the People, into a fufficient degree of Madnefs, to endure thofe grofs Attempts upon their Underſtandings and their Principles, which they have ſince made with too much Succeſs. The Arts to be exerted to theſe Ends, were a little ſlow in Operation, and to be practiſed at firſt tenderly.—However, they ventured to found the Ground they ſtood upon, and to make ſome Trial, what Abſurdities the Temper of the Times would bear. &c.

In Order to do this, almoſt as ſoon as the Parliament was met, they began to oppoſe every ſingle Propoſition that was made by the new Adminiſtration ; and though now thoſe very Meaſures were purſued, with the utmoſt Vigour, upon which they themſelves, and the whole Voice of the People, had ſo long and vehemently inſiſted ; and for not purſuing which an En-quiry was actually ſet on foot, into the Conduct of the late Miniſter, who upon this account was, according to their own Doctrine, to make attonement by no leſs a Sacrifice than that of his *Life*, his *Eſtate*, his *Honours*, and the *utter Ruin* of his *Poſterity* ; yet with a bare-faced Aſſurance, which raiſed the Deteſtation and Aſtoniſhment of all reaſonable Men, and which was a very Mockery upon Common Senſe, they oppoſed the ſending 16,000 of our Troops into *Flanders*, the taking 4,000 of the *Iriſh* Troops upon the *Britiſh* Eſtabliſhment, to be ſent after the former, and even in ſome degree obſtructed the Vote for 500,000 *l.* to aſſiſt the Queen of *Hungary*.—It was viſible enough, and it had been their own Form of Reaſoning but a few Weeks before, that Meaſures of this kind, nay more vigorous, if poſ-ſible, were neceſſary to be taken in that deſperate Situation in which we then ſtood, to convince the *Dutch*, the King of *Sar-dinia*, and all foreign Powers, that we were now in earneſt. —The Experience they had long had of our Councils would not ſuffer them to truſt us lightly :—The Form of the *Dutch* Government in particular, made them ſlow to reſolve, and their Situation made it deſperate to engage, till they were ſure of a ſolid Support :—The King of *Sardinia* had heartily and generouſly ſtept into the Breach, but his Circumſtances were, if poſſible, ſtill more critical :—The Kings of *Pruſſia* and *Poland* neither could have ſtopped, if they would, nor probably would if they could, and muſt have been hurried on where *France* ſhould have directed, or their own Ambi-tion have invited ; if by the gathering of this Cloud, a Storm had not been threatned from the Quarter of *Great Britain*, which might have created both Doubts and Terror as to the Event of their Quarrel ; this was therefore the only way to induce them to be more moderate and circumſpect in their Proceedings. It was certain, that nothing leſs than this could ſuſtain the drooping Spirits of the Queen of *Hungary*, and of

her

her diftreffed and faithful Subjects, in the defperate Condition to which they were reduced ; it was therefore paft all doubt, that if thefe Meafures were not purfued, fhe muft immediately accommodate with *France* upon any Terms ; and that *France*, having broken the only Power, which could give her any Diverfion in an Attempt upon *Great-Britain*, would have been immediately at Liberty to have joined her whole Power with that of *Spain*, and to have given Law to us :—This approaching Situation of our Affairs was but too vifible; nor was it at all extravagant, or very remote to forefee, that it would become much worfe ; that fome of the Northern Powers might be induced to enter into her Views, and that even the *Dutch* might, at length, be obliged to act as Inftruments to the long premeditated Defign of that dangerous People, to deftroy the Religion, Laws, Liberties and Commerce of this Nation.— This was plainly not to be averted by any other Means than thefe, and yet were thefe oppofed, though at firft in fo aukward a Manner, that it was vifible they were afraid the People would be fhocked at this fudden Turn, and detect their fhameful Inconfiftency,—which juft Effect indeed it had with fome ; yet with fo many it fucceeded beyond their Expectations, that it encouraged them to a Conduct of the fame kind, fo extravagant, in the next Seffions of Parliament, as will hardly obtain Belief in future Ages.—But the Order of Time, which is neceffary to obferve in this Narration, prevents my giving a farther Deduction of it in this Place.

I fhall take the Liberty however to follow them in fome other Branches of their Conduct, as far as they went for the Remainder of that Seffions, during which they acted conftantly with due Regard to one or other of the Rules of that Plan before mention.

The Lords having thrown out [a] *a Bill* which the Commons had paffed, and which was by them thought neceffary to be carried at that Time, they made a daring Attempt againft that Body, —they appointed a Committee to infpect their Journals, and grounded upon their Report a Vote of Cenfure upon that Branch of the Legiflature,—they fortunately mifcarried in that Attempt, in which, if they had fucceeded, the utmoft Confufion muft have enfued, and Confufion muft have been their only View, for what elfe could be intended, when under the Notion of obliging the Lords to follow their Opinion, without which they pretended the Nation could not be fafe in future, they openly made an Attempt for an immediate Diffolution of

[a] The Bill for indemnifying the Evidence againft the Earl of *Orford*.

the

the Conftitution.—Is the Conftitution now fo little underftood, or has Popular Fury fo deftroyed all Traces of it, that it fhould be neceffary to explain its Principles at this Day?—Is it not founded upon *this*, which is the *Corner-Stone* of the whole Buildding, that the *King*, the *Lords*, and the *Commons*, *fhould have an abfolute Negative upon the Proceedings of each other?*—With what Face then can they, who pretend to ftruggle in favour of the Conftitution, by endeavouring to make the Houfe of Commons more independant than it is, at the fame Time attack the Houfe of Lords, to deprive them totally of the fame Independancy, to which no man can deny that they have an equal Right; fuppofing that they were ever fo juftly founded, and entitled to procure further Securities for the Houfe of Commons, it is an incontrovertible Fact, that by this avowed Attempt, and indeed by all the Doctrines of late inftilled into the Minds of the People, they aim at the Deftruction of the Conftitution in another Part, which is equally Effential,—the beft Pretenfions they therefore have, are only thefe; that they build with *one* Hand, and pull down with *another*; and that while they ftop one Breach againft the Influence of the Crown, they open a wider, to the Democratical Spirit of the People, —the Conftitution *may*, nay, it *has*, fuffered equally from *both* —but what renders it doubly ridiculous, is, that the Crown will equally be able to enter in at the one Breach as at the other,— and every thinking Man may eafily foretel, that by what Steps foever this Conftitution comes to be deftroyed, an abfolute Power in a fingle Perfon, muft be the final Confequence, —this Conduct therefore plainly opens to us, how falfe their Pretences to the Conftitution were, equally falfe with every other they have made.—For however, at times, both the King, the Lords, and the Commons, in their Turn, may have obftructed what was for the publick Good by this negative Power. —Yet this is no more than what muft, and ever will be, the Confequence of a Divifion of Power in this Conftitution. — And if, whenever Power is in any degree abufed, it is immediately to be deftroyed.—No Government can ftand, for no Power can be given, but that it is liable to be fometimes exerted ill; yet furely no Man will venture to deny, that it is better to fubmit to fome unavoidable Events of Society, than to revert into a State of Nature; but this the People were too much heated to confider.—It was inculcated, that all Power ought to lie in the People, which, if it be righty underftood, implies, the People, including all its Magiftrates and Members, of which both the King and the Lords are undoubtedly a part.—But if it be taken in the confined Senfe of Fac-

H   tion

tion, imports a Republican Propofition, wholly contradictory to the Genius and the Principles of this Government; nay, if the People confidered this as they ought to do, fo far from being incenfed either with the *Lords* or with the *Crown*, for oppofing the Popular Points, which they have fometimes obftructed, they would not think themfelves intitled fo much as **to** repine at it,—they would confider, that as they have a Title by the Laws of this Country, to fuch Powers in the State as they now enjoy, they are under no fort of Obligation to part with them to the third Eftate,—that this impetuofity to force them to it, is not only the ftrongeft Provocation, but alfo no infufficient Reafon to keep the Ground they have, that naturally fpeaking, by their permanent Intereft in the Legiflature, their impoffibility of ever becoming Mafters of the State, and their evident Intereft to keep both the Crown and the People from too great an Afcendancy; the Lords are the Part of the Conftitution, who are moft likely to be fincere in its Prefervation, either from Tyranny or Faction, and therefore the moft proper to hold the Balance.—The Intereft of the Lords is undoubtedly to watch and carefully attend to both, for both may in fome Conjunctures, be fufpected to defire to engrofs the whole Power;—and whenever they throw themfelves into either the one or the other Scale, a rational Man would fooner judge by their Conduct, how the State of the Conftitution ftands, than by any other Circumftance.—It was intended, they fhould do this, and be at full Liberty to do it; though fuch muft be (and it ever was) their Fate, that which-ever Party they efpoufe, whether that of the Crown, or of the People, the Heat and Paffion of the other will infallibly find fome Pretences of Partiality or private Intereft to charge them with, as their Inducements to that Conduct.—But they are made to ftand to all this, and they muft ftand this, and be fupported in it, or elfe our Conftitution cannot ftand.—This defperate Meafure however paffed upon the People, like the reft of their Conduct, as a generous attempt for Liberty, and anfwered the Purpofe of Popularity, which, next to the View of Confufion, was their fecond Expectation from it.

We now come to the popular Bills, with which the People have been fo much inflamed; of thefe I fhall take the lefs Notice in this Place, becaufe I have referved my felf to fay fomething farther in the Conclufion with regard to them.—But, tho' I fhall not here enter much into the Merits of thefe Bills, I muft fpeak a little of the Conduct of the *Faction*, with regard to them which cannot be paffed over, becaufe their Impofition upon the People was extremely grofs, and their Difhonefty in imputing the Failure of them, (fo far as they have failed) to thofe who are

far

far more innocent in this Respect than themselves: They are chiefly comprehended in *a Law for the better Regulation of Elections*, another *to prevent Members from sitting in the House of Commons, who have Pensions from the Crown*, in *the Repeal of the Septennial Act*, and *a Law to exclude a certain Number of Placemen from sitting in the House of Commons*. - Now, as to the first of these, it is notorious to the whole House of Commons, that it was a Bill, as much laboured by the Gentlemen of the new Administration, and many of those, who now support the Measures of the Government, as it could possibly be,—and that they were sincere, is evident, by what has been since done with regard to the *Scotch* Elections in the last Sessions;—the true Reason therefore that a general Bill did not pass at that Time, was one which equally affected all Parties, and which will everlastingly prevent an effectual Bill of this kind; and this is the different Rights of Election, which are so numerous, that they distract and confound the different Interests of Gentlemen, which, to speak fairly on all Sides, induces them, by one plausible Pretence or other, for their private Regard, to *oppose*, or to *propose*, so many different Clauses, that such Bills at length become impracticable and impalatable to all—the Burgage Tenures too, which Gentlemen will neither part with, nor can tell how to regulate, are another invincible Obstruction; and the Powers and the Penalties create further Difficulties, which no Human Wisdom has yet been able to surmount.—For this Reason therefore, to impute the Failure of this Bill to any Set of Men, is notoriously unjust, unless it were by laying it in some Measure more severely upon some particular Gentlemen of the *Faction* itself, who contributed more eminently than others to confound that Part of it, which related to certain Counties, where they laboured to encrease the overgrown and almost unconstitutional Interest they have already. --*As to the Pension Bill*, it is a Bill allowed in private by all Parties to be impossible to take Effect, because the giving and taking of Gratuities of this kind are Transactions of so private a Nature, that Men must be downright Fools, and both Parties unite to make a Discovery against themselves, or the Law could take no effect.—Even in the Case, that Perjury must attend the Acceptance of a Pension, it might induce some profligate Men to double their Crime, — but it is not to be supposed, that he who would sell his Country, would hesitate to violate his Oath.—However, this was the only possible Provision, and upon this Footing, an honourable Gentleman now in the Administration, often presented it to the House;—but the great Care of the present Patriots would not trust it any more in his Hands, after he was taken into Employment, and a wise and busy

Man

Man among them took it upon himfelf, who being a true **Tory**, and therefore of a refined Confcience, and naturally prejud·ced to Oaths, purged it of its deteftable Whig Claufe, which reduced it to a mere nothing, a Law without a Penalty, fo that the Bill became a Jeft with all Parties, and many in that light voted for it *then*, who had always oppofed it *before*.—The Bill therefore fell into contempt, and was no longer regarded by any one, but him who had garbled it in this judicious manner.—Having thus related the fecret Hiftory of this popular Bill, I have only to add, that it is for the Intereft of the Publick it fhould never pafs into a Law, and was never defired by any Man of Senfe that it fhould ;—and yet that it is for the Intereft of the Publick, that it fhould be frequently propofed in the Houfe of Commons, which double Confideration may render it very confiftent for the fame Man, to vote for it at one time, and to vote againft it at another,—this may feem a Paradox ; but it is eafily ex-plained ;—for by frequently bringing it into debate, the De-teftation and Scandal of fo bafe a Practice, is maintained in its full Vigour, which is in reality the only Guard againft it.— Whereas, if the Bill were once paffed, the great Nothing, which is defired, being effected, there would be no farther Difcourfe upon the Subject ; thofe Oppoitunities of expofing the Meannefs and the Danger of the Thing, thofe animating anniverfary Speeches againft it would be loft ; and with them in a great degree, the Remorfe and Shame, that now attend the Crime.— We come in the next place to confider, the Behaviour of thefe Gentlemen with regard to *the Repeal of the Septennial Law*, in which they have deluded the People fcandaloufly : It is true, that they moved for this Repeal, and that fome of the Gentle-men in the Adminiftration oppofed it ; but they did it upon a Confideration, which ought to have, and will have the greateft Weight with every thinking Man ; they took juft Notice of the tempeftuous Temper of the People at that Time, and the yet unfettled Condition of our Affairs ; they then obferved, that the Repeal of this Law muft caufe a new general Election before it could be poffible that thefe Diforders fhould fubfide, and be-fore they could make any folid Judgment of the effects of the late Change ; that as every new Election hazarded, at leaft, the Syftem of the Time ; foreign Nations would not exert them-felves in this Conjuncture ; from a Dependance on the Principles of Men, who might probably be changed, and confequently new Politicks prevail, almoft as foon as they had been embarked with us ;——That as the like Confiderations had juftified the Meafures of the Septennial Law at the Time it was made, fo the Conjuncture of this Time might prevail, at leaft fo far, as

to

to continue till it might be debated fairly, and with lefs Heat
and Partiality, than it could poffibly be at this Period, whether
the prefent Eftablifhment of Parliaments fhould ftand ; and, if
that fhould appear improper, whether we fhould fix upon an
Annual or a Triennial Election ;—that a Triennial was objected to with ftrong Reafon, and that many thought an annual
would be lefs dangerous ; but that it was difficult to fettle either
in the prefent diverfity of Opinions upon it :—At the fame time,
fome of the *principal Leaders of the Faction* voted againft it
themfelves, and that *without giving any Reafon at all* ; fo that
the People were deferted in it, by thofe very Men, upon whom
they depended to carry it through, and who with a bafe Con-
cealment of this Fact, make no fcruple to lay the Mifcarriage
of this Bill, in which they had, at leaft, an equal Share, folely
to the new Adminiftration.—We now come to the *Place-Bill*,
in which their Conduct was deteftable, for jealous of the Honour and the Popularity, which the new Adminiftration naturally ought to have acquired by it, they not only falfely mifreprefented it in the moft outragious manner, but even openly
oppofed it : The new Adminiftration had acted in this with
the utmoft Prudence and Sincerity, and had done much more
than could have been expected of them.—The *Crown* and
the *Lords* are known to be jealous of the Growth of the *popular Intereft*, and it is by mutual Jealoufies of this kind, that
our Conftitution can alone fubfift ; the Violence and Extravagance of the Leaders of the Faction did not diminifh this Jealoufy ; the Courfe of the late Elections, and the Temper of
the People, not only fhewed it lefs neceffary than it had been
conceived before by many well-meaning Men, but their Demands were fo unlimited, and fo little Contentment fhewn
with former Compliances, that there was in truth very little
Profpect of regaining the good old Temper of the Nation by
any thing that could be done ;—this rendered it the more difficult to obtain any thing ; for it was well known, that no
Bill brought in by thefe Incendiaries, would be moderate e-
nough to gain the Affent of the three Eftates ; it was therefore
the only Method that could be taken to enter into a tacit Treaty
with the Lords, to agree upon fome Bill of this nature, which
they fhould previoufly engage not to reject.—It was furely better to procure fomething, than by pufhing for more to get nothing. The Lords agreed to this :—They confented not to
oppofe a Law, that fhould exclude above thirteen confiderable
Employments then actually enjoyed by Members of Parliament, and above two hundred fmaller Offices ; which, by con-
ferring three or four upon one Perfon, might have made a vaft
Number

Number of additional Preferments, a Thing still in the Power
of the Crown, notwithstanding any former Laws, to have
done.—But at the same time, they absolutely declared they
would go no further at that time, till they had seen how far
this would operate upon the Constitution :—This Difficulty
removed, it was necessary to gain the Consent of the House of
Commons too ; but the *Opposition*, by their Breach with the
new Administration, had been so weakened, and the Friends of
the *old* had now rallied to such a degree, that there was no
carrying any Point by Force against them.   Thirteen or fourteen of that Party, who were more than sufficient to have
turned the Scale against the Bill, were, as we have before observed, of the Number to be excluded by it ; it could not be
expected that they would abandon their Employments instant-
ly, to pleasure their Antagonists ; the only way possible to
gain their Consent, was to postpone the Execution of this Law
to the End of the present Parliament : The deferring its Execution for six Years was not material to the Constitution, and
it was thought by all moderate Men, a great Sacrifice in his
Majesty, a Condescension in the Lords, and an honest Acquiescence in the Persons possessed of these Employments ; in the
one to resign so much of his *Prerogative*, in the other to
strengthen the *opposite Side of the Balance*, and in the third to
part with their *Employments*, which they had a Prospect to
preserve much longer than that Term.   The Impossibility
therefore of gaining more, if more had been palpably necessary, must have justified the new Administration for getting
this : But what made it more infamous to reproach them upon this Head was, that it was actually more than was ever
gained by the People, at any one Time, or by any one Bill
before :—The other Acts for limiting the Number of Placemen in the House of Commons were all of them obtained one
after the other, and at different Periods ; though more therefore had been still wanting, they ought to have contented
themselves for a Time with this, as their Predecessors had done
in the like Conjunctures :—But the *popular Spirit* disgraced itself upon this Occasion, and suffering itself to be led away by
Men, who studied nothing but their private Ends, gave too
just handle for that Insinuation, which must be most fatal to
all *its Views*, and for a Charge upon the *People* of *England*,
which has been too justly laid against all others, that give
them one Thing it only leads them to expect more, and that
nothing but a total Translation of all Power to their Scale will
put a Period to their Clamour : What therefore was done by
the Faction in this Instance, was visibly done only with a View
to destroy the good Opinion of a Law, the most truly popular,

that

that was ever obtained by this Nation; if they could effect this, they did not care what the People loft by it, either in their real Security, or in the Suspicions, that would arise with thinking Men, of their dangerous Views against the Constitution; they knew (which is absolutely the Cafe to this Day) that not one Man in 500, whom they should enflame upon this Subject, would ever read, or consider the real Extent, of this Law; they suggested to the People, that the new Gentlemen in the Administration had formerly contended for *a total Exclufion* of all Employments; and thence imputed an Inconsistency to them, because they had now excluded what they *falsely* called a *few*, whereas this never had been the View, nor ever was intended by those Gentlemen at any time: They never contended for a Place-Bill much more extensive than the present is, and yet it may be justly supposed, that they did, and might honestly insist upon more than they thought sufficient, as the only way to obtain a Compromise at last, for that which was.

This Plan of creating Confusion was pursued in many other Respects, and by many other Misrepresentations equally gross and wicked; which are too tedious to be mentioned here :— The last I shall mention in this Place, is that with regard to the Enquiry into the Administration of the Earl of *Orford*.

We have shewn already how juft Offence his Conduct had given to the *Whigs*, and how by a fatal Series of pacifick Measures he had brought almost the fame Cataftrophe upon his Country, which fome day or other will too probably be effected by another Set of Men.—The *Whigs* avowed their Opposition to be levelled at this Man, not out of any personal Averfion to him, but because he was irreclaimable in this fatal Point; the *Whigs* had levelled at this Man for another Reafon, which was, during the Courfe of this neceffary Opposition, to prevent the Difcontents from taking a Turn to the Prejudice of the Royal Family, and had confined themfelves in their Attack to his Perfon, that by the Removal of one Man they might leave it in the power of the Government to reftore the publick Tranquillity again whenever they should think proper :—It was therefore upon an honeft, though political Principle, that their Opposition was thus perfonal; not out of thofe vindictive and fanguinary Views, which in the Courfe of the Opposition the *Tories*, who had allied themfelves with them, treacherously in private Difcourfe accufed them of, and which now they upbraid them with having departed from.— Yet allowing that fome Men in their firft Engagements in the late Opposition, had embarked upon perfonal Motives, and had

been

I

been heated to this Degree by their Refentments, or the Dif-appointment of their Ambition, fhall it be forbidden to Age, Experience, Reafon, Virtue and Reflection, to take their happy Effect, and moderate thofe Paffions, which are in themfelves wicked and unwarrantable; and fhall it be imputed as a Crime to any Man to have facrificed his private Views and his Refent-ments, as fome have greatly done upon this late Change, to the Peace and Tranquillity of their Country: But it is the Na-ture of thefe Men in their *Alliances*, to expofe the *Faults* of thofe, with whom they act, and in their *Enmity* to traduce the *Virtue* of thofe they act againft.

However, though the *Whigs* in the late Oppofition did not mean to purfue their Vengeance to the Head of this Minifter, they certainly did mean to deprive him of all his Power, and to fet fome Mark upon him that might prevent his Return into it again, and if poffible deter any future Minifter from the fame unhappy Conduct.—One Part of this they have been able to effect, and it is the moft immediately neceffary, and the moft material; and we fhall honeftly fhew the Reafons why they did not compafs the reft,—Reafons very fufficient to fupport them againft all the infamous Suggeftions of the Faction.—I fhall fpeak with Freedom and with Candour.

Whoever duly confiders the Courfe of the Mifmanagements of this Man, of which I have purpofely given a large Deduc-tion, will evidently fee, that the infamous Peace of *Utrecht*, in which it is well known he had no hand, naturally laid their firft Foundation,—the Diforders arifing afterwards from the unfettled State of *Europe*, brought on the *Quadruple Alliance*, that, in Procefs of Time, begot the Treaty of *Hanover*, and from the Treaty of *Hanover*, by the fatal Blunder of joining *France* againft the Houfe of *Auftria*, he became involved in fuch Difficulties, as he could never recover —But ruinous as, to fpeak fairly, all his future Meafures were, they were of fuch a Nature, as could not be imputed to any corrupt En-gagements with any foreign Power, upon which Ground a-lone the Publick think it warrantable to purfue him to Deftruc-tion.—I muft repeat it, the very Nature of his imprudent Conduct clears him from a Sufpicion of this; he proceeded round the Globe, obliging and difobliging every Power of *Eu-rope* in its Turn.—This he reiterated fo often, and provoked them all fo much, that it is morally impoffible, the Refent-ments of thefe Powers, fhould not have produced a Difcovery of this Treafon, if any fuch there had been.

This is palpably the Fact, this is honeftly the Truth, with regard to his *Foreign* Tranfactions, and every *Domeftick* Sub-ject of Complaint naturally flowed from the fame Spring.

For

For Oppofition grew infenfibly fo ftrong upon this untoward Step, that it drove him to practife any Art, to defend not only his Power, but his Perfon,—his pacifick Obftinacy became at length in a manner neceffary both to himfelf and to his Country;—he dreaded the Confufion which he apprehended from a Change,—the Event hath fhewn he had fome Reafon, tho' he blended his private Fears too much with his Apprehenfions for the Publick—an Error which every Man's Tendernefs to himfelf expofes him to,—he forefaw what has fince happened, that even a juft, a neceffary, and a fuccefsful War, nay, a War demanded by the whole Nation, would fecure no Minifter, who engaged in it, from the Difcontents, which the bare Expences, and much more the various Accidents that attended it, would infallibly create.—That private Views, and corrupt Principles, influence fo great a Majority in every Oppofition, that though the Points were complied with, upon which they then infifted, they would ftill, in general perfevere; that they would even mifreprefent the Conduct of their own Plan, and that however fcandalous it is for a Nation to prefs its Government into Meafures, and to defert them when engaged, yet that in the heated Multitude, the Majority are compofed of Men, in whom fuch Scruples are not found.—He foretold, what has been fo well verified, that the Enemies of their Country, however low and dead they may appear in Times of Quiet, revive in the Heat of War, like Flies and noxious Infects in the Sun. He therefore thought that in attempting to appeafe the publick Difcontents, by complying with their Demands for War, he fhould only furnifh Fuel for their farther Nourifhment.—He knew, that by the fatal Confequences of *Party*, National *Diffatisfaction* is, in this Country, very nearly allied to *Difaffection*,—as much as he at firft defpifed the *Tories*, he dreaded them as much at laft,—he juftly feared that the Succefs of the *Party* that oppofed, though led by *Whig Leaders*, and founded upon *Whig Principles*, would infallibly end in the Formation of a *Tory Faction*; and he dreaded, from that Faction, what every wife and honeft Man dreads from it in this Conjuncture, and what we fhould have already fatally experienced, if fome, from whom perhaps he leaft expected this Moderation, had not gallantly oppofed themfelves to the Torrent, thinking it the more incumbent upon them to reftrain its Fury, and confine it within juft Bounds, as they, (though honeftly and neceffarily compelled to it,) had been the Men who raifed it, preferring the folid Satisfaction of having twice faved their Country, to all the Noife of giddy Popularity, refigning it when they could no longer keep it by virtuous

Means, defpifing the Rage and Malice of a *Faction*, fincerely pitying, but determined not to follow an honeft, but deluded People, who after pafling many Dangers, and perhaps fmarting for their Folly, will live to do Juftice to the great Characters, they now licentioufly and injurioufly defame.

Thefe were the Principles upon which the Earl of *Orford* went, and this was the whole Myftery of his unfortunate Adminiftration.—It is eafy to point out both his *Follies* and his *Faults*.—His *Folly* was to lay down for this Country, a Syftem prudent for a petty State, but very improper for a Country, which bears fo great a Sway, and ought to take the Lead in *Europe*.—It is for a little State to purfue little Meafures, to temporize, to truft to Expedients and Events, to wait for Accidents, and the Activity of other Powers. But this is a Policy ill becoming us, and fatal ever in its Confequence, both to ourfelves and to our natural Allies, whofe Rank and Condition of Power compels them to confider an immediate Security, and can never admit them to exert their Force againft that *State*, whofe conftant Aim is Univerfal Monarchy, till we raife the Standard firft, and convince them, that under that Protection they may do it fafely. His *Folly* appeared in another Inftance, in not yielding fooner to what he could not hope long to prevent, an Evil which gathered Strength, and became more dangerous by Delay, and by the Means he was obliged to ufe in order to delay it.—His *Fault* lay in his Fondnefs to continue in his Power, which induced him, or mifled him, to overlook the true Intereft of his Royal Mafter, and his Country, and to purfue the Maxim of Peace to a ridiculous Extravagance. By this *France* was raifed,—by this our Allies were ruined,—by this the Safety of *Brittain* was reduced into the utmoft Hazard, —and by this his Country became contemptible abroad, and hateful at home ; till, to fupport his Syftem, and to preferve his Perfon, he was at length driven to make ufe of every Means of Minifterial Influence, to ftrain every Nerve of Power, allotted by the Wifdom of our Anceftors for the Security of Government, and to apply that Force to his own Defence.——By all this he has brought the neceffary Guards of our Conftitution into Difrepute, and has eftablifhed an Opinion in many, and a Sufpicion in more, that our Conftitution is impaired ; whereas, in truth, it has only been abufed,—a Difference extremely great, and fuch, as if not attended juftly to, may hurry us into the Ufe of Remedies much worfe than the Difeafe. In this Light does the Conduct of this Minifter appear to every moderate Man, and no doubt in a yet more favourable Light to thofe who were his Friends, who had concurred in his Meafures many Years, who owed him many Obligations.—Never

was

was a Man in private Life more beloved, and his worst Enemies allow, no Man did ever in private Life deserve it more:
—He was humane and grateful, and a generous Friend, to all
whom he did not think would abuse that Friendship.—
That he was false, and determined to the Prejudice of those,
whom he considered in this Light, is no more than will be
found in any Minister or Man,—and that he should be deceived in some Cases, by unjust Suspicions, is but human too.
—Many therefore have been unjustly treated by him, though
but few considering the Manner in which he was pressed, and
the great Length of his Administration.—This Character naturally procured that Attachment to his Person, which has
been falsely attributed solely to a corrupt Influence, and to
private Interest ; but this shewed itself at a time when these
Principles were very faint in their Operation, and when his
Ruin seemed inevitable.—The Violence with which he was
pushed, the Ferment of the People, who would content themselves with nothing but his Life, made these Men exert themselves in the extraordinary manner they have done to preserve
him.—Many, who condemned his Conduct, and would have
gone so far as to have deprived him of a Possibility of exerting
the same again, did not think it warrantable to take that severe Revenge, upon an obstinate mistaken Man, who had indeed violated the Interests of his Country, and trespassed upon
the Power in his Hands, but who had not exposed himself to
the Penalty of any one known Law.—This *Summum Jus*, appeared to them to be *Summa Injuria*, and the Laws must have
been more tortured to have reached him capitally, than he had
strained his Power to maintain himself·—Yet had he not been
defended in the manner in which he was, (offensive enough to
those who consider the *Manner*, and not the *End*) such a
Sentence, in the Rage of that Time, had been, in all Probability, his Fate.—Few were in their Hearts inclined to this
Extremity, though many, by the fatal Attraction of Party,
might have been drawn to have signed his Warrant, who would
have afterwards heartily lamented what they had done.—Had
it been even necessary to have taken this violent Step, there is
in *Englishmen*, as sure a Season for Compassion as for Fury: —
To the *latter*, they are easily *raised*—from the *former*, when
the Deed is done, they never can be *diverted.* An Administration *founded* in, or a Party *cemented* by *Blood*, would have
been the *Loathing* of this *Nation*, and in this case would have
been so *justly.*—If this be truly considered, was it not more honest, was it not more just, to stop short, without even that
Punishment, which perhaps very many think was due, than

to

to have carried that Punifhment fo far, as to have fixed the
Guilt of Murther upon this Nation.---And lefs than Murther
it can hardly be, to take the Life of any Man, which no Law
of this Land could have taken from him.---Thefe Confiderations operated with fo many, that had it been ever fo juft, it
was not practicable to have gone farther with him ;---the other
Members of the Legiflature reafoned firmly upon the Reflections I have mentioned, the Majority of the Houfe of Commons
thought fo too.---The farther Purfuit might have therefore been
an Amufement to the Multitude ; but it was not for *that alone*
reafonable to perfift in it, as no good End could follow from
it, the Effect could have only been Confufion, and a Handle to
blacken and reproach the Characters of Men, whom Gratitude,
Principle, and juft Scruple with-held, and who were fixed to
with-hold for ever.---All that I have here obferved is, not out
of any affected Tendernefs or Complaifance to him, or to his
Friends, but only to fhew how natural it was to have met the
Obftruction in this Point that has been found, and how impoffible it was, to have proceeded farther with this Minifter, than
was done by the new Adminiftration.---We have feen, that the
very Men, who reflect upon them for it, had been by their intemperate Behaviour the great Caufe why the Party of the late
Minifter had rallied. Their Violence in this Particular, was
the finifhing Stroke ;---no other Point could have united his
Friends in the fame Degree.---It was obvious, after the firft
Experiment, that this muft have been the Cafe ; opiniatring
this Matter further, therefore manifeftly proves, that they
meant nothing, but to make this Man's Caufe an Engine of Se-
dition, by which they laboured, to render a Perfon, who *in
Power* had done *great Prejudice* to his Country, the *total Ruin*
of it *in his Fall*. I fhall conclude, with regard to this Particular, with only one Obfervation, That of all Men living, the
Tories have the leaft Reafon to vilify his Conduct.---Firft, becaufe it was the Diforders caufed by their wicked Conduct in
the Peace of *Utrecht*, that firft laid the Foundation of all the
Errors of this Minifter.---Secondly, Becaufe the *Whigs* had not
proceeded in this fanguinary Way, againft a Minifter of their
Faction, whofe Conduct had been directly levelled againft his
Country, and who had affifted in a Plan for effecting that
which at leaft appears, to every *Whig*, the greateft of all
Crimes, the advancing a *Popifh Prince* upon the Throne, and
facrificing every Thing to *France*, to compafs this pernicious
View.---And, Thirdly, Becaufe they had *themfelves* ftopt fhort
but the Year before, upon a Motion which tended only to remove the Minifter from Power ;---their Behaviour therefore
againft

against the Minister in the present Time, shews, first, That they are without Shame; secondly, That they are void of Gratitude; thirdly, That they are false in their pretended Zeal, and consequently, that their Behaviour upon this Head ought to be odious to every Man, who has any Sense of Virtue, Honesty, or Honour; but their Point was to misrepresent the new Administration, and the same Desire of Misrepresentation, led them to fall soon after, without Mercy, on the Characters of the Members of the Secret Committee, some of whom, not long after, obtained Employments, which they thirsted after themselves, and the View of which was so apparently one of the Grounds of their own Opposition.----This they pretended to be a Proof of Treachery and Corruption, in the Persons upon whom they were conferred; whereas the just Reflection to be made upon it, was most pleasing to all well-meaning Men, since it was a convincing Evidence, that the Prince upon the Throne bore no Resentment even to those of his Subjects, who were engaged in the deepest manner against his late Minister, when he was once satisfied, that they were not tainted in their Principles, either to himself, or to the Constitution of their Country.

Thus it was, that the Faction proceeded as soon as they lost sight of their private Advantages, and the Prospect of a *Tory Administration*.—Every one of their Proceedings visibly appeared to tally with the Conduct of the same Faction in all former Times:—They could not be mistaken, and there wanted nothing to fix it upon them, but direct Attempts to poison the People, with regard to the Prince upon the Throne, and to the Royal Family.—This farther Evidence was not long deficient, for even before that Sessions was over, the Publick swarmed with such Seditious and Treasonable Libels, and impudent Productions, both in Verse and Prose, as never had been endured in any Age or Nation, which, encouraged by Impunity, have since risen to a Point that calls aloud for signal Punishment.— But to what it arrived at last, is not yet Time to relate; it was not till the next Sessions, that the Mask was compleatly taken off, and the Method I have laid down obliges me, first, *to observe the Conduct of the new Administration during the Interval of Parliament, the Success of their Measures, and the Difference that appeared in the Situation of our Affairs at the second Meeting of the Parliament.*

Now, as to the Conduct of these Gentlemen in the Administration, and those who have acted with them, it appears undeniably, from what we have already shewn with regard to the *Faction*, that they could act no other Part than to form the Measures of the Government.—First, Because these Measures were their own, they were directed by themselves, and it is a palpable Abfurdity for an Adminiftration to oppofe itfelf. Secondly, Becaufe nothing but Ruin could have enfued, either *at Home* or *Abroad*, if they had not defifted when they did.

For if they had not defifted when the Minifter was removed, and when the Direction of the Meafures was left to them,—one Month's Continuance of the former Adminiftration, muft have deftroyed the Houfe of *Auftria* without Redemption,—and they had been much more criminal even than the late Minifter himfelf, if they had neglected this Opportunity to fave it, and refufed when it was in their power to do it;—again, if they had declined the Acceptance of this Power when it was thus offered to them, what equal, or what other Benefit could have accrued to their Country by it?

It is obvious that nothing but Confufion at home could have been effected by it.—Their Party had been broken wilfully by the intemperate Conduct of the Faction; and it is abfurd to imagine that Parties thus broken can be ever reunited:—By the Effects of their Madnefs, the Minifterial Party, which had never been vanquifhed, and had only retreated, were now rallied, and as they were before equal, were now as vifibly fuperior in the Houfe of Commons, as they had been all the Time before in the Houfe of Lords, and in another Place;—the reafonable and the moderate Men had already, or certainly would have left them; and if a civil War had happened, every Man of Family and Fortune had been driven from them by it. Now that a civil War had been the Confequence, is the Opinion of every Man of Experience in this Country: The Symptoms of it never appeared fo ftrong in any Period of our Hiftory; many knew this who concealed it, and ridiculed the Apprehenfion, refolving to run all Rifques for their private Advantage, and many more becaufe it was the only probable Way of fucceeding in the great View peculiar to their Faction.—Convulfions of this kind are never forefeen by the Generality of Men; for if they were, they could not poffibly happen, becaufe Faction would be deferted before it could proceed fo far: The People of *England* were drawn on to the great Rebellion by the very fame Pretences, with which they were now encouraged to perfift; they were told that the oppofite Side would yield if they continued firm:—None or very few of the Parliament of 1641 thought that the King either would or could have refifted: Sir *Benjamin Rudyard*, a very leading Man in the Oppofition of that Time, upon his Death-Bed grievoufly lamented that he had been deceived by *Pymm* and *Hamden* into this Opinion; *Whitlocke*, another of that Stamp, ftrongly obferves this Management in the Faction of that Age; both Lord *Clarendon* and *Whitlocke*, and indeed

all

all the other confiderable Hiftorians of that Time, agree upon it, and remark the Aftonifhment of the whole Nation, when the King took the Field, and the Battle of *Edge-hill* was fought; that they began forely to repent, but it was then too late, and they were obliged to go on:—Now if a King of *England* at that Time, who had ftrained Prerogative fo high, who had manifeftly declared his Pretenfions to abfolute Power, who had galled both the Poor and Rich, and had ruled with a Rod of Iron, could have ftood his ground fo well, and during that Conteft frequently brought his Antagonift to the Brink of Ruin, and his People to the Verge of an irredeemable Bondage, what Man can think fo bafely of his Countrymen in this Age, as to imagine, that a Prince would now find no Friends, who has ftrictly made the Laws of this Land the fole Rule of his Government from the Beginning of his Reign; under whom no one Inftance of illegal Conduct can be alledged, and againft whom nothing was pretended to be urged, but the having upheld too long a Minifter, who was odious, (whether juftly or unjuftly, no matter which,) to his Country; when even this had been done in a legal Way, nay when that Minifter had been actually removed at the preffing Inftances of the People, and before the Majority of either Houfe of Parliament had pronounced him guilty of any Crime:—This Opinion therefore is very weak, and weaker ftill when we compare that Time with this. There was then no *Pretender* to the Throne, from whom a Change of Religion, and a Confifcation of Eftates might be expected, which Fears would operate upon many now, and cannot fail to tye a mighty Number fteady to this Family; that Prince had no Revenues, and he had no Army; the prefent Prince has both: And though he neither could nor would employ either to enflave his People, he undoubtedly would and could exert them in his own juft Defence, and in that of the Conftitution of his Kingdoms; and he would be warranted before God and Man to do it:—But would any Man of Senfe, any Man who fincerely loved his Country, defire to drive things to this Extremity?—It is vain to flatter and cheat the People with an affected Tendernefs for Liberty, when they prefs fo furioufly to put it upon fuch an Iffue:—It needs no *Solomon* to pafs a Judgment to which of the two Parents this Child belongs.

In truth there was no Poffibility for an honeft Man in his right Senfes to act any longer with this Party, when it was notorious by their Conduct, and by their Declarations in their Meetings to fupport what they called the *Broad-Bottom*, that their Conteft was not only fo in Fact, but avowed to be for private Profit and Employments. When in that Conjuncture, all the

Cry

Cry againſt thoſe, who were firſt taken in, was grounded ſingly upon the Non-admiſſion of all the *Tories*, and others of known worſe Principles ; had it been either wiſe or honeſt to have ſtopt that Settlement of our Affairs ſo infinitely neceſſary to prevent Ruin Abroad and Confuſion at Home, for the ſake of any private Men whatever, and much more for the ſake of Men of ſuch a Character? It had been already done in ſome Degree ; it was earneſtly wiſhed to have done it farther ; It might have been prudent in ſuch a Time, to have gratified even the private and corrupt Views of ſome for the Publick Tranquillity ; and it would have been done, if the publick Safety could have ſuffered it ; in proportion as the Moderation of Particulars could have allowed : But the Violence of the Faction put it beyond Diſcretion, and out of the Power of Government to do it. Their Conduct fully confirmed all former Suſpicions ; the Demand was too general to be complied with ; the Execution expected too ſuddenly ; the Nature of it too diſguſtful to diſpoſe the Heart of any generous Man to yield.   There is a Degree of private Intereſt, which may, which muſt be allowed to human Nature.   It is not Honeſty but Folly to decline any Advantages, which are not procured by any Sacrifice of Principle, or any other unworthy Means ; but when it appears barefaced and impudent, when it is regardleſs of all ill Conſequences, when it attempts to raviſh and over-power all juſt Authority, it then becomes deteſtable, dangerous and muſt be cruſhed at all Events ; was it not enough that the Miniſter had been borne down by the People ? that every Day produced new Changes in Favour of the new Adminiſtration ? Muſt the Government, the Privy-Council, all Employments in the State be canton'd out *ad arbitrium populi*, nay by a private Cabal, or at the *Tavern-Meetings* of a direct *Faction* ? What would the rational World think of this Conſtitution, if the Laws of this Country put this Power into the Hands of the People ; but how much more monſtrous, if it ſhould, or could be ſuffered to be done at their Caprice, without any Law at all, and by their own arbitrary Will ?

When a Combination viſibly appeared, to exclude all Men from a Re-election into Parliament, who accepted of Employments ; when the moſt expenſive Oppoſitions were created by all the worſt and moſt corrupt Means to turn ſuch Elections againſt the Perſons who accepted ; how was it poſſible for the new Adminiſtration any longer to purſue their View of bringing in their Friends, much leſs of making that Rout among the Placemen of the old Party, which was ſo vainly and abſurdly inſiſted upon?---When it was now on a ſudden become the wild Doctrine of the People, to let no Placemen at all into Parliament;

and

and when the Doctrine of the Faction was, that none should be suffered to come in but by their Consent and Approbation ; was not the Absurdity of *the first* a thing, that rendered it impossible ; the Conduct of *the other*, of such a Tendency, as no Government can or ought to bear ; preposterous beyond the Power of Words to express it, inconsistent with the Constitution, subversive of all Order in the State, and productive of such Consequences, as must have encouraged Faction to a Degree, that would not allow one Hour's Peace in future Time to this Country.

With Regard to the Popular Laws, the Leaders of the Opposition sincerely wished many Things amended in our Constitution, they had begun by a *Place Bill*, by the *Alteration in the Mutiny Bill*, with Regard to the Billetting of Soldiers in the City and Liberty of *Westminster*, have since proceeded by *a Law for regulating the* Scotch *Elections*, and by the *Abolition of the Pot Act*, which being under the Regulations of the *Excise*, and settled at the *arbitrary* Estimation of that *Commission*, was a heavy Oppression, and great Instrument of Influence through the whole Capital ; and they *still do honestly mean*, as fast as they can, to rectify all other Matters of *just* Uneasiness.—But was it possible, as Things were circumstanced, or would it be prudent, in any Time, to make every Alteration of this kind at once ? — If these Things be duly considered, they are great Points already gained. — These Things however are said to be nothing, but the little Content they have given is no Proof that they are nothing. — I wish it may not rather lead to prove, that nothing but a total Change to Popular Government will do. — In such an heated Condition, was it fitting that Popular Bills, be they necessary, or be they not, should be ravished by Force, when all those different Plans of Reformation, which, during the Course of the former Opposition, had been proposed by Men of different Principles, never approved by all, and assented too temporarily by the different Parties *only* for the sake of Union, — positively known not to be all necessary, but moved as *Succedanea* to each other ; when one was lost, to supply its Place by another, not in the View to procure *all*, but in Hopes at last to get *something*. — When all these different Propositions were now ignorantly and grosly confounded by the Vulgar, and blended into (what was never dreamed of, or intended in the greatest Fire of Opposition) one regular Scheme of a new Constitution, and when this was insolently made the *Alternative* of *Peace* or *War* between the *Governours* and the *Governed*,—when, among those who thought themselves most moderate, no two Men agreed upon what was necessary.—Some thinking that all Se-

curity

curity lay in a good Place-Bill, about the Degree and Extent of which they likewife differed.—Some in a *Penfion-Bill*, which others more juftly thought would fignify nothing.—Some in a Law for *Triennial Parliaments*, which all who did not delight in Riot, or in the Profpect of Corruption, thought both dangerous and dubious.—Some for *Annual Parliaments*, which others thought too frequent.—Some for what was called *Juftice on the Earl of* Orford.—Others not for fanguinary Views.—Some for *a Reduction of the Civil Lift*, which others thought unjuft to be taken away, having been legally given.—Some for the *Sale of all Employments*. —Others for allowing a few.—Some for taking *the Difpofition of them out of the Crown*, which others thought Anti-Conftitutional.—Some for *allowing them to fubfift*, but to be given only *to thofe who were not in Parliament*, that is, among *themfelves*. —Some to allow them but *to be given for Life*.—Some for making the *Army independant*.—Others for *no regular Troops at all*. In this Paffion, Irregularity, and Uncertainty of Public Opinion, if the Leaders of the Oppofition had ftood out till the People were fatisfied, it is plain they muft have ftood out for ever.—For what Conceffions foever had been made, the Bulk of that Set of Men, who, as I have obferved in the Beginning, compofe all kinds of Oppofition, would have ftill remained diffatisfied.—And this Set of Men, whether in the Right or the Wrong, always affume to themfelves the Title of *th' People*. Farther, whatever fingle Points had been obtained, it was now become a Maxim, that nothing was got, if all was not got, and at leaft thofe who had not been gratified in their refpective favourite Propofitions, would have ftill continued to abufe and villify in the fame degree.—And if all had been granted, which was impoffible, and abfurd, (becaufe, as I have obferved, all was never by any wife Men intended,) many others had been offended and terrified, at fo great a Change in the Conftitution, to the other Extreme.—They would have juftly complained, That the King and the Lords were rendered ufelefs, that an Anarchy muft be at length the Confequence, that the People would be raifed to the Power of doing tumultuoufly every thing they lifted, and that being arrived at this Power, they would naturally fall under the Direction of wicked and factious Men, who would lead them to purfue a thoufand wilder Projects, which would have daily opened in proportion to their Succefs. In confequence of this, a new Oppofition would have rifen upon quite contrary Notions.—This Oppofition would have naturally degenerated into thofe deep *Monarchical Principles*, which would have brought us back again to *Paffive Obedience*, *Non-Refiftance*, *Hereditary Right*, and all that *Train*

of

of *Nonsense*, which infested the *Reason* of this *Country* so many Years.—Great Numbers are to be found in this Nation, who will not trust to the limited Views of the People, who know, that when they gain one thing by Force, they are taught from thence to extort every thing by the same means; that as surely as *Princes* aim at *absolute Power*, the *popular Interest* equally drives at a *Democracy*; and when they are put into a Condition to enforce their Demands, never will desist in any Country till they get it.—This is not the Meaning of any honest Man, who would sooner keep this Constitution, with all its Faults, than put to Sea in Storms to search for another.—The People and Tribunes of *Rome* never rested till they got the Power of the Commonwealth into their Hands :—Their Ambition then became so notorious, their Views so corrupt, their Attempts so mad, that the Senate they opposed, and endeavoured to destroy, (though themselves not wholly free from Blame,) made Friends by the Extravagance of their Antagonists, to resist them.—In the Resistance, private Men grew too great for both, and the Contest ended in the Loss of Liberty.—It did so in *England* in the Time of *Cromwell*; the People never ceased pushing for the whole Power, till Reason came on the Side of the Crown ;—the *King* was then enabled to resist, which, when he did, if he had conquered, the Nation had been Slaves to him,—as it happened, the popular General became the Tyrant.—The unreasonable Opposition of the Cortez to the Emperor *Charles* the Fifth, compleatly ruined the Liberties of *Spain*,—it was worked up into Rebellion, and it would be good to remark the Pretensions of that Opposition, the Commencement, Course and Issue of that Rebellion, if we had time to do it here.

Yet no Man will deny, but that the People and Tribunes of *Rome* were in the Right to oppose the too great Power of the Senate to a certain Point.

The People of *England*, to oppose the weak and wicked Government of the Ministry of *Charles* the First, had they known where to have stopped.

The Cortez of *Spain*, to have exerted their Privileges, had they done it with Moderation, and without falling into Faction.

The *Error* lay, in not being contented with the just Concessions that were made to every one of these

The *Crime* in attempting by Force to alter their respective Constitutions, which ought ever to be deemed sacred :—Constitutions once established, can never be with Justice altered, but by the full and free Consent of the different Members of the Legislature.—It is intolerable for any one Member of it, to force the rest to concede any thing. Such an Attempt rarely falls to meet the Fate, which attends Injuſtice in all its Steps; it ſeldom ends, but in the Ruin of the Projectors, and in the utter Defeat of what they project.

As long as Men, by legal Ways alone, endeavour to procure Laws, which appear good to them, and quietly ſit down under their Diſappointment, if a Majority cannot be prevailed upon to come into their Opinions, and do not inſolently think themſelves entitled to model the Conſtitution of their Country to their own fantaſtic Whim, ſuch Endeavours deſerve no Cenſure, they may in time produce good Laws, and good Effects. —But when Men pretend to dictate to the Legiſlature, and impudently preach and juſtify Rebellion, if they meet with Contradiction, Government muſt anſwer ſternly to ſuch importunate Demands:—While ſuch a Temper continues, it is dangerous to grant any thing, one ſuch Precedent will beget a thouſand, and is ſufficient to overthrow the beſt eſtabliſhed Conſtitution upon Earth: When it ſhall ſubſide ſo far, that the People ſeem to be capable of Contentment, upon moderate Conceſſions, that Man is diſhoneſt, who will not exert himſelf to procure for them all that is fair, juſt, and prudent.—But till then, he muſt be mad, or worſe, who will yield one ſingle Point, which they never receive with Gratitude, but attribute always to themſelves, and conſider, as extorted by Force, an Evidence of their own Power, an Imbecillity in Government, and an Encouragement to all Intemperance.

When ſuch was the Caſe of this Country, when Men of the moſt infamous and factious Views, began to unmaſk, and ſhew themſelves without the leaſt Reſerve, when Treaſon was become a public Topic of Diſcourſe, when all Decency, Order, and Subordination, was in a manner deſtroyed, and the Populace indiſcriminately treated every Character of Dignity, Worth, and Honour with an outragious Inſolence and Contempt.— Had it been the Part of Patriotiſm to have ſtood out longer, to have further aggravated and inflamed this Extravagance, which threatened the Diſſolution of Government itſelf in all its Parts?

When it was manifeſt, that there was a Party, whom nothing could content but the Ruin of the preſent Family upon the Throne, and who would have ſtill continued to oppoſe, let what Changes ſoever have been made.—When by the moſt flagrant Inſtances of Paſſion, Faction, wicked Principles, both Republican and Jacobite, private Corruption, and an utter Diſregard of the Publick, were become thus manifeſt: when even popular Laws, as the Place-Bill, and the Rectification of all our Foreign Meaſures were oppoſed; when nothing but tearing the Government down, the Conſtitution up

by

by the Roots, putting the Adminiftration of all our Affairs into the Hands of the moft violent and dangerous Men, when no Time was given to effect any thing; but in the very fuft Week of the Change, a few Men difappointed of Places, which they had carved out for themfelves, had raifed the Inflammation to a higher Point than ever, when the Effect of their Labours upon the People had difcovered what a defperate Tempci they were in, when, in order to gain them to their Side, they had pawned, as it were, their Honour, *if they acquired Power* to yield every thing that the moft violent defired,——when, if this Compromife with them had been afterwards *broken*, the Nat' on muft have fallen into worfe Confufion; and if the Compromife were *kept*, the Government and Conftitution muft have been fubverted,—when they had openly drawn the Sword, and avowed Revenge, againft thofe Leaders who had wrought the Change, could thofe Leaders have ftood out till thefe Men were fatisfied, could they have refigned their Station, relied again upon thefe People, oi entertained any Hopes, that the Union broken, by the Violence of thefe Men, could have been reftored again, or could they have had any Piofpect with this difunited Body, to have pievented the Return of the foimer Minifter?

When by this mad, inconfiftent and wretched Conduct the honeft Leaders of the former Oppofition were in fo great a dégree difarmed of Power to do all the Good they wifhed to the Publick, or the Service they intended to their Friends; was it not wife and honeft to make the beft Ufe that they could of this Conjuncture? When the Madnefs of oihers prevented their making it better, was it not for the Intereft of their Country to act in fuch a way; as to keep out the former Minifter, and to employ the Influence of then new Stations equally to prevent the Continuance of the old Meafures, and to prevent the pernicious Defigns of a dangerous *Faction* in this unworthy Manner labouring to come in?—Weie they not juftified to join with thofe, who (upon various Motives, fome from Error, fome from Shame, fome from the Difficulty of quitting the Party, with which they had been fo long engaged, fome from a miftaken Principle of Gratitude, and falfe Notion of Honour, nay, fuppofe fome from Coiruption itfelf,) though they had done wiong before, were now ready and willing to change their Conduct, to rectify Miftakes, and to purfue thofe very Meafures, which were abfolutely neceffaiy, right in themfelves, which had been the declared View of all honeft Men till that Moment, and had been loudly called for fo many Years by the whole People? No worthy Man will deny that they

wcie

were not juftified in this Conduct ; no Man of Senfe can deny
but that they did both honeftly and greatly in what they did ;
*Cunctando reftituerunt rem, non enim ponebant rumores ante falu-
tem:* And by this temperate and fteady Behaviour under all
thefe galling Difficulties, of Infult, Clamour and unjuft Reproach, they maintained fo much Credit in defpight of thofe,
who laboured to deftroy it, that they changed the whole Spirit
and Conduct of the Adminiftration.

The Confequences of their vigorous Proceeding, quickly
fhewed itfelf in a wonderful degree ; the Face of Affairs turned in a moft merciful and happy Manner, beyond the moft fan-
guine Hope and Expectation of Mankind. The King of *Pruffia*
and the Queen of *Hungary* were brought to Terms ;   the one
to quit his Confederacy with *France* ; the other to yield a Part
of her Rights to induce him to it ;   the firft manifeftly from
an Apprehenfion of the Iffue of the Conteft, which grew
precarious upon the Exertion of the *Britifh* Power ; the other
in a Confidence of future Support from this Nation, in Return
for an extraordinary Conceffion.   The *Auftrian* Armies ra-
vaged, plundered and became entirely Mafters of *Bavaria*,
carrying the War into the Countries, and fuftaining themfelves at the Expence of the Enemy: Animated by the Profpect
of further Affiftance from *Great Britain*, and depending in
confequence upon that of the *Dutch*, (whofe Armies were actually augmented by 30,000 Men, and who begun in proportion as they faw they could confide in our Councils, to withdraw their Deference from *France*) they exerted themfelves
with a Bravery and Spirit, which carried every thing before it ;
the Supplies we had given the Court of *Vienna* enabled her, befides leaving 20,000 regular Troops in *Flanders*, to take the
Field with three Armies; one in *Bohemia*, another in *Bavaria*,
and a third in *Italy* ; which laft, in Conjunction with a Body
of *Sardinian* Forces, were fufficient to make Head againft a numerous Army of *Spaniards* in that Country ; the farther Supply given the King of *Sardinia* enabled him not only to form
that Army laft mentioned, but to compofe another ; at the Head
of which, with infinite Hazard to his Perfon, infinite Hard-
fhip and Fatigue, he defended his Dutchy of *Savoy* during
the whole Summer, and the greater Part of a long Winter's
Campaign againft another great and well-appointed Army
of *Spaniards* headed by a Prince of *Spain*, and in fpight of all
their Efforts, in which their beft Troops and immenfe Sums
were wafted, has to this Hour barr'd their Paffage into *Italy* ;
nor was this all, for by a ftrong Fleet of Men of War in the
Mediterranean and a proper Ufe of it, we ftruck fuch Ter-

ror, that the Court of *Naples* was obliged to agree to a Neutrality, and prevented an Army of 40,000 Men from succouring the Troops of *Spain*, which in the first Place, saved the Loss of the Ballance in *Italy*; in the second, proved the Ruin of the *Spanish* Army there . in the third, laid those Seeds of Discontent between the *Spanish* Court and that of *Naples*, (the former thinking it the strongest Instance of Ingratitude, to be deserted in this Extremity, by their own Son, who was so lately raised to that Dignity solely by the Expence of the Blood and Treasure of the *Spanish* Monarchy) as will probably never be removed, and may be the Foundation of great Advantage to us hereafter ; in the fourth Place, it has discoverd to us, of what Weight we may hereafter be in that Part of *Europe* in a higher degree than ever we knew it ; in the fifth, it has been the most severe Revenge, and was the most complete Method to distress the Court of *Spain :* For in a War with that Power, we could not have wasted her Treasure, and ruined her Reputation, in an equal Degree, or destroyed so many of her Troops in twenty Years, by any other Means, with this farther Advantage, that we rendered the Administration of the Queen intolerable to her Subjects, who were thus oppressed with Taxes, and drained of all their Men and Money to gratify ambitious Views, attended with these aggravating Circumstances, that they brought not only Ruin, but Disgrace and Scandal upon their Arms in every Instance : To this was joined an almost total Interruption of their Trade, and their Returns of Money from the *Indies*, which, as fast as their inexpressible Necessities obliged them to be made, were, in very many Instances, intercepted by the Vigour and Diligence of the Navy stationed, commanded and directed by the new Admiralty ; which Gains, if fairly accounted for, not only ballanced all the Losses, that our Merchants have sustained (notwithstanding the Number of their Privateers and the Extent of our Commerce) since the Time of the late Change, but have gone far to wipe off those Scores, which had been run up against them, by the Neglect and imprudent Conduct of the former Administration.

It could now be said no longer, that our Hands were tied by Fear, by Corruption, or by neutral Engagements.—We rode triumphant on the Ocean, our proper Element,—we confined the whole *French* and *Spanish* Fleets, who, tho' combined, dared not venture to oppose us, while we employed but a Part of ours to do not only this, but to keep *Naples* to its Neutrality, to insult their Ports, and barr their Privateers from issuing in any Numbers from the rest.—We restored the Honour of our Flag, and now returned the Insolence of *France,* whom we treated with the same Contempt, with which she, for many Years, had treated us. —We burnt the Ships of her Allies, and our Enemies, in her very Ports, we searched and rummaged almost every Vessel she put to Sea.—Our Fleets sailed from *Jamaica* with an avowed Design to attack, sink, burn, and destroy the Squadrons she sent into those Parts; and she knows the Orders of our Admirals, to sink, burn, and destroy, any other Fleet she shall venture to send out again; yet she has been obliged to pocket every one of these Affronts: If our Naval Dignity is not restored by these Actions, what can restore it? and if these Things cannot be denied to be true, as they cannot be, what Impudence, and what Wickedness must it be to villify the present Government, to poison and deceive the ignorant and unwary Multitude, with a perpetual Din, of the low contemptible Condition to which we are said to be reduced? It is a Shame to suffer ourselves to be abused in this gross Manner; the Leaders of the *Faction* themselves laugh at the Folly and Delusion of the People, that they have fooled to such a Point. They even now despise those Wretches who are thus seduced, they themselves loath and detest the seditious Tools of which they now make their Use, and when they have served their Turn, will assuredly turn their Backs upon them: But let me return to say one Word more upon our Conduct with Regard to *France*:—Let any Man look back upon the insolent and imperious Treatment, which towards the Close of the last Administration we received from that Power. Let him then consider what we have since done, and let him answer, if he can, whether this Nation has received no Benefit by the late Change.—*France* has found, and proclaims it by her Conduct, whatever *we* may stupidly and ungratefully do at Home, that she trembles at the Power and the Measures of this Nation. If publick Contempt be publick Weakness, as it is with Nations known to be; what Applause is due to those, who have shifted that Contempt from themselves, and cast it upon the Enemy, and who have consequently procured that Weakness to *France*, which the former Minister had by twenty Years tame Administration with Pains procured for us; if there be any Sense left in this Nation, they must see all this; if there be any Honesty, they will confess it, let their private Views or Disappointments be what they will; if there be any Warmth of Heart, Love, or Regard, for the Honour, the Dignity, the Safety and Well-being of our Country, they will proclaim it in despight of Faction, popular Ferment, or any private Danger. The Maxim of *Tacitus*, however applied by him, will hold true with every State, *Majus famâ potentia quam*

quam sua vi nixa : Great as the Power of *France* may be, it is the Fame, the Opinion of that Power, that has so long supported her in her ambitious Views, enabled her to trample upon the Rights and Liberties of all *Europe*, and to sport with the most sacred Ties of Truth and Faith of Treaties ; it is this, that encouraged her, after so many solemn Declarations in the last *German* War, *that she would acquire nothing,* to grasp that mighty Acquisition of *Lorrain* ; it was this, that induced her, in that perfidious manner, to violate her Engagements to the *Pragmatic Sanction,* which were the Condition of that Acquisition ; it was this that terrified every Potentate in *Europe* into a Submission to all her Indignities, and into Non-Resistance under the Yoke she has imposed so long upon many Nations, and under the Prospect of the Chains she was forging for all the *European* World. Is it not therefore a mighty Point, gained by this Nation, in the space of little more than one Year, to have reduced that over-bearing Power into this deficient State of Credit, and to have restored that Credit to ourselves, which was so totally lost ?—It is not an empty Vanity, but a solid Benefit.—Can any Thing tend more, hereafter, to lighten the Expence of future Struggles for the Liberty of *Europe,* than this Reduction of the Credit of that Nation, and this Restoration of our own ? Can any thing prevent so much the Occasion of taking up Arms, as that Discovery, which will induce all the Powers in *Europe* to be less afraid to do it against *France ?* And can any thing give so great Weight to our Negociations without Recourse to the Sword, as the general Opinion, that whenever we draw it, we are able to curb that Power? This Conduct visibly must have this fortunate Effect, that if it be unhappy for us to be reduced to the Necessity of engaging in Land-Wars upon the Continent, it will render that Necessity less frequent ; if the Greatness of the Expence is grievous, and drains us of our Specie, it must make it less in future, as it must secure us more ready Assistance and stronger Alliances, than if we wanted that *Fama potentiæ,* and that *Opinion,* which by the Providence of God, and the Conduct of our Affairs has been now restored again.

Thus, we have undeceived the World as to the Power of *France* ; not *that it is not great,* which would be delusive ; but that it is not *omnipotent and irresistible :* And thus we have in a short time gone far, not only to restore Things reduced both at Home and Abroad to an almost desperate Condition, but even turned the Errors of the former Administration to Advantage ; which is visible in the highest Degree, by the Effects

L

O

of our Meafures in the *Mediterranean* already mentioned —
Without all doubt, one of the moft fatal and unhappy Steps
of the late Adminiftration feems to have been the neutral Con-
duct there (though whether, all Things confidered, it was
avoidable, is not perhaps fo eafily determined) by which the
Spanifh Armies were enabled to be landed fafely in a Time of
War, in Sight of our Squadrons, in *Italy*; and to form a
Junction with the *French* yet by the Vigilance fince, the
Neutrality of *Naples*, and the driving both Fleets into one
Pound, we have enclofed all the Land-Forces of *Spain* far from
Home, and in great Meafure out of the Reach of Recruits,
Neceffaries and Supplies, and we have our Padlock upon the
greater Part of the Maritime Force of thofe two Powers,
which would have haraffed us exceedingly had they been in
different Parts; kept us in perpetual Alarms, diftreffed our
Trade; and fo divided our naval Force, that notwithftanding
our Superiority at Sea, we fhould have fuffered many Inconveniences, nay, even Danger from them, to our own Coafts,
and fome of our Settlements abroad.—It will yet have a farther
Effect, it difpirits and brings down the haughty Spirit of that
People, who are ever preffing for War, it difcontents them
with their own Adminiftration; and if we can do it as
effectually as their former Conduct has done it by us, *there need
not be a greater Curfe upon that Government, a greater Plague, a
greater Obftruction to their Views, nor a furer Way to bring them
to their Ruin.*

By the Advantage that we have made of our Fleets in thofe
Seas, we have derived another great Advantage, for by tem-
porifing with the King of *Naples*, we have fecured the Elector
of *Saxony* and King of *Poland*, who, befides the Hazard of his
own Dominions, has, by his Alliance with *that Prince*, his
Intereft to confider too, and who may be juftly fuppofed to
fuffer fome Weight in the Scale of his Determination, from a
Reflection of the Condition to which his Daughter might be
reduced, by any Rafhnefs he might be guilty of, in this Conjuncture

By thefe providential Succeffes, which all the vile Sarcafms
of Faction can never prevail, to have attributed to any other
Caufe than the manifeft Revival of the *Britifh* Spirit, directed,
as it now is, the *French* were every where fo foiled, that the
Auftrians were enabled to act upon the offenfive, and to befiege
Prague, where they confined no lefs than 24,000 of the beft
Troops of *France* for the whole Summer, with two Marefchals
of *France*, and prevented them with the reft of their broken
Army, from receiving any Supplies, or from doing any confi-
derable

derable Mifchief,—till, by the Neceffities into which they were at length brought, the Court of *France* was compelled to withdraw the Army under the Command of the Marfhal *Maillebois*, from the Circle of *Weftphalia*, where 35,000 of their Troops had been employed to awe the Electorate of *Hanover* and the *Dutch* at the fame time. This was one of the firft Steps they took in the Beginning of their Attempts on *Germany*, and one of the wifeft, as the Confequences of their Inability to continue it, have fully fhewn.—By this they effected three great Ends, they diverted all the *Hanoverian* Forces from the Affiftance of the general Caufe; they awed the *Dutch*; they prevented the Conjunction of the Troops of *England*, and of *Auftria*, in the *Low-Countries*, with thofe of *Hanover*, and thofe of both the former with the *Dutch*.—*Hanover* was obliged in Prudence, for the common Good and Safety of the *Allies*, to confent to a temporary Neutrality; for if they had hazarded the Event of War, (inferior, as they were, in Number) and if they had been defeated, that Body of Troops, which, as we have fince feen, were intended to more important Purpofes, had not only totally been rendered ufelefs; but there could have been no Poffibility of compofing afterwards that grand Army which was neceffary to be compofed, if we effectually intended to affift the Queen of *Hungary*, and to deal roundly with *France*, and which has been fince compofed, notwithftanding the pofitive Affertion of the *Faction*, *that it could never be*, to whom the Devil has owed a Shame, and has fairly paid them, by giving them the Lye in every one Point that they have advanced.

This Neutrality of *Hanover* having made fo great a Noife, I muft have Leave to enlarge a little farther on this Subject; (for though my prefent Purpofe is not to defend the Meafures of any Time antecedent to the late Change, it is honeft to do Juftice to every Man, and not at all neceffary to add more Errors than are due to the former Adminiftration.) To fpeak fairly of it, however malicioufly it has been made the Matter of Ridicule, it was the only Step that in that Circumftance could have been taken with any Judgment or Difcretion, from this known and general Principle, that you fhould never rifque a Divifion of your Forces, if you can avoid it.—The Court of *England* confidered the *Auftrians*, *Heffians*, and the *Englifh* in the Netherlands, together with the *Hanoverian* Troops, as one Army, difperfed in remote Quarters, but intended to be affembled, and to act together when conjoined; they were then capable of making a formidable Army, and might be able to act or undertake any Thing, and we had great Reafon to believe, and

received

received the ftrongeft Affurances from the Leading Men in *Holland*, that when it was affembled, they would concur with a large additional Body of *Dutch* Troops; — if therefore the *Hanoverians* had acted fingly, and been defeated fingly, the other divided Corps of Troops had been of very little Ufe, (as we have juft now obferved) and might have followed their Fate. But a farther certain, and yet more fatal Event muft have followed from it. The *Dutch* Miniftry would have never been able to have procured the Affent of the States, or to have engaged them in a Caufe fo hopelefs, as it would have then appeared, when the Electorate of *Hanover* fhould have been reduced into the fame Condition with *Bavaria*, and have proved the fame Acceffion of Strength to the *French*, that the other Electorate now affords to the Queen of *Hungary*. This might very poffibly have been the Cafe; and any Man, who has not been thoroughly drench'd with the Poifon of the Times, muft be fenfible, how ruinous fuch an Incident muft have been, independent of any private Regard for thofe Dominions, to the common Caufe of *Europe*. — Whoever is the leaft converfant in publick Affairs, or has even common Senfe, muft be able to judge of thefe Reafons, which were rendered infinitely ftronger by this Circumftance, that they actually did, by their Neutrality all that time, afford the Houfe of *Auftria* a moft material Affiftance, depriving the *French* and the *Bavarians* of fo great a Force, — to which, under God, was owing the Prefervation of the Houfe of *Auftria*; for by this means the happy Turn was effected in *Bavaria*, and that Superiority acquired to the Arms of the Queen of *Hungary*, which, had this Neutrality been never made, and had this Body of Troops been joined to the *French* and *Imperial* Armies in *Bavaria* and *Bohemia*, could have never happened, and they muft in all probability have ruined her in one Campaign. — While the twenty-fix or twenty-eight thoufand *Hanoverians* were upon their own ground, they were a Match in the defenfive Part for a greater Number; but if drawn from thence, they had been equal only to the Numbers, of which they actually did confift themfelves.

So long therefore as the *French* continued upon the Confines of the Electorate of *Hanover*, there was neither Prudence or Neceffity to act any other than a neutral Part; for by their Situation, and the Advantage of their own Country, it is demonftrable, that twenty-eight thoufand anfwered the End of an actual Aid to the Queen of *Hungary* of 35,000 Men.

But when the reduced Condition of the *French* obliged them to quit this Meafure, it was neceffary for us to change our Plan —
the

the *Hanoverian* Troops, had they remained in the Electorate, were then of no longer Use. In such a Conjuncture, no honest Man in *Britain* would have wished, that so great a Body of the best Troops in *Europe*, which by good Fortune were under the Influence of this Nation, should be unemploy'd.—The Question therefore was, in what way they might be most advantageously employ'd,—some imagined, that it had been proper to have followed the *French* Army, and the wise Politicians of the *Faction* bellowed loudly against this Neglect of Policy, as they pretended it to be; but many invincible Reasons opposed themselves to this Advice; some time must have necessarily been spent in settling a Point, which was of so nice a Nature, both in our own Councils, and in those of the Imperial Court;—and by that time (tho' it was very short) the *French* Army had got a great way upon their intended March.—It was to be considered again, that the *Hanoverian* Troops could by no means follow with the same Expedition, that the others went;—they had no Magazines, the *French* had exhausted the Provisions, and though they had passed through the same Country, when fresh and unannoyed, yet even they, from want of previous Preparations, suffered much in their March, and dwindled greatly;—how much therefore more must those, who trod the same Ground after them, have suffered; how much must they have been delayed? The Season of the Year began to be advanced, and the Summer must have been consumed, before they could have reached the Enemy; who in all Probability must have effected (if it was to be effected) whatever they could have proposed, before we could have come up with them.—Again, if the Enemy upon the Pursuit of the *Hanoverians* had turned short upon them, and waited in some strong Post, they might have engaged them to great Disadvantage, being superior in Number;—and they might have obliged them to stay and face them in a Country, that they had left behind them ruined;—they had the strong Town of *Egra* to befriend them, which the *Hanoverians* could not have neglected, nor have taken.—Thus the Effect of their March would have probably been fatal to that Body of Troops, who must at best have wintered far from home, in a ruined Country, liable to all the Inconvenience of a Winter's Campaign, and we should have put ourselves with a much smaller Force, and in a much more helpless Condition, near our Enemies, to have endured yet greater Hardships, than those, by which even their great Armies, inured by two Campaigns, and much better provided for the Event, have been in a manner mouldered into nothing.—Yet even this Risque would have been run, if it had been insisted upon by the

Austrian

Austrian Ministers, with whom we acted with the strictest Harmony.—We laid before them all these Ill-conveniencies, and the irretrievable Prejudice that an Accident to this Body of Troops must have occasioned in the next Year's Operations.—The Impossibility in that Case, of bringing into the Field, or forming a sufficient Army, to deal with that Force, that might be brought against us by the *French*:—That our *English* Troops, (which were not even then all landed) and the *Austrians*, in the *Netherlands*, were too remote to join the *Hanoverians* in any reasonable Time, had they set out upon that March immediately; that they were not yet accustomed and hardened to the Fatigues of War, and must therefore have been intirely ruined by such a March, at such a Distance, and at such a Season of the Year; that if it were possible, by the Means of the difficult Passes in the Mountains of *Bohemia*, by withdrawing the Troops from *Prague*, (leaving a sufficient Number to form a distant Blockade, and to distress the Garrison,) to prevent the Junction of the two *French* Armies, *Prague* must fall of course, the *French* must be disheartened and confounded by their Disappointment, and both their Armies suffer terribly, as they always did in the following Winter, while the Armies of the Allies united, much more numerous, strong and vigorous, might enter into Action fresh, and with infinite Weight in the ensuing Spring.—These Reasons had their just Effect, they were proved solid by the Event. —The *English* Councils directed the *Austrian* Operations upon this Occasion, and they felt the happy Consequence.—The Army of *Maillebois* never could penetrate through the Passes of *Bohemia*; but there involved, were miserably butchered and destroyed, by Sword and Famine;—while the Garrison of *Prague* were reduced in prodigious Numbers, by vain Attempts to escape, their Parties continually cut off, and their Provisions and Supplies so effectually obstructed, that they were at length necessitated in the severest Season of that cold Climate, and after the most insufferable Hardships, to abandon the Capital of *Bohemia*, and the whole Country, to their lawful Sovereign, (excepting *Egra*, on the extreme Borders of it,) bringing off with them not 10,000 Effective Men, the miserable Remains of at least 30,000, who had triumphed in that Country in the Beginning of that Year.—But upon their Arrival, Diseases broke in upon them, and swept off so many, even of that small Number, and of the Army sent to bring them off, that they could not remain there, and must have perished for Want, if they had been still harrassed by the *Austrians*.—In fine, they were reduced to such Distress, by a Series of Calamities, that left it might be said, of *two great Armies*, amounting together to more than 70,000 Men, not one should live to return, the *French* Court

recalled

recalled their shattered *Remains*, and of *both*, not more than 20,000 Men had the Felicity to see their Native Soil again ; where the few that survived the incredible Fatigues they had sustained, brought back, rather Weakness to their *Master*, than Security to his *Frontier*, filling his wretched Subjects with Grief, Dejection of Spirit, Detestation of the Views of their ambitious Monarch, and Terror of the Miseries they have endured ; which every Man, capable of bearing Arms, by the absolute Power of their Government, and the Distress of their Affairs, sees himself likewise hourly in Danger to undergo.

Thus far we have observed how much Folly, Ignorance and Villany have concurred to misrepresent two important Points; the Neutrality of *Hanover*, and the Conduct of our New Councils in not marching after *Maillebois*'s Army : To prosecute this Deduction of our Affairs during the last Interval of Parliament, we come now to shew the Part acted by our Administration upon the Removal of that Army. The Deliberations we have mentioned took up no more, as I remember, than three Weeks ; and the Point being agreed between the Ministry of *Austria*, and our own, *that the* Hanoverian *Forces should not follow*, the next Step was obvious : If our own Reason could not have shewn it to us, it was dictated and pointed out by *France* ; it was evident, as we have before observed, that the View of *France* in sending her Armies to the Frontiers of that Electorate was no other than to prevent the Junction of the *Hanoverian, Dutch, British* and *Austrian* Forces : if that was so favourite a View, that she put herself to so vast a Charge for it, opiniatred that View so long, and submitted to all the Ill-Convenience of weakening her Armies in every other Part for it ; would it have been excuseable in us not to have profited by such a Lesson, and to have lost the Opportunity, which the Absence of that Army gave to form the necessary Conjunction of all our Forces,—the only Person, who could have Reason to demur upon the Point was the Elector of *Hanover* himself ; who by detaching such a Body of his Troops, and breaking his Neutrality, left his Country exposed to some Hazard, that if the former Troops should change their Destination, or succeed in their Attempt, they might return to take a severe Revenge upon his Dominions with Impunity : When therefore his Majesty agreed to this Proposition, the Ministers of *England* could not have answered it to their Country, if they had not availed themselves of this Body of his Forces.

They therefore took 16,000 of these Troops into the *British* Pay ; not, as it has been maliciously insinuated, in a Method contrary to the Constitution, and unknown before ; but in a

Method

Method warranted by all former Examples both in the Reign of King *William* and Queen *Anne*, when in the Interval of Parliament it became neceſſary from any Event to hire Foreign Forces, the Buſineſs was concerted by the Crown, the Treaty for the Subſidy agreed, and the Eſtimates refered to Parliamet; where the Liberty ſtill remained entire to reject them: The ſame Method was purſued in this Inſtance, the Parliament had the Eſtimates laid before them, and might have refuſed to confirm the Meaſure, if it had appeared to them improper or unjuſt; ſo that of all the Debates that ever paſs'd in Parliament, none ever violated more the Heart of every fair and honeſt Man, than that with relation to theſe Troops; in which this Point was with equal Confidence and Malice urged to the moſt indecent Extremity, in Defiance of all Truth and Candour, and with a manifeſt View to impoſe upon the Underſtanding of Mankind; there was not a Man of the leaſt Experience, who did not know that this was a Part of the known Prerogative exerciſed in innumerable Inſtances, and a Prerogative not like ſome others, which may be thought to have been a Relique of bad Times in Government, when the Conſtitution was leſs pure; or crept gradually in, when the Power of the Crown was ſtrained too far, but a Prerogative founded upon the ſupreme Law of all Neceſſity, without which no Government could ſtand ſecure one Hour: for what muſt be the Condition of this Country, if in no Dilemma, no Exigence whatſoever, (and ſurely none was ever greater than that of which we are now ſpeaking) during the Interval of Parliament, the Crown might exerciſe a Power of this Nature? What Opportunities in the moſt critical Conjunctures might be loſt? What Ruin muſt our Armies be expoſed to, in caſe of any ſignal Defeat abroad? But it is a Point too obvious to be longer inſiſted upon, and the Abſurdity of denying it is equalled by nothing, but that of debating *one whole Day* to prove *a Meaſure illegal* and *unparliamentary*, and to condemn it becauſe it had not the *Authority of Parliament*, which was *that very* Day ſubmitted to the Judgment and Power of the Houſe *whether it ſhould be a Meaſure at all or no.*

But to ſhew farther how tender his Majeſty was of exerting his Prerogative, beyond what the Neceſſity of our Situation required, his Majeſty hinted it to his Parliament at the Cloſe of the antecedent Seſſions.——After ſpeaking of the Supplies which had been already granted, *for the Support of the Queen of* Hungary, *and to reſtore and ſecure the Balance of Power, ſo particularly recommended by his Parliament*; he added farther, *And if it ſhould become neceſſary for me to contract new Engagements, or to enter into farther Meaſures, I rely upon your Zeal and Perſeverance in ſo juſt a Cauſe, to make them good.*

When

When the Prince foresees that an Exigency may possibly arise, at a Period of Time in which he cannot possibly take the Council of his Parliament —If in such an Exigency the Nature and the Practice of the Government permits him freely to take what Measures he may judge necessary for the Interests of his People, without any Form or previous Notice whatsoever, if yet that Prince reminds his Parliament of such a possible Contingency, as far as the Nature of the Thing can possibly admit, instead of a Stretch of Prerogative, it must appear, to every candid Man, the strongest Mark of Tenderness to the Privileges of his People, a manifest Inclination to decline the exercise of his Prerogative, and in fact, the greatest Condescension.— There is no Man of Candour, who will consider this, but must see, that the most open, most frank, most generous, and most respectful Conduct, next to the direct Request, *to be permitted to take the Measure*, was *to hint it to the Parliament, that it was intended to be taken.*

Now, that his Majesty could not lay this Scheme before his Parliament, or open his Design more directly than he did at that Time, is proved by the stubborn Evidence of Facts and Dates, which though misrepresented by the *Faction* upon every Turn, and concealed, when they do not serve their Purpose, cannot be totally denied.—It is confess'd, that this Measure might have been, in all Probability, intended before the Dissolution of the Parliament.—But could it be then resolved? In the Nature of the Thing, it could not, because it was a Contingency, which could only happen if the *French* Army marched,—it may be said, that some Steps had been already made by *France*, that convinced the King and the Administration, that they intended to march;—and if not, it is probable his Majesty would not have touched at all upon it.—But these Steps might have been only taken as a Feint, at least Accidents might have intervened to prevent the Execution of that Project.—Unless therefore his Majesty had been not only King of *Great Britain*, and Elector of *Hanover*, but King of *France* at the same Time, he could not have told his Parliament, that his Electoral Troops should march to join the National Troops of *England*, when this Measure depended upon an Event which was not in his Power, and which actually did not happen in a considerable Time, the Parliament rising upon the 15th of *July*,* and the March of the *French* Troops not having taken Effect till several Weeks after. As therefore it was impossible to have communicated that as a *positive Measure*, which in its Nature

* The *French* Army did not march from *Frankfort* towards *Bohemia*, till the 30th of *August.*

M

could

could not be then resolved, so must it have been an Absurdity, visible to all Mankind, to have told the Parliament, *eventually*, which was the same thing as to have told *France*, and all the World, what we intended to do in case they marched —The Politicks of these Times are of a very extraordinary Nature, when the Government is not only pressed, from Day to Day, to discover, by Motions for Papers, every secret Transaction, every Negotiation, and Plan of Operations, even while they are still depending; but when we are to forestall the Measures of our Enemies, and to tell them, *Gentlemen, take Care what you do—if you do so, we will do so,—if you march from* Hanover, *we will certainly use that Opportunity to unite our Forces as soon as possible after you are gone.*

The Prudence of the Administration appeared likewise in the *Time,* the *Place* to which they marched, and in the *Nature* of this Bargain —As to the *Time,* it had been Madness to have slipped this Opportunity, to form our Army, which might have afterwards been impossible; had we deferred it till the Spring, as some have taken great Pains to persuade the People we should have done, *France* might have taken such Measures, or such Events might have happened, as would have rendered it then impracticable,—again, (which would have been a Matter very near as fatal in its Conseqence) the World might have been convinced, that it was never intended to be done at all; it was of the last Importance to shew the *Dutch* a powerful Support to induce them to engage as soon as possible. As to the *Place,* another Point of Importance was to give the *French* Alarms upon their own Frontier, to prevent their sending any farther Force to *Germany,* or to prevent their assisting the Infant Don *Philip,* who was already very superior to the King of *Sardinia,* for which our National Troops were by no means alone sufficient : And it had its Effect; the Letters of *Van Hoey* shew, that *France* did not slight those Measures, which our own People ridiculed. They have since discovered what the *Dutch then thought,* and what the *Dutch* have now *publickly declared.*—The *French* encreased their Troops in *Flanders* with all the regular Troops they could draw together, and much of the Militia from the remotest Part of their Dominions, they sent but faint and insufficient Succours into *Germany,* and none at all to the *Spanish* Army.—By the March of these Troops into *Flanders,* we had therefore visibly these several Advantages —First, That they were a great Encouragement to *Holland.*—Secondly, That they were a Security to the *Barrier,* and to the *Netherlands* in all Events.—Thirdly, That they created the most distant Diversion that could be made. — Fourthly, That, as far as possible,

they

they prevented the Neceffity of a Rupture, becaufe *France* would not probably attempt to attack us there, unlefs compelled to it, as long as the *Dutch* had not yet acceeded, and was yet obliged to prepare and arm in the fame Degree, as not knowing how fuddenly they might take the Refolution, which they were then *inclined to*, and have fince *refolved*; whereas if they had marched to the *Rhine*, where, as others of our wife Politicians have for the only Alternative fuggefted, that they fhould have gone afterwards, *France* would have been induced, either by Neceffity, or Prudence, to have attacked us there, when only half our Force had been aflembled, and at leaft we had been engaged precipitately in that Extremity, while there was yet a Poffibility, that the Difficulties of the *French*, and Encreafe of our Ability and Succefs might have brought about a Termination to thefe Troubles. We reaped another Advantage from the good Quarters in thofe Provinces, which kept our Troops in better Health, and in more Convenience; being in a plentiful Country, and in that of an Ally; whereas we could have quartered no where elfe, without the greateft Inconvenience.—We were there equally ready (confidering the Seafon of the Year) to perform any Service that the prefent or future Exigencies fhould require; befides the Difference of being united near to our own Country, where Supplies could be furnifhed with more Eafe and Expedition; and where all the Money, that was confumed, contributed, though indirectly, to affift the Houfe of *Auftria*; as it enriched her Provinces, and enabled them to pay more punctually, and to furnifh greater Sums to their Sovereign's Aid. Laftly, it enabled us to amufe the *French*, and gave us an Opportunity to pretend a Defign on *Dunkirk*, which drew down a great Body of their Troops to the very greateft Diftance, from whence they could annoy the Enemy· A Point fo artfully conducted, that every other Power were ferious at it but our own People.

As to the *Nature of the Bargain*, much has been faid upon this Head, to prove it not only *bad*, but *criminal* in the higheft Degree. In order to the fetting this Matter in a clear Light, it is neceffary to obferve, that during the long War of 1702, great Numbers of Foreign Forces having been hired, the Method then purfued, and the Conditions then obferved, have been the Rule by which we have gone ever fince; our fubfidiary Treaties therefore run all upon the fame Plan, and contain the fame Conditions, that they did then; (excepting in two or three Articles of a trivial Nature, which the Change of the univerfal Difcipline and a particular Circumftance made it neceffary to differ in, as we fhall have Occafion to fpecify

M 2

hereafter.) This Expence is conftantly fummed up in *three* Articles,—That of *Levy-Money* for the furnifhing and compleating both Horfe and Foot, that of the *Pay* of the Forces, and that of an *annual Subfidy* befides, in a certain Proportion, according to the Number of the Troops ; thefe three Articles of *Levy-Money*, the *Pay of the Forces*, and the *Subfidy to the Prince*, make the general Charge common to all the Forces, that we have hired for a Space of above forty Years.—This is the Bill always brought us in for mercenary Troops,—*Not that any of thefe Articles is literally the Sum applied to the Account of the Charge of that Article, of which it bears the Title, but the Deficiency of the one is made up by the Exceedings of the other, and many Contingencies and Neceffaries are accounted for under this Form ; upon the grofs Amount of which, thefe Princes are enabled to make good their Engagements with us.* There is likewife another Condition, for they always tie us to contract for a certain Number of Years, whether we want the Troops or not ; without which they would find no Account in their Bargain.— When the Conjuncture of Affairs obliged our Minifters to take the *Hanoverian* Forces into Pay, if they had had the mean Inclination to have paid their Court to his Majefty, they were therefore warranted by all Precedents to have made their Bargain upon this Footing, as thefe Troops were in a Manner the only Troops we could have hired at that Time; as they were as good as any in the World, as they were fituated the moft commodioufly for our Service, and as they muft have been ufelefs to the common Caufe, and have been disbanded, if we had not paid them, his Majefty's Electoral Dominions, not being fufficient to maintain both them, and the other Troops he had raifed in this critical Situation of Affairs, efpecially with the great additional Charge of Marching: The Minifters therefore could have deferved no Cenfure, nay, might have even merited Applaufe, for taking a Meafure, which would have been juft, fair, and equitable, and beneficial to this Country, even upon the common Foot of other mercenary Troops; nor could this Nation have had any Title to have complained of his Majefty, if in his different Capacity, as Elector of *Hanover*, he had defired to be confidered on the fame Footing as any other *German* Prince.—But *his Majefty*, with a *Generofity*, for which he has met with a very *ungrateful* Return, declined thefe Pretenfions, and to fhew his own Zeal for the Service of the Houfe of *Auftria*, and his Defire to make the Burthen to *Great Britain* as light as poffible, he confented to Conditions, to which no other *German* Prince would have fubmitted, and which were both in prefent, *certainly*, and in profpect, *probably*, a great Reduction

of

of the Charge to this Nation; for whereas in all other Treaties of this kind, part of the Sums stipulated are paid, and commence before the March of the Troops—He consented, that their Pay should commence only upon the very Day they began their March from *Hanover*, viz. the 31st of *August* 1742.—He insisted upon no Terms, *as to the Time that we should pay them*, so that if the Troubles, in which we were involved, should have determined in the Space of *one Year only*, we were bound to keep them *no longer*,—a Circumstance that might very possibly have saved a *Million* of Money to this Nation, and which might have proved (were this a Bargain of neat Profit to his Majesty, as these Incendiaries suggest) a Loss of as much to his Majesty, in his Electoral Capacity.—Nor was this all; but his Majesty entirely remitted that Article of *Annual Subsidy*, which every other *German* Prince has done, now does, and ever will insist upon; and which, according to the Proportion paid to the King of *Sweden*, as Landgrave of *Hesse-Cassel* (who besides Levy-Money * and the Pay of his Troops, receives an annual Subsidy of 33,000 *l.* for only 6,000 of his Forces) his Majesty had been entitled for 16,000 of his Troops, to near 100,000 *l. per Annum*; which Saving to this Nation, together with the other Particulars we have mentioned, make so vast a Difference between the Charge of these Troops, and those of any other we could have hired, that it is an Impudence beyond Example to have treated this Point in the Manner that it has been treated by the *Faction*, as we shall farther shew hereafter.

But though it may not be strictly regular in Point of Time or the Order we have laid down, to take full Notice of the Proceedings of the *Faction* upon *this Head* (till we come to *the next*, viz. *their Conduct in the next Session of Parliament*) yet it will not be illconvenient to clear the Way, by removing the Rubbish of those Objections, with which they have flattered themselves, to cover the Malignity of their virulent Scandal upon this Measure, because this Scandal was of a Nature so uncommon, desperate and dangerous, that it will be greatly for the Advantage of the Publick to present it naked, stripped of that delusive Garb in which they have used so much wicked Art to dress it, and void of any other Matter that may divert the Publick from the full View and Contemplation of its Iniquity.

To proceed therefore; under this Head of the Nature of the Bargain for the *Hanoverian* Troops, it was objected, *that by taking these Troops into* British *Pay, before we marched into* Germany, *we paid full one half Year before we had Occasion for them.*—As to this, it has been already answered, that we might

not

* See the Votes of the House of Commons, *April* 14, 1740.

not have been able to have joined at all, if we had not done
it when we did; it has been likewife fhewn, how many other
Advantages we both did reap, and expected juftly to reap from
it. By Parity of Reafoning, we fhould not have begun to
embarque our National Troops for *Flanders*, till the Beginning of this Campaign.—And if Troops are not to be affembled,
till the Moment they are to enter upon Action, or if an
Adminiftration is to be condemned for being in Readinefs to act
as foon as Circumftances will admit, or for not acting, before
either Time, Circumftances, or the Seafon of the Year will give
them leave; and if an Army is expected to fight whenever it is
in the Field, without regard to any Event or Situation of things,
we have to deal with Politicians, whofe Ignorance or Prejudice
render them unworthy of any reafonable Anfwer.

Another Objection was to *the granting Levy-Money for Troops
already raifed, and again, to the granting a greater Levy-Money
than is paid to other Foreign Troops.* As to the *firft*, we have already given a fufficient Anfwer, by obferving the Nature of all
thefe Contracts, viz. *That no one of thefe Articles litterally contains the Sum applied to the Charge of that Article of which it
bears the Title: but the Deficiency of the one is made up by the Exceedings of the other, and many Contingencies, Neceffaries, and
extraordinary Expences, are accounted for under this Form; upon
the grofs Amount of which, and not otherwife, Foreign Princes can
be enabled to afford their Troops to us at the Rate they do,* and upon
this Foot it was allowed lately to the Troops of *Denmark.* As
to the *Second*, the Levy-Money of thefe Troops is in the fame
Proportion with that of all others; but the Sum was the larger,
becaufe the Body of Troops, hired in this Inftance, confifted
One-third of *Horfe*, whereas in moft of our other Contracts of
this Nature, the Horfe have ufually amounted only to *One-fixth*;
and particularly in the Cafe of the *Danes* and *Heffians*, which
lately were and now continue in our Service.

It was again objected, that we *are charged with a new Article for the Officers of the Artillery*; and it is true, that it is a
new Article, but it is an Article which arifes from an Improvement in the Military Difcipline, and one of the moft remarkable of any that have been made in modern Time. Every
Regiment, in the Service of all the *German* Princes, carrying
with them two Field Pieces, which they manage with a very
extraordinary Addrefs, firing incredibly often in one Minute;
and no Man can pretend to fay, that it was not neceffary to conform ourfelves to the Difcipline of the Age we live in, and to
avail ourfelves of any new Advantages in War, which might either give us a *Superiority*, or put us upon a *Level* with the *Enemy*.

We

We were accufed again with making a bad Bargain in *charging the Exchange, by the Eftimate laid before the Houfe of Commons at the Rate of ten Guilders ten Stivers the Pound Sterling, which is fuppofed to be an Exchange of eight Stivers to our Difadvantage,* and an unneceffary Expence of 26,000 *l.* But this was fully anfwered in Parliament, though all the Writers of the *Faction* made no Scruple to conceal it in their fubfequent Productions.—
" They were there told, that in the Nature of thefe Things,
" all Eftimates muft be formed upon fome pofitive Rate of Ex-
" change ; that this Rate was mentioned in the Eftimate, be-
" caufe from the Variation of Exchange, it might have amount-
" ed to that, and to prevent a Deficiency if it fhould ; but that
" this Eftimate did by no means fix the Rate of the Exchange,
" and that all Savings that arofe or might arife upon that Head,
" were conftantly, and would, according to ancient Cuftom,
" be certainly accounted for to Parliament."—This Objection therefore has no other Foundation than the Ignorance or Malice of the *Faction*.

It was likewife objected, that *in all Contracts of this Nature during the former War, there was a Deduction of Two and one-half* per Cent. *to be applied to the Ufes of the War,* which amounted to 16,447 *l.* and which was not deducted in this Contract.— This Objection favours ftrongly of the Party from whence it comes,—they had been fearching after Precedents from the Conduct of their *Faction* in the Reign of the late Queen *Anne,* when their Predeceffors made no fmall Difturbance upon this Head, and when the fame *Faction* attacked that great Man the Duke of *Marlborough* in Parliament, for having taken this Deduction of Two and one-half *per Cent.* from the Foreign Troops under his Command. *In the Report of the Commiffioners for taking, examining, and ftating the publick Accounts of the Kingdom* at that Time, which was intended as an Inquifition upon that General, they then infinuated this Abatement of Foreign Pay *to be a Deduction for the Ufes of the War :* But the Nature of the *thing* was fully explained, fuch a Deduction has been always made and is made at this Time ; but it neither then did, nor confequently does now, appear in any publick Account. It is a Sum which was firft obtained by Confent of the allied Princes in the Reign of King *William,* in the Nature of a voluntary Tax upon their Subfidies, afterwards continued in the Time of the Duke of *Marlborough,* and in the Reign of Queen *Anne,* always allowed by Warrant from the Crown to the General in Chief for procuring of Intelligence, and other fecret Service, but never laid before Parliament in Diminution of any Eftimate. Nothing more therefore

foreneed to be said to shew the Fallacy and Malevolence of this Objection, or to wipe off the Imputation of Excess in this Particular.

For a farther Aggravation, a Comparison was attempted to be drawn *between the Charge of the* Hanoverians *hired in the late War in* 1702, *and those now taken into our Pay.*--- But no such Comparison can properly be made, because we have not the Materials for it,---the *Dutch* first took them into their Service, and they were afterwards turned over into *our* Pay. --The *Dutch* therefore paid the first Expences of Levy-Money, *&c.* and unless we had Access to the Archives of that Republick, neither *they* nor *we* are qualified to ascertain this Point, though it is not reasonable to believe, that these Troops were then hired upon different Terms, than such as have been the general Rule in Cases of the same Nature.

The next Matter of Cavil was the *extraordinary Charge of a Regiment of* Hanoverian *Guards*, which being equal in Expence to twice their Number of common Men, is reckoned another Instance of exorbitant Expence. But, surely, there is no Man who will dispute this to be a proper Expence, when the Prince commands in Person, and he must be very much abandoned, who will think it decent to urge it now, when this Nation has so lately obtained so great and so manifest a Benefit from his Majesty's personal Appearance at the Head of our united Army.

The last Objection, which has made the greatest Noise, tho' it deserves the least Notice, *is to the hiring of* Hanoverian *Forces at all upon any Terms.* It is demanded, how an *English* Administration dare advise the Hire of Forces the most obnoxious, Forces that must create so great a Discontent, Forces that must establish that dangerous Distinction of *Englishmen* and *Hanoverians*, and a Measure that must shake the Interest of his Majesty upon the Throne, and poison the Affections of his People? ---But let us have the Liberty to put a few Questions to these Gentlemen in our Turn.---Could we have composed a sufficient Army without these Troops? **Why is** it more criminal to hire these Forces in the present **War, than** in that of Queen *Anne*, when we constantly entertained a great Body of them in our Pay without any Objection? **What is it** that has rendered these Forces *now* obnoxious **which were never** so *before?* What has created any Discontent upon this absolutely necessary Measure? What has established that dangerous Distinction of *Englishmen* and *Hanoverians?* What is it that has shaken the Interest of his Majesty, or poisoned the Affections of his People (*both* which have been indeed strongly endeavoured, but I thank God *neither* yet affected) no other Answer can be given to any of these Questions, but that there is in this Country at this Time,

a

a Faction deftitute of Principle and Shame, and void of all Remorfe, who taking Advantage of the Ignorance and vulgar Prejudices of a heated People, have glaringly attempted, by fallacious Arguments, vile Mifieprefentations, and downright Falfhood, covered by a popular and confufed Jargon of feditious Rhetoric, to gratify their Revenge, to advance their private Interefts, and to promote their pernicious Views, at the Expence of facred Truth, and moral Virtue, at the Hazard of the Liberties of *Europe*, the Peace of their own Country, and the Security of a Prince and Family, upon whofe Eftablifhment the Conftitution of thefe Kingdoms can alone depend.

We have now pretty fully gone through with a Deduction of the Meafures taken by the Adminiftration during the Interval of Parliament; we have explained the Nature and the Neceffity of thefe Meafures; we have fhewn the Succefs, and almoft miraculous Alteration in the Situation of our Affairs; which were vifibly their Confequence. But whether they were the neceffary Confequence of them or not—the Face of Affairs was in fact fo wonderfully changed, that inftead of that Profpect of almoft inevitable Ruin, which appeared before our Eyes, in the Beginning of the previous Seffions of Parliament, there was, at leaft, a great Probability of faving the Houfe of *Auftria*, and of reftraining the Ambition of *France* from profiting by her immenfe Expences, and the Labour fhe had taken, to move the whole Earth to the Deftruction of the only Power, that ftood between her and the virtual Poffeffion of the Univerfal Empire.—Let us inculcate this happy Alteration by a fecond Recapitulation of it.

Saxony and *Pruffia* were disjoined from the Alliance of *France*, and with Circumftances, that in a great degree fecured us from a Poffibility of their uniting with her again during the prefent Contention; *Bavaria* was not only incapable of affording any material Affiftance to the Views of *France*, but actually a confiderable Part of it in Poffeffion of the *Auftrians*, two great *French* Armies of veteran Troops totally deftroyed; Difeafes and Defpair, the vifible Companions of the remaining Forces of the Emperor and *France*, inferior to the *Auftrians*, who were now flufh'd with Succefs, enrich'd with Plunder, enured to Arms and Victory. Thefe remaining Forces coup'd up in a Corner of *Bavaria* and *Bohemia*, in the utmoft Diftrefs for Provifions, not to be recruited till the Spring, and then, from the vaft Loffes of the regular Troops of *France*, only by new Levies of a raw and difheartened People, forced, driven and preffed into the Service, with the moft manifeft Dread and Terror of it, the *French* Government, detefted and defpifed by

N

its

its own People, for its ill Success and ruinous Measures; the
Queen of *Bohemia* repossessed of the greatest Part of her Dominions; and of a Treasure inestimable, the united Hearts of all
her Subjects, moved to the utmost Degree of Tenderness by her
Danger and the Injustice of her Enemies, warmed with the
most fervent Zeal, by her gallant, firm and prudent Conduct;
the King of *Sardinia*, steady to his Engagements, and infinitely
serviceable to the common Cause, the *Spaniards* check'd,
foil'd and disappointed in all their *Italian* Views, the King of
Naples bridled by our Fleets, the *Swedes* confounded by *French*
Councils, and by the just Arms of *Russia*; courting the Mediation of *Great Britain* for their Preservation, who but the Year
before had been led by *France* to disturb the Peace of the *North*,
in Contempt of *Britain*, and probably not without a remote
View to her Destruction: the *Dutch* potently armed, visibly
able, and secretly inclined to join us in the Quarrel, a very
great Army in the *British* Pay of the best Troops in *Europe*;
fresh and ready to enter into Action, whenever Necessity should
require, the *Turks* incapable of being moved by *France*, thinking of nothing but their own Preservation against the Attempts
of *Persia*:---These were the happy Circumstances into which,
by the Providence of God, and the Prudence of the Administration, our Affairs were brought, when his Majesty opened his
Parliament upon the 16th of *November* last.

*We now come to the next Head of our Discourse, the Conduct
of the Faction at the next Meeting of the Parliament* ---They,
who had been longest in an Opposition, and had conducted it,
and know the most of it, even they were unable to conceive in
what manner their former Colleagues would behave, upon what
Footing they could oppose the Support of Measures so lately
popular, conducted with so much Judgment and Vigour, and
attended with such providential Success, or thwart the Prosecution of his Majesty's further Views to take Advantage of this
happy Change. They knew indeed the Men by long Experience, they were well acquainted with their Views, and that they
would stick at nothing to obtain that Share in the Emoluments
of Power, which their Madness had so lately deprived them of;
but they were at a Loss to comprehend how they would betake
themselves to screen their Views from the Detection of the People, without whose Assistance they could do nothing; a People
brave and honest, endued with more Understanding too, with
more Lights and Knowledge from the Nature of our Government than any other People in the World, and in general never
wrong, but when seduced by Fraud, or heated by Passions; the
Success appeared too notorious to admit of those Frauds, with-

out

out Misrepresentations too gross to be even supposed; and the Grounds of those *Passions* had been too justly removed, in all Instances, that it was practicable to be done, it was therefore thought impossible, that any such Attempt would meet with the least Encouragement, since the *previous Step* must be to eradicate *the old Principle* upon which the Safety of this Nation has ever depended; which it has never departed from without Shame and Misfortune, and which the People ever recurred to again, however temporarily seduced, viz. *that this Nation must eternally oppose the Advancement of the Monarchy of France.*

The *Faction* saw all this, and considered their Game at first as desperate, but their very Despair obliged them to persist— they knew that Opposition could never want some Allies from such as had been duped by them, and knew not how to retreat, and from such as, by the same Errors, were in the same desperate Condition with themselves, from such as were avowed *Jacobites*, and such as were of beggarly Circumstances, who had a Probability of bettering themselves by the Confusion of their Country, which though far short of a Probability, was yet better than a Certainty of *Ruin* and a *Goal*, which flared them in the Face.

They had a farther Dependance upon the Liberty of the Press, which is always a mighty Engine, of equal Use to *Liberty* and *Faction*, they took Advantage from the Knowledge that the Ministers they now opposed were tender of it, and knowing this, they thought themselves secure in the most monstrous Abuse of it that was ever known in any Age or Nation.——A Use which their former Leaders, when it was under their Direction, never put it to themselves, in the same degree, *nor pointed to the Mark, at which it has been since wickedly levelled.* ——This was the Spring by which they proposed to set the whole Machine in Motion, and by this they depended to retail Scurrility and Treason with Impunity (for Argument they had none) upon a wretched Set of People, who with Education just sufficient *to enable them to read*, spend all their leisure Time, and sometimes more than they have conveniently to spare from behind the Counter, in some blind Coffee-house, and thence retiring to their Tavern Assemblies, retail it out again, to Men still below them in this *great Qualification*; where, to shew that they understand the true Spirit of every libellous Production, they enter into all its Sentiments, and become, in their own great Opinions, and in the Opinions of their Auditors, after a little Habit in this Way, consummate Politicians, judging of the Interests of all States and Kingdoms, and of all Ministers and Princes, as well as of their own, *whom they constantly take*

N 2

for

*for granted to be the worst of all, and the sole Authors of every Ca-
lamity and Disorder of the whole World.*

With these *Troops,* and with this *Artillery* of *Faction,* they
still thought themselves enabled to take the Field.—They had,
it is true, seen all Squadrons of Opposition intermixed with
Bodies of these, but never led by such Generals, nor consisting
of these Troops alone: However trusting in their Numbers,
and depending upon their Noise, which, though it would produce no Argument from their own Quarter, prevented those
that came from another, from being heard, they commenced
the second Campaign, confiding more in the Division of their
Enemy, than in their own Strength, and trusting that some unfortunate Events, or some unhappy Errors, might, in Time,
afford them better Colours, than (in spight of all the Varnish
they could put upon it) their Cause would for the present
bear.

Of late Years, by the vast Encrease of Trade, and the Custom of living in the Capital, for the greatest Part of the Year,
London and *Westminster* had vastly encreased,—all great Cities
are the Seat both of *Liberty* and *Faction,*—in Proportion to their
Numbers and their Wealth, their Abilities either to defend the
one, or to exert the other, encrease.—For the Means of one,
and of the other, are the same, and they differ only in the Extent to which they are carried, and in the Lengths they go.—
From this Encrease it was, that the late Opposition derived its
Force, and it was by the Influence of these two Cities, in great
measure, that they routed the late Administration.--*Westminster*
had in a particular Manner exerted itself to maintain its Freedom
of Election, which had been, with unaccountable Imprudence,
invaded with very strong and odious Circumstances at their
Choice of Members for the present Parliament.—The Administration still, with greater Rashness, were determined, if they
could, to make this irregular Election stand, which so much offended all, as well violent as moderate Men, that there arose a
Conjunction of all Interests, and of all Principles, which created
an Opposition so formidable, that it was not to be resisted, and
such as, it is hoped, there will never be the same Occasion
to see again.—The Justice of the Cause, and the Consequence
of its Issue to the People, made Men exert themselves with an
uncommon Spirit, and caused them to appear in vast Numbers, and in very frequent Assemblies, by which Men of all
Tempers became acquainted, who would otherwise never have
known each other.—The most *warm and violent* consorted together, who when they had carried their Point, and found the
Sweets of Victory, (from a kind of Turn natural to that Order

of

of Mankind, and to Perfons of fuch a Difpofition) knew no longer how to confine themfelves within their own proper Sphere, and thought themfelves equally qualified and equally entitled to direct the Nation, as to conduct their own Election. Thus when the *Moderate* and *Wife*, contented with having done their Duty, and carried the only Point with which they were intitled to interfere, retired peaceabl to reap the Fruits of an Event, which produced many other beneficial Confequences to their Country *Thefe*, though *a more Honeft*, ftrengthening themfelves with Numbers who had no Right to vote, and laying hold of every Man they could draw in, ftill continued to maintain the Shadow of their former Meetings. *Thefe* were the firft applied to by the *Faction*, and affuming the Title of a numerous, powerful, and worthy Set of Men, who had lately made fo great a Noife in the World, under the Stile of the *Independant Inhabitants of Weftminfter*, were, in Conjunction with proper Inftruments in the City of *London*, to take the Lead, and to fet the Example to all the other Cities and Corporations of the Kingdom. Through this Canal, the Ice was to be broken to the People in general, and Inftructions were drawn up, in which three or four were out of Form confulted, and which about *fourfcore* out of 16,000 Electors in *Weftminfter*, and *two or three hundred* out of 6000 Liverymen in *London*, fanctified with their Approbation.—Thefe being publifhed in the printed Papers, were, with Diligence and Expedition, fent into the Country, as the Senfe of this great Metropolis, to be thence taken for the Voice of the whole People of *England*; and for Fear, notwithftanding this Suggeftion, that the People in the Country would not fufficiently refent it, if their Reprefentatives did not literally conform themfelves to this pretended Senfe of the whole good People of *England*, they publifhed a Pamphlet, to convince them, that it was the Duty of every Member of Parliament, to vote in every Inftance as his Conftituents fhould direct him in the Houfe of Commons,—a Thing in the higheft Degree abfurd, for *it is the conftant and allowed Principle of our Conftitution, that no Man, after he is chofen, is to confider himfelf as a Member for any particular Place, but as a Reprefentative for the whole Nation,*—without which there could neither be Freedom of Judgment, or Speech, without which all Debate muft be entirely unneceffary, and without which the Legiflature would be torn with Faction, Nonfenfe, and Contrariety of Interefts, to a degree of Confufion that muft deftroy all Government—Hence it is that Parliaments have never allowed the Right of Inftructing to be in the People; and it has accordingly been a Practice, which, introduced firft in the

Times of the *great Rebellion*, has never since been exercised but in Times that threatened *the same Confusion*.

Yet when these Instructions appeared, they were far from answering the first End of inducing all others to follow their Example. Some few Corporations did it; but no Endeavours of the Faction could extend it far: Nay, some addressed their Members, and particularly *Bristol*, the *third City* in the *Kingdom*, in direct Opposition to them; nor is it to be wondered at, for the Instructions from *London* were not only a direct and scurrilous Libel upon the Administration, but the most seditious Instrument, that ever was penned, and very little short of Treason both against the King and Constitution. Those of *Westminster* were less fruitless in personal Abuse, which they hinted only, that they kept in Reserve till they saw whether their Ideas were complied with; in many other Respects they went *as far*, and in some, *viz.* with Respect to the Constitution, *still farther* than the City of *London* itself.

The distinguished Points of these ever memorable Performances may be reduced to the following Heads, *1st*, the *Abuse of Persons* without the least Reserve or Decency: *2dly*, The *Place-Bill: 3dly*, The *Triennial Law* *4thly*, *Justice* upon the Earl of *Orford: 5thly*, *Granting no Supplies* till the 2d, 3d, and 4th Point here mentioned were complied with.

Now if every one of these Points be duly considered, we can be at no Loss to discover what their View was, and from what Quarter their Instructions came.—With regard to the first, as I have observed before, *the Abuse of Persons* was the Fort of the Faction in all former Opposition; but as they were very sensible that to answer any View by it, they must carry it to a greater Excess; and do it with greater Injustice and Confidence than was ever done before, it was very prudent to be able to quote for their Example, what they termed the Sense of the whole Nation —As to the second Article, the *Place-Bill*, they knew no *wise Government* would think it prudent to strengthen the popular Interest in such a time of Inflammation, that therefore *King*, *Lords* and *Commons* would refuse to pass it, as they had the more Reason to do, a Bill of the same Nature very considerable in its Consequences (though misrepresented grossly) having passed in the last Sessions. As to the *Triennial Law*, they were sure that could not be obtained, because they knew there were not ten Men seriously for it, in the whole Parliament, and their most flaming Patriots had themselves voted against it in the last Sessions. As to *what they called Justice* upon the Earl of *Orford*, they knew that they had already by their own Conduct put it out of the Power of any Set of Men to ef-

fect it ; which was the Reason that in Truth they infifted upon
thefe three laft mentioned Points ; being fure from thence,
though Things fell out the beft for this Nation, and the worft
for them, never to want Ground and Pretence for Oppofition,
and for a feeming Juftification of the *grand Point of all, the
diftreffing of Government, by granting no Money to the Crown* ;
which without this Addrefs and thefe Arts, the People would
have looked upon them, not as *Patriots*, but as *Monfters* and
Madmen, in the then critical Situation of Affairs, to have oppofed, when *the Ballance of Power*, that Point with Juftice fo
much favoured at all Times by this Country, lay at an immediate Stake.

It was thus by heating the Minds of the People, and by fetting them in a vain Difpute, that they endeavoured to bring
the Nation off from the true Scent, and to pave the Way for
the Revival of their *Tory* Principles again .—By inculcating thefe
popular Points, and fpreading a certain general Maxim very
fallacioufly applied, that *It was of no Confequence what became of
the Liberties of* Europe, *if we did not firft fecure our Liberties at
Home*, they difguifed their Attempts of deftroying both the
one and the other.

The *Faction* having now no Means to gain upon the Reafon,
fought only to depend upon the Madnefs of the People, and
having laid a Foundation by *thefe Inftructions* before mentioned, upon the firft Opening of the Seffions, oppofed *the Addrefs to his Majefty in Return for his Speech from the Throne*,
in which were enumerated feveral of thofe Advantages, which
called fo loudly for the Gratitude of this Nation both to *God* and
Man ; but they difcovered no Temper of that kind to *either :*
Nay, as if the Senfe and Memory of all their Auditors had been
totally loft, they difclaimed againft the prefent State of things,
as it equally bad and defperate, with that out of which we had
fo happily efcaped, retailing by rote the fame Imputations to
the prefent Conduct, and the fame Reflections upon the prefent
State of our Affairs, as they had learned of their Leaders before,
when the Situation of Affairs was totally the reverfe : Notwithftanding the vifible Importance of convincing the World abroad,
in this critical Conjuncture, (efpecially after the great Confufion of this Country and the Change of the Miniftry) that the
Publick were united to fupport the Common Caufe ; though
it is well known, as an able Foreigner obferves, *que fur tout
depuis le Commencement de ce Siecle, les Harangues des Rois de la
Grande Bretagne à l' overture du Parlement font confiderés comme
des Efpeces d' Oracles touchant la Situation generale des Affaires de
l' Europe :*

P Europe * :—And though, whoever has travelled abroad is sensible how the Expectations of all Nations are raised or depressed according to the Sentiments expressed from the Throne, and according to the Reception of the King's Speech in the first Debate of Parliament; it was in vain to reason from hence, that what gained Credit with all Foreign Nations, ought to meet with some Respect at home.—That the Consequences of not corresponding with the Sentiments of the Crown, must either be a Suggestion of *Falshood* in his *Majesty*, or of *Ignorance* or *Madness* in *ourselves*, that in such a Situation this must throw Things back again into all the first Confusion—that any Coldness expressed in such an extraordinary Conjuncture, must convince the World, that a second Revolution of our Administration was to follow,—that as the Confidence arising in all our natural Allies, and Dejection in our Enemies, proceeded only from the Prospect of the Change of Measures consequential to it, both would infallibly be defeated by a Prospect of the Discontinuance of that Administration —That these Reflections must convert the Confidence of the one into Despair, the Dejection of the other into Confidence,—that this must infallibly induce the King of *Sardinia* to listen to the Invitations of Advantage thrown in his Way by *France* and *Spain*; intimidate the *Dutch* from entering into Engagements with us; compel the House of *Austria* to submit immediately to any Terms which *France* should impose, and irrecoverably sacrifice all *Europe* to be cantoned out at the Will of that imperious Power; induce *Prussia* and *Saxony*, who had just receded from that Confederacy, to pursue new Views of Advantage to themselves, at the Expence of that distressed Princess; sacrifice all the Sums already expended in this Cause, and totally defeat all the Views, we now so reasonably entertained, of restoring the Balance of Power. In fine, that it would inevitably drive us back into the Steps of the last Administration, which even the *Faction* still affected to condemn and punish —All this had no Effect; these Arguments could have no Effect on Men, who had Views to which they bore no Relation, and who, by their original Principles, wished secretly the very Thing that others, by their Reasoning, endeavoured to prevent; at last the Sense of the House being taken by a Division, it appeared, not less to the Amazement of themselves, than to that of all honest Men, that so many were of their own Principles, so many defeated in their Expectations, so many fettered in Apprehensions of the Spirit of the Time, the Hazard of their future Elections, the Fear of Personal Abuse,

* Rou_____

the

the miſtaken Shame of deſerting what they called their Party, (though they knew them in the wrong, and wiſhed to be out of the Enchantment) ſo many led away by the ſpecious Pretence of imaginary or irremediable Grievances, and ſo many weak and deluded Men, that they were joined by a very great Number.

This Degree of Succeſs elated them ſo far, that they gave a Vent to all their Rage and Malice againſt every one, who had differed from them in this Vote;—painted it out to the People in every Colour of Inconſiſtency; - they had treated thoſe, who acted with the former Adminiſtration, for twenty Years paſt, without Mercy, as the greateſt Villains for entertaining for a Principle, *that they ſhould vote with their Party in all Queſtions whatſoever, right or wrong, and that Party could be no otherwiſe maintained*. Yet, as much as they had condemned this Principle a little while before, they made no ſcruple to adopt it now, and for this ſingle Vote, branded every Man, who gave it, at once, as a Deſerter of the Cauſe of his Country, exerting every *low, mean* and *infamous Art*, to *injure, blacken,* and *defame* him.

The *Faction* now obſerving, that they were abetted, not only without Doors, but within, by a larger Body of People than they could have at firſt imagined, determined in the next Inſtance, without Reſerve, to try how far that Deluſion had extended, and could ſupport them.—When therefore the Eſtimates for the 16,000 *Britiſh* Troops in *Flanders* came to be conſidered, *they oppoſed, with the utmoſt Vehemence, the granting the Supply for this Service, inſiſting upon their being recalled home, and diſbanded*;—and now they began to appear in their full Colour the Men they were; they not only trod in the Steps of their Predeceſſors, in the Reign of King *Charles* the Second, King *William*, and Queen *Anne*, but they travelled that Pace, which none of them had gone before.—None had ever ſo openly avowed the Views of leaving the whole World to the Mercy of *France* · No *Engliſhman* before could have dared to make a Propoſition of this Nature, when our Armies were actually united in the Field, and *France*, bending its utmoſt Force to the Ruin of our moſt potent and conſtant Ally abroad.—Even in that infamous Scene in the Reign of the Queen, they were contented, for the firſt Step, to agree to a Ceſſation of Arms, and to ſeparate from their Allies —They made a Peace, ſuch as it was, before they brought back a ſingle Regiment;—they had then the Pretence of ſome Conceſſions from *France*, ſmall as they were, compared with the Advantages in our Power at that Time to have procured :—they had the Plea of a dangerous Intereſt, that the General had acquired in the Army, and of

O   ambitious

ambitious Views, in a great Subject, which a Princess, *the laſt of her Race,* had no Ability to contend with ;—they had Pretences, from the immenſe Sums which had been already expended upon the War, and which People naturally wiſhed to be eaſed from almoſt at any Rate ;—they had even ſome Shew of Conſiſtency in their Conduct ; for they had been long at work to obſtruct and oppoſe the Continuance of it.—But for theſe People, all Appearance of Reaſon and Conſiſtency was as remote to juſtify them in what they did, as their Deſign was manifeſt to ruin the Intereſt, to pervert the Principles, to inſult the Underſtandings, and abuſe the Weakneſs of their Countrymen.

We can never recur too often to this Point, that whoever knows the Hiſtory of this Government, can judge of its Intereſts and its Dangers, muſt know, that it has been, and ought to be, the conſtant Principle of Politicks, by which this Nation muſt be ever governed.—To keep down the Power of the Houſe of *Bourbon,* that if ſhe now acquires ever ſo little an Addition to it, *In its Conſequences, the Trade, the Liberty, the Religion, the Indepedency of this Nation, will be inevitably undone*—*That to prevent this Power from Encreaſe, we muſt ſupport ſome great Power on the Continent, capable to ſtand for a Time, till Confederacies may be formed againſt her* ;—that for Ages paſt, and ſtill at this Hour, *no other Power is in any Degree equal (or caralle in any reaſinable Proſpect of Time to be made equal) to that Taſk, but that of the Houſe of* Auſtria.—And that *therefore the Sum of all the Politicks of this Nation is to ſupport, by all the Means in our Power, the Houſe of* Auſtria.

The Nation has ſo long ſeen the Force of theſe Maxims, has ſuffered ſo much from every temporary Departure from them, and inſenſibly advanced into ſo manifeſt Danger, by every Relaxation from theſe Principles, that there was not a ſingle Man, who did not profeſs them, and upon this was grounded that univerſal Clamour againſt the late Adminiſtration. The Author of that worſt and moſt malicious Label that ever was publiſhed, entitled, *The Caſe of the* Hanover *Troops,* himſelf confeſſes, that the univerſal Diſſatisfaction of that Time was principally owing to this weak, and, as he adds, wicked Conduct of our Foreign Affairs, and Neglect of theſe Principles. I may ſay more, there was not a ſingle Man of this Nation, who was not fully convinced, that they were true, though ſome were ſorry for their private Views againſt the Government, that they ſhould be purſued for no other Reaſon, than that they knew them to be true ·—And therefore, upon the late Change of the Adminiſtration, it was reſolved, by the almoſt univerſal Senſe of the whole

2

Nation,

Nation, notwithstanding the first impotent Attempt of these Gentlemen to prevent it, that these 16.000 National Troops should be sent into *Flanders*.—When this was done, however, the Affairs of the Queen of *Hungary* had already providentially begun to mend, by a fortunate Winter's Campaign, and our Spirits were a little raised, by seeing her Ruin a little protracted. —Yet it was then evident, that these 16,000 Men were far from being able alone to prevent that Ruin. Had the Nation therefore been ripened enough into a fatal Distraction, much more might have been *then* urged, with greater Plausibility, against this first Step, than against the Continuance of it, after it had been made.—The Prospect of being able to compose an Army sufficient to act against *France*, was then in some Degree precarious and remote. It might have been, (as it has been since) urged, that this could only operate by way of a Diversion,—and hardly that, because the *French* could not fear Hostilities from such an Handful of Men ;—yet, I say, the Measure was even then approved by the almost universal Sense of this Nation,—as it was a Beginning, as it maintained the Faith of Treaties, as it was a Pledge of the future Intentions of this Country, and a Proof of our Change of Politicks, as it was a Root and a Foundation for other Troops to be gathered to, as Time or Incidents, or the common Danger, might induce ,—and as it was conformable with *an established Rule of Politicks, that he that gains Time, gains every thing.*

The Sense therefore of these fundamental Principles brought, as I have said, in a manner, the whole Nation to be willing, at a Time, when two of the greatest Powers in *Germany* were embarqued, and in the Field, in Conjunction with *France*, against the Queen of *Hungary*,—at a Time, when *Hanover*, and the *Dutch*, were both awed by a *French* Army ; and when no certain or immediate Prospect appeared, of Assistance on any Side, but from the House of *Savoy* in *Italy*, to adventure this Experiment, an Experiment of 6 or 700,000 *l.* They thought every thing was to be tried in such Extremities, and no Expence to be considered, where the *Trade*, the *Liberty*, the *Religion* and *Independency* of this Nation, were visibly at Stake.

How then could this scandalous Opposition to the Continuance of this Measure be swallowed by the Publick in the very next Year, when the Face of our Affairs was changed in so wonderful a manner in our Favour, when *Prussia* and *Saxony* had desisted from being Enemies to the House of *Austria*, when the *French* Armies had been so greatly diminished, when the Queen of *Hungary* had almost cleared her whole Dominions from the Enemy, when the *Dutch* and *Hanover* were no longer awed by

France, when inftead of a naked Body of 16,000 Men, by the Junction of *Heffians*, *Hanoverians* and *Auftrians*, we had actually an Army collected in one Body of 50,000 Men : The Anfwer to this Queftion is eafily made, the Ardour of the Nation had, by infamous Arts been converted into the Heat of a *Faction*, Oppofition, which was before conducted by *Whig* Principles, was now led by Incendiaries and *Jacobit s*; who never did, nor ever will lead the People but to Meafures inconfiftent with their Interefts and Safety.

But though the Wicked abound in this and in all other Countries, yet they are never numerous enough alone to attempt the Ruin of their Country, they muft have a vaft Acceffion of the Honeft to affift them, and they muft impofe upon their Weaknefs to abet their Views ; they muft have fome Pretences to prevail upon them.—Let us now confider what thefe Pretences were.

" They firft began tenderly to infinuate that our firft Prin-
" ciples of Policy, however long maintain'd, were in them-
" felves erroneous, and that confidering the former immenfe
" Expences of this Nation, the little Fruit that we had reap-
" ed from them, and the Probability of being ftill from Time
" to Time engaged in new Quarrels, it was fit to be confider-
" ed, whether it was not proper to enter upon a new Syftem ;
" that it was vifible we could never make any Acquifitions up-
" on the Continent to reimburfe our Expences; and that we
" therefore confumed ourfelves only for the Benefit of other
" Powers, that our Navy was a fufficient Protection for us a-
" gainft the whole World; that the regular Troops, which
" thefe Views obliged us to maintain would prove the Ruin of
" our Liberties; and the vaft Taxes produce the Ruin of our
" Trade ; fo that it was thrown out as a Doubt fit for the Na-
" tion to confider, whether it was not better to leave the reft
" of the World to fhift for itfelf as well as it could, and to
" entrench within our own natural Boundaries, take our
" Chance, and defend ourfelves the beft we could " They
were obliged to venture thus to fhake the eftablifhed Principles
that they might afterwards debauch the Underftandings of the
People, in which they proceeded exactly upon the Plan of their
Brother Politicians, the *Jefuits* and the Church of *Rome*, who
begin all their Practices on thofe they mean to feduce, by raifing Doubts as to the Fundamentals of their Faith, which when
once departed from, expofe their unwary Pupils to be driven
from one Point to another, till they at laft refign their Senfes
to their infiduous Guides ; thefe Political Seducers could not
have failed to learn the Craft of a Set of People of whom they
followed

followed the Views; and like those by whom they had been taught their Leſſon, they applied theſe Inſinuations with great Caution at the firſt, and only upon ſuch Objects as by the Weakneſs of their Underſtandings were too dull of Apprehenſion to detect their Views, and who by their Ignorance could not be able to know, that theſe were the conſtant Practices of the *Jacobites, Enemies* of their *Country* and *Friends* of *France* upon all Occaſions.

There is always much Ignorance and much Weakneſs in the Bulk of Mankind, ſo that they were not long before they found their Effect in this ſecret Management; and they were further aſſiſted by a certain Temper, which every thinking Man muſt have obſerved in human Nature of the lower Claſs, *that they delight in any thing that is new, and in the marvellous*; theſe Refinements upon our Policy were ſtrange to them; and they admired at the Sagacity of thoſe, who had ſtruck out thoſe new Lights; which they were proud to appear the Inventors of, or at leaſt, to ſhew their ſuperior Judgment in comprehending as ſoon as hinted, and to diſplay this ſuperior Sagacity, farther inculcated all theſe Doctrines, upon the common People, who are always prone to reliſh a Diſcovery, which promiſes a Reduction of their Taxes and of an Army.

But alas! how ſhallow are the Underſtandings of theſe Men, who can be impoſed upon by this ſuperficial Reaſoning? Can the Wiſdom of this Age entertain the Vanity to think, that their Anceſtors have for ſeven hundred Years perſiſted in an Error, which the bright Genius of the enlightened Vulgar have now at length diſcovered to be ſuch? ſhall every Cobler in his Stall pretend a Knowledge of political Affairs, ſuperior to that of the beſt, the wiſeſt, the greateſt Men of this and all former Ages, whom their Education, and whole Turn of Life have adapted and dedicated to the Study of Politicks and Government? What ridiculous Vanity is this? and what Folly, to imagine that Men, who have no Intereſt in the State, but the Profits of their daily Labour, ſhould be more anxious for the Well-being of their Country, than thoſe, who have vaſt Properties to take Care of; who really feel the Burthens, which are but imaginary upon the reſt (becauſe in the Nature of things they caſt off the Load of all publick Charges from themſelves upon the Rich, by an Advance both in the Price of their Commodities and Labour,) and who alone ſuſtain all the Taxes of the Nation? Whoſe Lands are ſaddled directly or indirectly with the whole Expence; who, if Ruin falls upon their Country, muſt, by Forfeitures and Confiſcations, loſe their Eſtates, their Titles, and perhaps their Lives, while theſe, living by the

natural

natural Occafions of all Mankind, muft ftill be neceffary to
every State, tranform it how you will, muft be from that Neceffity preferved, and carry with them, through all Difafters
of their Country, a certain Method of Subfiftence. Shall this
Order of the People, from the falfe Oratory, and Declama-
tions of a few feditious Leaders, be perfuaded to oppofe their
new-fangled Sentiments to fuch Men as thefe, prefume to fet
up for Leaders of Political Opinions, and by a few Inftances
of temporary Neglect in Great Men, (warped perhaps on fome
Occafions from their Duty to their Country, by the Allure-
ments of great Offices in the State,—or mifled into the Support
of wrong Meafures, for a time) be carried away, to think their
Affairs more fafe under the Direction of Men of defperate Fortunes, low Rank, and even of the very Commonalty themfelves ;—or becaufe all the Inftances of frantick Management
in Princes, have been collected together, to make a Bundle of
Infamy againft Government by Monarchy, and to expofe the
Errors and Wickednefs of fome crowned Heads ,— are they to
conclude, from thefe partial Informations, that Monarchy is
no longer to be endured, or trufted with any degree of Power,
however legally entitled to it by the Conftitution of their Country ?—and that neither the Prince, who derives his Glory from
the Greatnefs of his People, his Security and Affluence from
their Profperity, nor the Nobility, whofe Titles and Eftates
depend upon the fame Source, are proper Judges of the Intereft
of the Publick, while they deem themfelves the only knowing,
wife, and honeft Politicians of the World.

Again,—Will this Nation be feduced to fuch a Point as not
to fee, that neither this, nor any other in the Word can ftand
alone, and without Allies ?—That Maritime Power is precarious, neceffarily divided often, and capable of changing from
one State to another, when protected only by itfelf —That
when the *Romans* gained the univerfal Empire on the Continent, though much in a lower Condition in their Marine than
France now is, the *Carthaginians*, the only State of the whole
World then potent in this refpect, were in the End deftroyed.—
That we ourfelves only by one fortunate Defeat ruined the Naval Force of *Spain* in 1588, and acquired the Dominion of the
Sea.—That every People almoft in *Europe*, have now fome degree of Power upon that Element, and that a little Acceffion
of Influence to *France*, muft put her in a Condition to compel
that whole collected Power to contend with ours,— that fhe
might, with *a little Extent* of her Barrier, and *Arrondiffement* of
her Dominions, reduce half of her Armies, and employ half of
her Revenues to encreafe her Fleets.—That the Experience of

all

all our Hiſtories ſhews, the utmoſt Care of the moſt numerous
Squadrons inſufficient to ſecure us againſt being inſulted, nay,
even actually invaded;—and that ſuch Invaſions have never
failed to put us to great Expence, and have always given us
great Alarms, and ſometimes proved ſuccesful;—that we have
rarely wanted a Faction, at any time, to back and to abett Attempts of this Nature; nor that, from the Nature of our Government, we ever ſhall,—and that when they were thus backed,
and thus abetted, they hardly ever failed of their Deſign.—The
very Government, and Monarchy and Conſtitution of this Country, owe their Origin to theſe Invaſions;—not to ſpeak of the
Romans, whoſe Conqueſts are very remote, the *Saxons* conquered this Iſland, from the *Britons*, by their Fleets; the Empire of the *Saxons*, who, in Proportion to thoſe Times, had very conſiderable Naval Forces, was, for a while, entirely over-
thrown by the *Danes*;— and ſcarce had the *Saxons* recovered
their Ground, but that the *Norman* Invaſion compleated all,
and made an entire Conqueſt of this Nation.—From thence forward is it forgot how we have ſuffered by Deſcents from *France*;
how the Contentions for private Title were perpetually carried
on by foreign Aids, to the Perturbation of our State; how frequently every Party ſucceeded in their Turn; how near the
Spaniards, as I have before obſerved, came to make a Province of this Iſland; how the Revolution, in the Memory
of thoſe now living, ſucceeded, in ſpight of all the Vigilance of Government; how *Ireland* was upon the very Point
of being loſt; how the *French* invaded, and retreated thence
with Impunity; how, ſince that Time, many Deſcents have
taken Effect; when our Navy was in its Zenith, and thoſe
of other Powers at their loweſt Ebb,—how vaſt a Number of
our Ships have been found inſufficient to anſwer all our ſeve-
ral Purpoſes of Defence, of Trade, the Annoyance of our Enemies, and Protection of our own Coaſt, againſt one inconſi-
derable Enemy, and one hollow Friend?—If we have not forgot all this,—we muſt be mad, to think, that, at any Time,
or in any Situation, this Nation can, with Security, alone confide in their Naval Force, much leſs when the reſt of *Europe*
ſhall be reduced to the dread of, or to a provincial Dependance
upon a great Empire, within three Hours ſail of ſome Part of
our Dominions, and within ten of our Capital itſelf.

Will this Nation, however careful of its Liberty at Home,
out of a remote and, honeſtly ſpeaking, little to be dreaded Danger of the Influence of a ſmall Military Force, expoſe itſelf to
thoſe Inſults, which muſt deſtroy all Peace and Quiet, interrupt

all Commerce, and may, upon every Turn, ruin the publick Credit of this Country, which gives Life to every Thing, in which we find either Profit or Security at home :— But much more shall this Nation, from these imaginary Dangers, be distracted enough to disband her Armies in the Time of actual War, and run headlong into the manifest, immediate and certain Dangers of a Foreign Yoke ?— Are we to put ourselves to immediate Death for fear of dying hereafter ?—What Folly is it, (out of a magnified Misrepresentation of Distresses, imaginary, and falsely pretended, Decay of Trade, or Suggestions of Poverty in the midst of immense Opulency, greater than either we or any other State in *Europe* ever yet enjoyed,) to refuse Succour to *those Allies*, whose (*Standing Armies* awe that Power, which, when once unrestrained by them, can never possibly be resisted, but by such Standing Armies at home, as would indeed be ruinous both to Trade and Liberty. By these occasional and temporary Expences, we secure the future and constant Assistance, and avail ourselves of the Benefit of Standing Armies of numerous and potent Nations, which answer, upon any Emergency abroad, that Want, which we otherwise should have of them at home, and without which our Country would infallibly, sooner or later, be the Seat of War,—without which our Inhabitants, instead of Manufacturers, must universally become Soldiers,—and our Battles be fought within our own Bowels, and by our own Countrymen, instead of being fought in the Countries of our Enemies, and to the Depopulation of other Nations.— No Expence can be too great to secure us these Advantages, or to preserve us from these Evils,—and to pretend, that the Benefits of our Situation are to be carried further than this, or to be secured by any other Means in the present State and Politicks of all the Powers on the Continent, is a *Presumption* upon the Goodness and Felicity permitted us by Providence, and *a Nonsense* that will destroy it all.

However evident this Reasoning may be, yet it's contrary met with Advocates, and enlarged *their Bottom*; but, *broad* as they affected to call it, and *broad*, as it really became, by the Folly and Passion, and the Ferment of the Time, the Foundation, upon which it was built, was too bad to admit it to stand without it was yet much *broader*, to which End they employed their Sophistry, upon the Head of our Troops in *Flanders*, still much farther. This they urged in the Debate of that Day ; but afterwards, according to their Custom, retailed among the People, in a Pamphlet, intitled, *The Question stated with regard to our Army in* Flanders. At the Close of which, they summed up all their Argument, corrected by the Debate, inlarged by the

Col-

Collection of the various Reasonings of their Orators, and reduced by Leisure, into the Method best adapted to impose upon the Publick.

These Reasonings were drawn into the Form of Questions most falsely and fallaciously composed, and as falsely and fallaciously answered by themselves, which I shall take the Liberty to answer in a different Manner.

The first Question was in these Words; 1*st*, Why, with one War upon your Hands, will you draw yourselves into another?

2*dly*, Why will you make yourselves Principals in a War, in which you ought only to be Auxiliaries?

3*dly*, Why do you run yourselves into Expences you can't bear, into Difficulties you will find it so hard, if not impossible to get out of, into Inconveniencies you see no End of, Pursuits where there is nothing to gain, and Struggles in which you have so much to lose?

4*thly*, Why, if the Queen of *Hungary* is to be farther assisted, do you, instead of sending her Money, which might assist her, expend treble the Money she would be thankful for in raising Forces that can't assist her?

5*thly*, Why did you dissuade the Queen of *Hungary* from listening to all Offers of Accommodation the last Summer, and particularly at the Siege of *Prague?* Why did you endeavour to prevent her accepting the Terms proposed of reciprocal Evacuation of *Bohemia* and *Bavaria*, leaving other Claims and Pretensions to future Negotiations and civil Decision, which is the End they must come to, unless these Squabbles last for ever?

6*thly*, Why did you embarque in this Measure, without the Junction, Consent, Approbation, or even Participation of *Holland?*

7*thly*, Why have you alone taken upon you the Hazards, Burthens and Expences of a Scheme, which all the Powers of *Europe* combined, would not perhaps be able to execute, and which no Power in *Europe* will assist you in?

These Questions are, by the Confession of the Author, who was known to be a capital Writer, the Substance of all they had to offer upon this Head, —and we shall now come to shew their flimsy Texture; —they are intended to pass as so many solid Facts, attended with so many irrefragable Reasons, how much they differ, from either Fact or Reason, appear by the following Reflections.

As to the first Question, we entered into the second War, because we were bound by the strongest Ties of Treaty and publick Faith to do it; —because the first War could never have been brought to a happy Conclusion without it, —because the second Enemy supported the first; —because the second Power,

with-

without entering avowedly into that War, supplied, encouraged, and fomented the Difference between us and the firft; and becaufe there is more Safety in an open Enemy, than in a falfe Friend.—becaufe the Views of the firft and fecond Enemy coincided with each other; and becaufe we were certain, that the fecond Enemy would have joined the firft, with her whole and an irrefiftible Force, when fhe had finifhed her Work in *Germany*, and that then we fhould have had to deal with both thefe Powers, without any one Ally in the World, --- whereas, by joining againft the fecond, at the Time we did it, we were able to act in Conjunction with fome of the greateft Powers in *Europe*, and a reafonable Expectation of the Aid of more;---becaufe the rafh Attempts of the firft Power, partly to gratify her own wild Ambition, and partly to affift the Plan of the fecond, had afforded us the Means, if we engaged againft the fecond, of ruining the Armies of the firft, of confining her Fleets from any Poffibility of doing us any Harm, and in fine, of difappointing her moft favourite Views, of exhaufting her Revenues, and of throwing her Government into Confufion in one Campaign, more than by any other way of waging War with her to the End of the World - -All this could be only done, when we had the one War upon our Hands, by engaging in the other.

As to the fecond Queftion, it will fcarce admit of any Anfwer, becaufe the Affertion it implies is abfolutely and notorioufly falfe in Fact, for we have hitherto not been Principals in this War in any Senfe whatever. We have acted only as Auxiliaries to the Houfe of *Auftria*. --- And this it feems I need not take the Pains to juftify, fince in acting as Auxiliaries, we are by Confeffion of this Author only what we ought to be.

The third Queftion contains a complicated Charge, to which I fhall diftinctly anfwer· 1ft, It is as happily as it is palpably untrue, *that the Expences into which we are involved, are fuch as we cannot bear.* For to the heavy Difappointment of the Enemies of this Country, the great Supplies of the laft Year have been raifed upon Terms as low, notwithftanding all the Arts of monied Men, and all the Terrors fcattered by the *Faction*, as they ever were in Times of the moft profound Peace, while the Enemy, we are engaged with, cannot raife the Sums he wants, at twice the Rate of Intereft we pay: Nor are they likely to reap any greater Satisfaction, with refpect to the Supplies in the next Seffion 2. *As to the Difficulties, which are foretold to be fo hard and impoffible to get out of,* it is now vifible that by the Steadinefs of this Parliament, and the Bleffing of God upon our Arms, we have already proved the *Faction* to be lying Prophets, and what has already happened, fufficiently promifes us a full Detection

of

of the Falsity of every one of their Predictions. 3. *As to the Inconveniencies we see no End of*, it is undoubtedly true, that no human Reason can prescribe an exact Period to any War, the Inconveniencies of which must last till such War is determined; but if this be an Objection, it is such a one, as must make against engaging in any War, however just or necessary, in any Country or Conjuncture whatsoever. 4. We are charged *with Pursuits, where there is nothing to gain, and Struggles, in which we have so much to lose* --- But can these Men pass for Patriots upon the Publick, who say, we have *nothing to gain*, by restoring that faithful Ally, which is alone able to stem the Ambition of the *French* Monarch, the implacable and ever dangerous Enemy of this Country? or can they be thought to have either Common Sense or Honesty, who contend, that we should lie by in time of such Danger? --- *When are Men to struggle, but when they have so much to lose, as the Trade, the Independency, the Religion, and the Freedom of their Country?*

The fourth Question demands, *why we did not assist the Queen of* Hungary *with Money only?* I cannot but observe, that this Question, considering the Tendency of their *former* Insinuations, is a little unnecessary, unless they doubted of the Weight they might have upon the Publick, --- for the general Turn of their Discourse has been, that it is vain to assist her, either with Men or Money. --- In good Truth, if the Subject were not of too serious a Nature, it would be impossible not to laugh at the miserable Shifts they have been put upon to defend their wretched Cause. Whenever any Man of Sense and Knowledge kept them close in Argument, and urged the Faith of Treaties, the Danger of *France*, the Ruin of the Ballance, the Case of the Earl of *Orford* (censured by themselves for neglecting these Considerations,) they confessed all this, and denied, that they opposed it; they said, that they agreed in the Necessity of assisting the House of *Austria*, and that they differed only in the Means, yet, if ever they could fasten upon any weak, ignorant, or ill-disposed Person in private Conversation, it was their whole Labour to convince him of the Danger, Impracticability, and Inutility of doing it at all. This was the Topick upon which their Tools and Emissaries were instructed constantly to entertain the People, --- nay, they came at last to talk publickly in Parliament in the same disingenuous manner, and with the same Inconsistency --- It will not be soon forgot, in what Manner, or how in the Debate of this very Point, their most eminent Directors argued, *some* grounding their Harangues upon this Position, " That the late Success of the House of *Austria* had reduced " *France* so low, that she could not carry on the War with

" any

" any Prospect of Success; that the Queen of *Hungary* might
" therefore make a Safe and an honourable Peace, and that to sup-
" port her any longer would be to abet her in a War of Acqui-
" sition and Ambition, with which we ought to have no Con-
" cern; either declaiming upon this direct contrary Principle,
" that the House of *Austria* was never reduced so low, that she
" could never more be relied upon as a proper Power to be
" maintained for the support of the Ballance against *France*,
" and that consequently, the Expence of assisting the Queen
" of *Hungary* in this View was fruitless and destructive, and
" tending only to encourage *her in the Project*, and to plunge
" *ourselves* into *the Certainty* of more immediate *Ruin.*" It is
unnecessary to make any Remarks upon the Difference of the
Premises, it is enough, that the *Conclusion* was the same from
both. This kind of Reasoning therefore, as I have already
observed, seems to have rendered this Question (*why we did not
assist the Queen of* Hungary *with Money, only of little Importance*)
because, according to the Doctrine we have mentioned, the
proper Quest on should have rather been, *Why do we assist the
Queen of* Hungary *in any way whatsoever?*—However, we shall
follow our Gentlemen for the present in their own Way,——
and answer first, because, though she might have been thankful for a third Part of the Money, which our Troops cost us,
as any Power in her late deplorable Circumstances would have
been, it was not *her Thanks*, but *her Preservation* from immediate Ruin, it was not *her Gratitude*, but *the Recovery of
her Power*, to ballance *France*, which it was our Business to
procure; it must have been an Aid that would be *effectual*, or
we should have left her worse than we found her. Now this
Insinuation, that a pecuniary Aid would have been alone effectual, is far from being true, though the whole Money, which
our Armies cost us, had been remitted to *Vienna*.----First, because such immense Sums, exported out of this Country thither, would have distressed us greatly, and would have none of
it return'd; it would have therefore been impracticable to have
continued this Expence for any time. Whereas, by Experience
of the last War, it was manifest, that very near two-thirds of
the Charge of the Armies we maintained within a nearer Distance of this Country, returned to us again: and we have had
a Proof that we can support a War in this Method without any
vast Diminution of our Specie. 2dly, Because such immense
Sums must, from the Nature of that Court, have been much
wasted or consumed; but, however applied, could not so conveniently have answered our End, because we should have lost
the Advantage of a Diversion to the Forces of *France*, which

is a Measure of the greatest Benefit in War. 3dly, Because we should have lost the Advantage that resulted from the Security of the Barrier, from the Encouragement of the *Dutch*, from the Protection of the States and Circles lying upon the Confines of *France*, and the Influence we have since manifestly gained upon the Diet of the Empire. 4thly, Because no other Measure could have put it in our Power to attack and penetrate into *France* itself, if God should prosper our Arms with any remarkable Success, and because by this Apprehension the Flower of her Armies have been consequently retained at home, and she more likely to be brought to Terms of reasonable Accommodation 5thly, That by this means we availed ourselves of two great Points, *first*, of the Cavalry of the Allies, which is the best in *Europe*, and must have been for the greatest Part unemployed in this Quarrel, if the War had not been carried on in this manner, and, *secondly*, of the natural Superiority which Confederated Powers have over a single Nation, and what was our manifest Advantage in the last War, *viz.* that the Loss of Men on our Part will fall more equally, and will be less felt; while the whole Loss of *France* falls upon her own Nation, from whence alone she is able to recruit; which Circumstance, all other things supposed to be equal, must enable the Queen of *Hungary* to sustain the War longer, and with less Inconvenience than the *French*.—For whatever the Vulgar have been taught to think, the *Austrian* Dominions are by no means inexhaustible of Men;—tho' the *French* have suffered more, yet the *Austrians* have lost a great Number, and it is a certain Fact, that *France* alone contains more Inhabitants than all the Countries of the Queen of *Hungary* put together.—As to the last Assertion, *that we have raised Forces that can't assist her*, it was founded upon an infamous, wicked, and abominable Falshood, *That the Troops, with whom they acted in Conjunction, could not, nor would not, march in the Empire*, now as fully laid open, and disproved in every Respect, as it was impudently and maliciously maintained.—In fine, a full Answer to all this Trash and Ribbaldry is contained in one Word *Dettingen*, which, had they their Deserts, should be branded in the Forehead of every Member of the *Faction*.

The fifth Question is grounded upon and conveys the Assertion of a Fact, which to this Hour they cannot tell whether it be true or false; that we dissuaded the Queen of *Hungary* from listning *to all Offers of Accommodation, the last Summer, particularly at the Siege of* Prague, &c. To this I reply only, that if we did it we did wisely. None but Politicians, such as these, would have consented to a Cessation of Arms; (for these Offers of Accommodation in effect amounted to no more) the only View of which was to prevent the Ruin of 30,000 Regular Troops of *France*, and all the ill Consequences she suffered in the ensuing Campaign. Let us farther see upon what Terms ;—— *Why you, the Queen of Hungary, are Mistress of Bavaria, which we cannot recover ; we, the French, are Masters of half Bohemia, which we cannot keep ; give us therefore up Bavaria, and you shall have Bohemia ; saving only to the Emperor, our Ally,* (that is to say, both to us and him, a sufficient Pretence to attack you again immediately, when we have got out of our present Scrape, with an additional Force) *his Pretensions to all your Dominions, the present Possession of Part of* Bohemia, *and the Town of* Egra, *which is the Key to the whole, giving up moreover to him your Interest in* Swabia, (which is little less than the third Part of that Circle, and has, by the Number of its Votes, the same kind of Influence in the Diet of the Empire, as Cornwall *in the* British Parliament ;) *together with the* Forest Towns, (which as soon as you have parted with, your ancient and permanent Alliance with the Swiss, by which they are tied never to act in any Capacity as Enemies against you, will be dissolved ;) *then will we deliver up the City of* Prague *into your Hands.*---Now, that this City of *Prague* (out of which 10,000 of 30,000 that were there, and their best Cavalry a Part of that Number, never lived to return, which did not long after, and was then every Day expected to fall into the *Austrian* Hands,) was all that the Queen of *Hungary* could have gained by this Cessation, is too visible to be denied ; and it is therefore no Wonder, that she was so obstinate as she is represented by the *Faction*, she was not inclined to trust to a new Capitulation with that very Body of Troops, who, had they not, contrary to all military Faith and Rules of War broke a Capitulation, by which they saved their Lives at *Lintz* a few Months before, could not have been at *Prague* in that Conjuncture to have demanded a second Opportunity to abuse the Mercy of this generous Princess. Yet, shortly after, it was made a Pretence against her for not accepting these absurd Terms. The *Faction* abused her for it, and proclaimed that she no longer merited our Assistance, that she was vindictive and ambitious, and that she had changed the Nature of the War, that it was now become offensive instead of defensive on her Part ; that she deserved to perish for her Folly, and our Ministers to be hang'd for advising her to it.---To what?--Not to trust to the insidious Offers, to the Faith of that perfidious Power, Offers, that gave no Assurance of any Accommodation ; Offers plainly calculated to enable her Enemies to fall upon her immediately after, with redoubled Force, tending only to deprive her of the happy Op-

portunity, which God had prefented, to give the greateft Blow
to *France*, that was ever given to her in one Campaign ; Offers
to bribe her by an *Advantage, which was, in Fact, already in her
Hands,—to be guaranty'd to her, by the Honour and Honefty of*
France,—confirmed by the additional Power of her releafed Army,
and fecured by the Refervation of the Emperor's Title to all her Do-
minions, which the Emperor has, by his Memorials, fince actually
avowed as his Intention never to have departed from. The Acceptance of fuch Offers may be advifed by *Jacobite* Counfellors, and
abetted by inconfiderate and never-to-be-unblinded *Tories* ; but
no honeft *Englifhman* can bear fuch flagrant and manifeft Difcovery of a Confederacy in this Country to promote the Views of
France ; or fuffer himfelf, by any Pretence, to affift in the Advancement of fuch a Party into the Adminiftration of Affairs,
as could recommend it to be done.

Indeed thefe Endeavours to prevent us from availing ourfelves
of every Advantage againft *France*, thefe outragious Attempts to
prejudice our People againft their natural Allies, this heaving
with fuch exceffive and unnatural Efforts againft the Principles
of Reafon, Safety and Juftice ; all this puts it out of our Power,
to deal more gently with thefe Men. And were it in our Power
their Malice and Inveteracy to all who differ from them, de-
prives them of all Title to any better Treatment.—But to proceed—

Our Minifters therefore acted honeftly and wifely (if they did
give the contrary Advice) and unlefs they had been of the Principles of that *Faction*, which abandoned the *Catalonians*, and the
French Proteftants of the *Cevennes*, made the feparate Peace of
Utrecht, facrificed their Allies, and all the Advantages of the late
War, the Glory, Intereft and good Faith of this Nation ; and
unlefs they had entertained the fame View, the Prefervation of
the Houfe of *Bourbon*, for the Service of the Pretender, they
could have given no other. If this Step had not been taken, by
this Time indeed we fhould not have had an Army in *Flanders*,
nor would there have been a fingle Army in *Europe*, that could
have ventured to have oppofed the Views of *France* ; the Queen
of *Hungary*, attacked by the collected Force of *France*, would
have clearly underftood what was meant by the *future Negocia-*
tions, and the *civil Decifion* then propofed to her, fhe muft have
fubmitted long e'er now to the Will of that relentlefs Power ;
and we fhould have had all our Thoughts turned vainly, and without Effect to execute the pleafant Scheme of thefe wife and honeft
Patriots, that of *entrenching ourfelves in our Ifland againft the*
united Power of France *and* Spain ; how long it had been before
thefe Entrenchments had been forced, every knowing Man can
eafily fee and underftand.   The

The next Question is, *Why did you embark in this Measure without the Junction, Consent, Approbation, or even Participation of Holland.*—This Way of infinuating Falfhoods with an *If,* and in this Manner, has the fame Effect upon the People, as fo many certain Facts, and give thefe Men the Opportunity, when the Infinuation is proved falfe, either by the Reafon of their Adverfaries, or the Event, to fay they only fuggefted what feemed to them the Cafe, and that they never pofitively afferted thefe Things.— But as they have all the Effect of pofitive Affertions, and as they reafon upon them always, as if they were to be taken for granted, and for fo many undeniable Truths, we have no other way to treat them, but to take them on our Part, as the People are intended to take them on theirs. ---Thefe Affertions then, are all of them either falfe, or fallacious, but if ever fo true, the Meafure was fuch as the whole People (for the Reafons I have mentioned, when I firft entered upon this Head) with all its Inconveniences, and thefe great Uncertainties, thought themfelves reduced to an abfolute Neceffity, by way of Experiment, to undertake. --That we did it without the Participation of *Holland,* is a glaring Untruth, for it cannot be foon forgot how our Minifters were ridiculed by the *Faction,* for the preffing Inftances we made in *Holland,* to engage them to join with us at that Time.---And that it was without their *Junction, Confent,* or *Approbation,* is very fallacious, becaufe thefe Words convey an Idea, which is abfolutely falfe, *that they refufed to join at all, that they gave us Reafon to believe, that they never would confent, and that they had given us to underftand, that they condemned our Undertaking.*---Whereas the Fact was only this, that they would not join in the Inftant that we firft defired, ---that they would not confent till they found that they might depend upon the Vigour and Stability of our Adminiftration,--- that they would not publickly approve of a Meafure, in which it was not fafe for them to engage, till they faw a Force fufficient to protect them, and till they were convinced, that the Efforts of a *Faction,* which had betrayed them once before, were too weak to defeat its Effect, and to caufe them to be left, as they were formerly, at the Mercy of the *French.*---Thefe appear to have been their only Reafons.---This we knew at that Time by the Affurances of their Miniftry to ours;---this the *French* then equally underftood (as any Man may fee by *Van Hoey's* Letters;) and this is now fo clearly demonftrated by their actual Acceffion to our Views, that for the future the People, if they are not infatuated, muft be convinced, how little Dependence they ought to have upon Men, who fcruple no wicked Arts to render them the Tool, to effect their ftill more wicked Defigns, and

2   that

that *there may be a Neceffity, in fome Conjunctures, to repofe a Confidence in the Abilities, Integrity, and Intelligence of thofe who who direct their Affairs.*

The feventh Queftion afferts three monftrous Facts, equally falfe, and equally tending to the Ruin of our Country :---1ft, *That we have taken upon us alone the Hazards, Burthens and Expences of this Scheme* ; that is, of preventing *France* from being Miftrefs of all *Europe* :---2dly, *That all the Powers in* Europe combined would not be able (perhaps) to execute this Scheme .---3dly, *That no Power in* Europe *will affift us in it.*

I am already wearied, and it is impoffible to find Variety of Terms to exprefs the Iniquity of the Conduct of thefe Men.--- All their Affertions are fo exactly correfpondent with each other, that the fame Epithets muft be perpetually repeated, when we reflect upon them ; yet it is impoffible for honeft Men to let fuch Advances pafs unanfwered.---What Impudence can be fo great as this, to fay, that *England* alone has taken upon itfelf the Hazards, Burthens and Expences of this War ?---The Houfe of *Auftria* has now in different Parts, and in different Armies, no lefs than 180,000 Men :---Under Prince *Charles* 63,000 ; under other Generals in *Germany*, employed in the Sieges or Blockades of *Egra, Ingolftadt,* &c. 30,000 ;---with the King of *Sardinia* and Count *Traun* 27,000 ; in *Flanders*, and upon the *Rhine*, 20,000 ; in the *Trentine*, and the *Tirol*, and adjacent Parts of *Bavaria*, 15,000 ; upon the *Adriatick*, ready to fuccour, either the *Italian* Armies, or to be carried into the *Neapolitan* Dominions by our Fleets, 12,000 ; and at leaft 13,000 Men in the Garrifons of *Auftria*, the different Parts of *Bohemia, Hungary, Moravia, Servia, Croatia, Sclavonia, Carinthia, Carniola, Stiria,* and other Provinces which, bordering upon the *Turk*, can never be totally left unfurnifhed ;---the King of *Sardinia* has above 40,000 and with his Militia above threefcore, which amounts at leaft to *Two hundred and forty thoufand Men*, towards which we contributed no more than the Vote of 500,000 *l.*---Can it then be faid, that we alone have taken upon us the Hazards, Burthens, and Expences of this Scheme, this genuine and incontrovertible State of our Confederacy, even at the Time of this Debate, evinces better than any Scheme of Argument or Words can do, the Falfity of every one of thefe three Affertions.---*That we bear the whole Expence---that it is impoffible for all* Europe combined to prevent France *from becoming Miftrefs of the World---and that we have no Allies---*fo far untrue, that fince the Acceffion of the *Dutch*, though as yet with no more than 28,000 Men, and his Majefty's Quota for the Electorate of *Hanover*, (both which the *Faction* impudently afferted we were

Q   never

never to expect,) together with the *English, Hessians,* and *Ha-noverians,* in the *British* Pay, we have now in this Confederacy, and actually in the Field, little less than 320,000 of the best Troops in *Europe,* which is a greater Force than *France* alone will be ever able to bring against us, which she cannot maintain, and which, as her Troops consist at present of the very Reliques of her exhausted People, if they are once defeated, her Country cannot recruit again. And we are farther morally sure, should the War continue, of a much greater Assistance from other *German* States, certainly from *Russia,* and not impossibly from even *Saxony* and *Prussia.* So that as our Affairs now stand, considering the total Ruin of *Bavaria,* the Inability of *Spain,* the immense Losses and Expences of *France,* which have been all wasted to little Effect, the Security of the *Turk,* the deep Resentments, and the Stake for which the House of *Austria* now contend, the *manifested Perfidy* and *detected Views* of *France;* we are in a much fairer Situation, if we avail ourselves of it, as we ought, to reduce *France,* than we ever were in any Period of Time. The only Danger therefore to which we are now exposed is from the Wickedness of this *Faction,* and the Levity and Folly of our own People, who may, by their intemperate Conduct and Impatience, induce our Ministers to accept of indifferent Terms from *France,* (though they know that she now lies in a manner at our Mercy,) rather than be compelled after yet greater and more clear Advantages to sacrifice still a fairer Prospect. Let me therefore adjure my Countrymen, by all that they hold most dear and sacred, not to concur in obstructing and defeating this glorious Opportunity, which God has thrown before us, which if properly improved is the only likely means to secure us for Ages yet to come, (most certainly for many Years,) against all those Expences, that have been so long heavy on us; against the Necessity of those standing Armies, which are so odious; and against those Taxes, which, by the necessary Methods of their Collection, so greatly, though unavoidably, harrass the People, which create that Dependency of which they are so jealous, and prevent the Diminution of that Debt, which is at present so great a Clog upon our Lands, our Commerce and our Influence abroad.---The natural Consequences of that Success, which it seems at this Time so much in our Power to ensure, will far more effectually secure the Constitution of this Kingdom, than all the Paper Guards of popular Laws. These are but palliative and vain Remedies, if carried too far, tend only to aggravate the Differences and Jealousies between *Prerogative* and *Privilege,* and may compel Government to invent new Arts of a more secret, and consequently of the most dangerous Nature to the Liberties of every Nation.

We

We have now done with our Reflections on the Conduct of the *Faction* upon this Head of the 16,000 Troops in *Flanders*; and I hope with some Advantage to the Publick, by the clearest Vindication of that Measure, and by the manifest Detection of the Views of those, who opposed it, and seduced the People to be discontented with it. Wicked as their Conduct was in this, I know not how to describe its dangerous Tendency with relation to the next Point, upon which they shewed themselves. There are some Crimes so horrible, Designs and Views so infamous and so pernicious, that they secure themselves from Detection by the Honesty of Mankind, whose Ideas can scarce rise to the Suspicion that Man should be guilty of them. Of such a Nature was the Opposition of this *Faction* to the Question of the *Hanoverian* Troops.

In all the Course of the former Opposition, (though no rational Man will attempt to excuse every passionate Conduct of any Party,)—yet being conducted by Men, who ever strictly maintained their Affection to the Royal Family upon the Throne, who knew, that its Security was the Security both of *Liberty* and the *Protestant Religion*, it may be affirmed, that they never endeavoured to poison the *Affections* of the *People* to the *Prince* upon the *Throne*.---It was the *Minister* they attacked only, and a *Change* of his *Person*, and his *Measures*, as we have already observed, were all that they encouraged the People to expect.---Had their *Prince* been guilty of any *Errors*, or subject to any *Infirmities* to which human Nature is exposed, as well upon the *Throne* as in a *Cottage*, they would have thought it their Duty to have covered and concealed them all, rather than have hazarded one Grain of the Affections of the People to the Family upon the Throne.---If any Thing of this kind ever escaped, (and very little of it did in that Opposition,) it was the secret and never-to-be-traced Venom of *Jacobites*, who united in their Party, and abused the Liberty of the Press; but for any one of those Men who are now taken into the Government, or who now act with it, who were the Leaders of the Party at that Time, they neither acted nor countenanced, nay, they kept down and destroyed that Tendency wherever it appeared.---Their Opposition was upon true *Whig Principles*, their Writings all tended to fix the People to these Principles, and one of the Reasons why they encouraged the Spirit of Popularity and Republicanism, perhaps too far, was to divert the People from a contrary and fatal Turn another way.---But the Dregs of that Party, stripped of their Leaders, gleaned of the *Whigs*, by whom they were then governed, are now fallen into the Hands of Men, whose Principles are the very reverse,—who

labour

labour to deſtroy every Seed of Affection, or good Opinion in the People, towards the Royal Family.

To render this deſperate Deſign more practicable, they had thus begun to deſtroy the Senſe of the People, as to the Neceſ-ſity of the War, and the Aſſiſtance of the Houſe of *Auſtria*, in the manner we have ſeen, that they might (and it was im-poſſible to be done without it) with more Effect inſinuate, in due time, the pernicious Belief, that it was a War engaged in merely for the Intereſts of *Hanover* alone.

They flattered themſelves that the Time was now come.--- The Preſs ſwarmed with ſuch treaſonable Pamphlets, as were never ventured, or ever known to be publiſhed in any Age or Nation.--The King's Perſon was in Ballads, and Libels at-tacked with a Licence, which never was taken, even in the great Rebellion, when the King and the Nation were in actual War upon each other. It was now aſſerted publickly, and in Print, [a] *That the Intereſts of* Britain *had been ſteered, ever ſince the Acceſſion of this Family, by the Rudder of* Hanover.--[b] *That the Intereſts of* Great Britain *had been conſtantly and manifeſtly ſacrificed, for many Years, to that of the Electorate.---* [c] *That the Intereſts of* Hanover *had been the Touchſtone of all our Mea-ſures ſince the Acceſſion.---* [d] *That* Great Britain *had been hitherto ſtrong and vigorous enough to bear up* Hanover *on its Shoulders, and though now waſted and wearied out with the continued Fatigue, ſhe was ſtill goaded on, as if already ſold to Vaſſallage, and by Compulſion obliged to perſiſt in the ungrateful Drudgery, without Hope of, or Title to, Redemption,--- and forced* [e] *to ſubmit to the Ignominy of becoming only a Money Province to that Electorate.-- That nobody could or did indeed wonder at the Affection his late Majeſty expreſſed for his native Country, and nobody blames the Tenderneſs his preſent Majeſty preſerves for it : Both of them had their Beings and their firſt Impreſſions in it. Nor would it be ſur-priſing,--if the Succeſſor ſhould have ſome Prædilection for the Meri-dian in which he was born and educated, but it is a terrible Doctrine, that of being a pecuniary Province to a little State upon the Con-tinent, deſtined only to bolſter up its Pride, ſupply its Indigence, and gratify its frivolous Ambition, to laviſh away, upon a puny hopeleſs ſtunted Child, the Nouriſhment neceſſary to ſupport the healthy and thriving one---* [f] *Exhauſted and beggared as we are al-ready, a ſervile Submiſſion, and the breaking and taming of the true* Engliſh *Spirit, may poſſibly be thought the next Thing neceſ-ſary;*

[a] Caſe of *Hanover* Troops, fol 30.　[b] The Intereſt of *Hano-ver*, fol. 19.　[c] Ibid fol. 51.　[d] Caſe of the *Hanover* Troops, fol 71.　[e] Ibid. fol. 83.　[f] Caſe of the *Hanover* Troops, fol 54.

fary ; in order to which, the Interest and Influence of Hanover are no longer now to be disguised or concealed, but openly avowed as the Rule of our Conduct, and the Spring of our Actions.--[a] *Lured by an insatiable Thirst of Gain, in whatever Shape ; in love with military Spectacles, and to make a Soldier-like Figure in the Field, Hanover may proceed as far as a March, or a Counter-march more would be too much.---*[b] *Will you lose the Affections, and exhaust the Strength of your Kingdom, for the Addition of a Bailliage to the Electorate.---*[c] *We have too much good Sense to be so imposed upon, too much Spirit not to resent the very Attempt, and too much Discretion to beggar ourselves for the sake of an Infant, which has been a Snare and a Curse to us from the Beginning.*——This is the venomous Stile, these are the very individual Words and Language of this detestable Set of Men, set forth not only in their Speeches, both within the House and without, but published in the Face of Government, and to the World, delivered to the People as their Creed, inculcated as the Fundamentals of their Political Faith, written by their most eminent Men, avowed by them, recommended, and with amazing Industry spread through the remotest Corners of the united Kingdom. I have referred to the Pamphlets themselves, and to the Pages, that I may not be accused of Misrepresentation ; (the Books are in every Man's Hands,) for they who are capable to assert this, are base enough to deny it when they have done it.

Let us now see upon what Pretences, and upon what imminent Danger, this Fire, Fury, and Treason, dared to avow itself, to expect Countenance of the People, or to escape its Punishment.--It was for this, and this alone, because *the Ministers had taken* 16,000 Hanoverian *Auxiliaries into* British *Pay, to serve in the Quarrel against the House of* Bourbon, *and to support the House of* Austria. Without which we have so fully demonstrated that it could not in that Conjuncture have been supported, or the Ballance of *Europe* saved from utter Ruin.

The Articles of Impeachment drawn up against the King of *England*, (for the Attack was now pushed to the Foot of the Throne itself) were these :

1st, *That the King and his Father, Electors of* Hanover, *having no Regard nor Paternal Affection to their* British *Dominions, had falsely and treacherously, to their People of* England, *betrayed their Interests, and by a corrupt Majority in Parliament, had sacrificed the Wealth, Treasure, Security, Liberty and Reputation of this Country, by one continued Series of uninterrupted Measures, to the contemptible Interest of their* Hanoverian *Dominions.*

[a] A Vindication of the Case of the *Hanover* Troops, fol. 29.
[b] Ibid fol. 54.　　　[c] Case of *Hanover* Troops, fol. 72.

2dly,

2dly, *That to give the finishing Blow, to perfect this long-laboured and indefatigable Undertaking, and to gratify an Avarice insatiable, his present Majesty had hired* 16,000 *of his* Hanoverians *under a Pretext of composing an Army of Auxiliaries for the Service of the House of* Austria.

3dly, That at the Time he did this, [a] *he was convinced of the Impracticability of raising this Phantom of the House of* Austria, *to be again in a Condition of ballancing the House of* Bourbon.

4thly, That at the same time,—[b] *He knew too well, that it is against the Interest of every Prince in* Germany, *and even of the King of* Sardinia *himself, that such an Event should take place.*

[c] 5thly, That he had done this :—*When the Queen of* Hungary *became not only successful in her own Enterprizes, but found Means to disengage* Prussia *and* Saxony *from* France, *nay, even* France *herself became perplexed and entangled to such a Degree, as to find herself obliged to offer Terms to the Queen of* Hungary, *for the saving both her Forces and her Honour.*

6thly, [d] That he had been guilty of a Conduct *to the last Degree impolitick, to say no worse, not to advise that Princess to accept the Offers of* France, *(viz. to save both the Forces and Honour of* France,) *with which Terms,* Prussia, Saxony, *and every Prince in the Empire, but one, are satisfied.*

7thly, [e] That he had persisted in this Scheme of hiring 16,000 of his *Hanoverian* Troops, *though from the Moment that the Queen of* Hungary *rejected these Offers, the Interest, and (of course) the Policy of the* Dutch, *was changed, the Dread of* France, *and its being to be paid, at the Expence of their Barrier, was lost.*

8thly, That therefore he had violated *the invariable Maxim* (i. e. the Maxim laid down by the *Faction* to serve the present Purpose) *never to enter into a Land War, but when the* Dutch *Barrier was in Danger :* And that *he knew very well,* because the *Dutch* stood out, *there was no real Necessity for our medling at all.*

9thly, That he had done this, *when he knew the* Dutch *would never join us, which it was evident they would not, because they had not.*

10thly, That he had done this, though by the Laws of the Empire, *he knew that these Troops neither would nor ought to march into* Germany *in Aid of the Queen of* Hungary, *and tho' he knew they could be of no Use to her in* Flanders, *nor any where else.*

[a] Case of *Hanover* Troops, fol. 51.   [b] Ibid. fol. 52.   [c] Ibid. fol. 49.   [d] Ibid. fol. 53.   [e] Ibid. fol. 49.

11thly,

11thly, That he had done all this *contrary to the Senfe of Parliament, and in a manner that violated the Conftitution and Privilege of Parliament.*

There are but three Inftances in all the Hiftory of this Country, of Articles of this Nature brought by the Subject againft the Prince; in the Reigns of *Edward* the Second, *Richard* the Second, and *Charles* the Firft; and in every one of thefe it was by Parliament, and after the Prince was virtually or actually depofed; but fuch an Arraignment of any Prince, while he fat upon his Throne, and had the Approbation of his Parliament for every Meafure that he took, was never paralleled in this or any other Country.

And when we confider, not only the malevolent and defperate Tendency of this Charge, how the Facts have been mifreprefented, how the Events have fhewn the Falfhood of almoft every Article that is here laid down, and how obvious the Anfwer is to every one of the reft; when we confider the Views (to which they directly led) of Ruin to the Peace and to the Intereft of this Country both at home and abroad;—who can fay, that the Authors of this wicked Conduct, who now ftile themfelves by the gentle Term of *Oppofition*, are charged by too harfh an Appellation, when they are proclaimed by the Name and Title of *a Faction.*

A Faction they are and muft appear to every cool and honeft Man the worft in their Defigns, the moft daring in their Attempts on Government, and the leaft warranted by any Pretence or Shew of Reafon, that ever reared its monftrous Creft his Nation.

To obferve, as it might be done, upon the *Inconfiftencies, falfe Conclufions,* and *Abfurdities,* contained in each Article of the Charge above-mentioned, would be to provoke *Mirth,* inftead of that *Horror* which ought to arife upon this Proceeding, and would divert that *Attention,* and *deep Reflection,* which the Nation ought to have upon the *Danger* they are in from the Practices of thefe Men.—As to every Point that may feem to have the leaft Colour of Objection, I have purpofely anfwered before, in the former Pages of this Work, that I might not interrupt that Reflection, and for the fame Reafon I fhall here clofe my Account of the farther Conduct of thefe Men, with refpect to this *memorable Queftion of the* Hanoverian Troops; to which Conduct nothing could add Aggravation, fince its pernicious Intention manifeftly was no other, than *by one uniform Proceeding, to dethrone his Majefty in the Hearts of his People, that they might the more eafily detrude him afterwards from the Throne itfelf, and to preferve the Houfe of* Bourbon, *in a Condition to place a*

Succeffor

Succeſſor in his ſtead. In which View, they likewiſe gave all Obſtruction in their Power to the Supplies, and to every Way and Means to raiſe them.

But we are now, by farther Circumſtances of the laſt Seſſion, to ſhew how they have impoſed upon Mankind; —particularly in thoſe three Points, by which they had duped the Publick to adhere to them, and to give up their Senſes like an infatuated People with Regard to Foreign Affairs; *viz.* the *Place-Bill,* the *Triennial Law,* and the Inquiry into the Conduct of the Earl of *Orford,*—as to the *laſt* it is notorious, that they moved it only as a *Matter of Form,* and ſupported it in a Manner, that ſhewed it was a *mere* Farce; nay, they actually attempted, to take Advantage of the Union, which could not at once be rendered perfect between the Members formerly attached to his Party, and thoſe that were lately admitted into the Adminiſtration, by giving ſufficient Hints of a Diſpoſition to treat with him not only for his Indemnity, but for his Readmiſſion into Power again, upon Condition of being employed themſelves; to which they applied themſelves in an open and unguarded Manner, diſcovering in no one Point (after this Form was paſſed) the leaſt real Inclination to prejudice him further; on the contrary treating his Friends with an affected Diſtinction of Reſpect, directing all their ſcurrilous Speeches and Invectives ſolely againſt the *new Part of the Adminiſtration,* nay, comparing *their* Conduct with *that* of the former Miniſter, not only with an Advantage, given in the Compariſon, to the former, but with Encomiums from the Mouths of their Principal Orators, upon his Wiſdom, Moderation and tender Regard to the Intereſt of his Prince and Country. Whoever ſat in the laſt Seſſions of this Parliament will bear me witneſs as to what I aſſert; but they did it ſo groſsly, that it is almoſt paſt the Belief of thoſe, who did not ſee and hear it, and ſo as to ſhew manifeſtly that they conceived the Capacities of their Audience in Parliament, to be as dull and capable of Impoſition, as thoſe of the Herd they had ſo fatally and ſucceſsfully practiſed upon without: But they were miſtaken here; they had there to deal with *Whigs,* who can never be impoſed upon by theſe Men, who have experienced them too long, and know them too well, to truſt them in any Shape, which *Proteus-*like they are ready to aſſume to attain their private Ends. Even the Miniſter himſelf was contented with what he thought a better Security, the *Affection* of his old Friends, and the *Principles* of the new Part of the Adminiſtration, which would not ſuffer them to inflict any Puniſhment or to take Revenge upon any Man whatever, whoſe Deſtruction, from a Chain of Conſequences,

and

and the Ferment of a Nation, thus inflamed by thefe Incendiaries, muſt have brought Confuſion upon their Country. He thought it more fafe to rely upon the good Senſe and Honeſty of his declared Enemies, than to confide in the Faith of a *Faction*, whofe Practiſe and Principle it was to deceive and to betray. The *old Part of the Adminiſtration*, though (from a natural Exultation in the Security, which the Folly and Wickedneſs of ſ fe Men, had beyond their Expectation infured for them they might divert themſelves, and expreſs fome Pleaſure to this Turn in their Favour, and to find the Burden of Abuſe retorted upon thofe, who had not long before been very liberal of it to them, ſtill knew this never-to-be-forgotten Truth, that neither they nor the Nation could be fafe at any Time, without the Union of the *Whigs*; and could not ſtand without it for one Hour, in the preſent State of Things. The fame Knowledge induced the *new Part of the Adminiſtration* to bear with Patience all this Malice of the oppofite Party, and the difagreeable Circumſtance of being not entirely well treated by thofe they co-operated with: they confidered thefe things to be as unavoidable, as it was certain, on the other hand, that Time would by Degrees redreſs this temporary Inconvenience; and they comforted themſelves with this happy Reflection, that the Benefit which had accrued to the Nation, was fingly owing to the *Firmneſs* of their *former*, and the *Moderation* of their *preſent* Conduct; that any *Good* unattained, or any *Evil*, likely to enfue, was the Off-fpring of the Wickedneſs, Paſſions and Folly of other Men; and that the Succeſs and Prudence of their Meaſures, had maintained the Balance of Power *abroad*, and the Intereſt both of their King and Country *at home*. By this viſible Infincerity of thefe pretended Patriots, the Publick ought, and will, if they are not wholly blinded, fee that *the further Succeſs of this Enquiry is an impracticable thing, that it is not owing to thofe upon whom they caſt the popular Odium of it, and that it is now palpably kept in Reſerve only for a Subject of Diſtraction and Diſunion of the honeſt Part of this Nation.*

Now as to the *Place-Bill.*—How ridiculous it is for thefe Men, (who embarked in the preſent *Faction* avowedly upon the Account that they had not been the very firſt of the late Oppoſition taken into Employment) to be the Perſons entruſted by the People of *England* to obtain for them what they deſire, in this Reſpect, wants nothing to give it Illuſtration; yet, if it wanted any, it would receive it from the faint Attempt of the *Faction* to compaſs this Point, which was viſibly no more than to maintain the Shew of their Profeſſions, and far from being carried on with that Warmth and Spirit which they

R   exerted

exerted in the other Purfuit of diftreffing the Government in every Step and Shape in the Profecution of the neceffary, juft, important and practicable View of recovering the Weight, Influence, loft Honour, and Security of this Nation, with Regard to its Affairs abroad —How therefore can the People be deluded with their Pretences to procure what thefe Demagogues have put it out of the Power of any body to procure for them, and what fo manifeftly appears they have no real Intention to procure themfelves, were it in their Power? ---It is therefore evident, that this Point is likewife now only maintained for the fame Views of Difunion and Diftraction.

Their Conduct, as to the Point of a *Triennial Parliament*, clears this up yet more plainly.—Thefe Men have not fo much as followed the *Inftructions*, which they themfelves *inftructed* the People to infift upon ,—for they never once attempted, or made any Motion, during the whole laft Seffions, towards the Repeal of the *Septennial Law*,—which is to be accounted for no other Way, than that they found an infinite Majority difpofed againft it, or that they themfelves were not fincere in their Profeffions for it.—Both thefe were indeed their Reafons, and either might be fufficient to open the Eyes of Men.—But as to the latter, we have already fhewn, that their chief People voted directly againft it themfelves, when it was propofed in the preceding Seffions,—and they muft either have acted counter to themfelves, which would have expofed them too much, while their former Votes were frefh in every Man's Memory, or have detected this great Truth, to thofe whom they laboured ftill to deceive, that they never themfelves intended it fhould pafs.—What Dependance then, or what juft Profpect can the People have to compafs this favourite View, by the Aid of thofe Men to whom they have abandoned their Senfe and Reafon, and every Thing that is moft dear, from the idle Expectation that they will obtain it for them?

If then the People of this Country may fo clearly fee, that thefe Points are, from every Circumftance, and above all, from the former Imprudence, and the prefent deceitful Conduct of this Set of Men, not poffible to be attained —Why do they perfift *to imagine a vain thing?*—If their Oppofition, as from what I have obferved, is moft undoubtedly the Cafe, cannot tend to procure thefe Things for them ;—for what is their Perfeverance in that Oppofition, *but for Oppofition fake?*—Or what Effect can it produce, but the Prevention of a certain important Good, *the Eftablishment of a perfect, permanent, and almoft defpaired of Security, as to our Foreign Affairs?*—Which would any rational Man reject, (confidering moreover the irretrievable

trievable Condition we shall be reduced to if we should lose this happy Opportunity) for the sake of the Pleasure of *Opposition only?* —Can any Man justify this delusive Entertainment of the Multitude, with Projects, which in his Soul he knows *impracticable,* and which, if *practicable,* are undoubtedly both of the *nicest Nature,* and of very *dangerous* and *uncertain* Operation, from the unforeseen Consequences that attend all great Alterations in the Government of all Countries?—Or will any honest Man think himself intitled to lay the Seeds of such Divisions and Discontents in this Nation, as manifestly tend to shake the Foundations of the Monarchy, and the Constitution of this Country, for the sake of *Opposition only?*—This is all the Fruit the People can at this time hope to reap from it,—their Leaders indeed may hope another,—what that is, the Tenor of their Conduct plainly manifests, and that it is both of a *publick* and *private* Nature.-- But will the People be allured to abet such Views for the *Publick,* or is it worth their while to hazard and to sacrifice so much for the *private Views* of such pretended Patriots?

I might content myself, if I only wrote to reasonable Men, and to Men in their right Senses, with this full Detection of the corrupt and pestilent Views of this Faction, and with this Evidence of their Want of Capacity, as well as Inclination, to compass any thing but the Ruin of this Nation both at Home and Abroad. But as I write to Men heated and inflamed with Passion, to a giddy and unthinking Multitude, elated with their late Success, and thence liable to misjudge of their Abilities, and to think that practicable which in a cooler State they will plainly see to be wholly out of their Power,— as, so long as they shall think their Pretensions to be just and necessary, they will never desist from the vain Pursuit; and as, by this Means, the Nation will be harrassed with the most fatal and endless Confusion, I shall now, with the utmost Candour, Honesty and Truth, endeavour to give them a juster View of those false Opinions, which in some very important Points, they so vainly, and yet so passionately entertain ; though it may clash with the Popular Opinion, so as to draw down the worst Inconveniences upon myself ; though it may even disgrace the Judgment, or create some unjust Reflection upon the Sincerity of others, as subjecting them to the Imputation of having maintained Doctrines which were in themselves erroneous, or even such as they knew to be such. Candour, Honesty, and true Patriotism, will make it rather a Matter of Honour than Shame in these Men, to submit to these Inconveniencies ; nay, even to make a fair Acknowledgment, either of their Mistakes, or Faults, rather than by a

false

false Desire of appearing *consistent*, to be really *inconsistent*, in their most capital Profession, and Intention, that of *supporting*, *in every Event, and at every Hazard, the true Interest and Happiness of* Britain.

We have already observed in another Place, that the Views of the *Jacobites* had been so universally exploded by their infamous Conduct during the last four Years of the Queen, and by the P oof that arose of their dangerous Designs, from the Rebellion, that broke out soon after, and the Nation was so universally convinced of the Danger of that Faction, had seen such Consequences from their pretended Patriotism, and thought themselves so happy in that critical Deliverance; that our Government enjoyed a Tranquillity beyond the Experience of any former Time. The *Jacobite* Spirit and the *Republican* Temper of the People, both seemed in a Manner to have been annihilated by the different Inconveniences they had in the Space of threescore Years, alternately brought upon the People; the Concurrence therefore of the whole Nation made the Government so strong, and the Administration of Affairs so easy; that it tempted the late Minister to wanton in his Power, to disoblige many able and considerable Men, to despise the People, to be guilty of Mismanagement in the Conduct of our Revenue, and to form Projects for the raising of Money, without due Attention to the Tenderness and Suspicions of the People upon any Encrease of Influence or Power, till by this Conduct, by attempting to engross more than he could execute, and by undertaking to manage Foreign Affairs, which he little understood; our Condition insensibly grew very desperate both at home and abroad, and yet the People seemed insensible of this to such a Degree, and made so constant a Choice of those he recommended, that most Men thought their Spirit greatly changed and broken, and that it was necessary to rouse them from the Lethargy they seemed to be in This honest Apprehension made them not afraid to animate the People by Discourses of a *Republican* Turn; —the Liberties of *Europe* were upon the Brink of irretrievable Ruin, and if these were lost, the Liberties of *Britain* could not stand·— Any means, that were not more dangerous than immediate Ruin, were thought lawful to be used, to effect this Change, the Means they used, far from seeming dangerous, appeared false to them, and to have a Tendency to bend the People from that Pile, which, upon all our late Disorders, had appeared to cast very dangerously another Way.--But their Zeal undoubtedly hurried them too far in this Respect. We have spoken freely of the *Faults* and *Errors* of the *late Minister*; we

shall

shall not scruple to speak with the same Freedom of the *Opposition to him.* This was at least an *Error,* if not a *Fault* in them, ---and the Publick at this Hour feel its bad Effect.

For the People have been so heated with Discourses of this kind, that they have taken that, which was the *Means* to be the *End* and *View* of Opposition. The great and original End and View of their Opposition, was to *change the Minister,* and to *change the Measures;* but the People now having got these *Ends,* and carried this *View,* consider them only as the Means to get in effect what no prudent Man ever wish'd or intended they should get, *the whole Power of this Government, and the whole Constitution into their own Hands.*

Moreover, by the Ferment that has arisen in this Nation, it has manifestly appeared, that neither the Spirit of the People is so low, nor the Power of the Crown so high, as both were imagined by many to have been during the Course of that Opposition. It appears, that the People are still able to remove a bad Minister, and to force a Change of Measures, whenever it becomes the universal Sense, that the Minister and the Measures are really wrong; the Liberty and Power therefore of the popular Interest in this Country is incontestible, and as great as it is necessary or ought to be in any. To change the Ballance of the Constitution is not their Right, nor ought those Alterations to be made, which would enable them to do it.

It appears further, that the Views of the popular Interest, inflamed, distracted and misguided as it has been of late, by those into whose Hands it has unhappily fallen, are such as they were never imagined to have been; a Party of Malecontents (by the Sufferance of the most ignorant and uninformed) assuming to themselves, though very falsely, the Title of the People, claim with it a Pretension, which (were their Title just,) no People could have a Right to claim, erecting themselves into a new Order in the State, affecting a Superiority to the whole Legislature; insolently taking upon them, to dictate to all the three Estates, in which, the absolute Power of the Government, by all the Laws of this Country, has indisputably resided ever since it was a Government, repining at every Decree they make; endeavouring to animate the People, in effect, to resume into their own Hands, that vague and loose Authority, which exists (unless in Theory) in the People of no Country upon Earth, the Inconvenience of which is so obvious, that it is the first Step of all Mankind, as soon as formed into Society, to divest themselves of it, and to delegate it for ever from themselves:—A Power, which could not be permitted

mitted even in a Society of 500 Families, impracticable in a
great Empire, and therefore an ideal Doctrine, tending to no
Point or Purpose whatsoever, but to cast this Nation into the
most horrible Confusion, and to throw it back into a State of
Nature. That has likewise appeared, which nothing can discover but Revolutions or Conjunctures, that approach so near
them as this has done; viz. *that though the Influence of the Crown
has seemed for some Years to have increased visibly, the popular Interest has been for many Years invisibly encreasing in a far greater
Proportion.* The greatest Changes in all States are wrought by
certain Alterations in the Circumstances and Properties of the
People; which escape the most penetrating Eye, till Time and
Accidents have ripened them to a proper Crisis. The Convul-
sions of Nations are like the Shocks of subterraneous Fires,
formed by an Assemblage of combustible Materials, long collecting, and unsuspected till the very Moment of their fatal
Explosion; the *Effects* are therefore the only means by which
such *Causes* can be learned: The *Republican* Spirit so strangely
risen as we have lately seen it, that to work its Ends, it has pre-
posterously joined with its Antipathy the *Jacobite*, directs us
surely to this *Cause*, which can be no other than the great Encrease of Property in the People. The *Revenues of the Crown*,
however magnified, we shall presently come to shew, have borne
no Proportion to it, the *Encrease of the Peerage*, either in *Property* or *Number*, (notwithstanding the Additions that have been
made since the Revolution,) partly from the great Caution of
the Crown for many Years past, and partly from a weak and
mistaken Prejudice in their own Body to the Extension of Honours, have in no degree kept pace with it; and the Lords are
hardly now of any Poize in this Government. Induced by the
Circumstances of the Time, to examine the Point, it is visible
beyond all Power of Contradiction, that this has been the
Case.—At the *Revolution* the Numbers of the People were
computed nearly at *Six Millions*, and by the long Peace, and
necessary Encrease of Procreation, this Number cannot be *at
present* less than *Seven*, or in that Proportion; the Expence of
the People per Head was about *Seven* Pounds at the *Revolution*,
at *this Time* it is universally agreed, that this Expence amounts
to *Ten*. Now as the Revenue of the People must infallibly
be at least as much as the People spend, it follows, that
the Revenue of the People was at the Revolution *Forty-two
Millions*, and that it is *Seventy Millions* now: The People
have therefore encreased in their annual Income *Twenty-eight
Millions* (or in that Proportion) since the Revolution; and as it

is

is a Maxim inconteſtible in Politicks, that Power always follows Property, which muſt ſooner or later operate in every Country, it is manifeſt, that the People have acquired in the Space of fifty Years, more ſolid Weight in the Scale of this Conſtitution, than they could have gained, or can gain by all the popular Laws, that ever were made, or can be made in their Favour to the End of Time.

Before I proſecute this Argument, to the Concluſion which I intend from it, perhaps it may be thought neceſſary to explain a little, how it came to paſs, that this Growth of the Popular Intereſt ſhould be ſo little perceived till now.—It happens in all ſuch Caſes as it has happened in this, and for the ſame Reaſon,—the Spirit of the People riſing with their Circumſtances, creates Difficulties to Government, of which it feels the Effects, long before it apprehends the Cauſe. Theſe Difficulties in a manner drive Government to exerciſe all its Authority, and to uſe many Arts in its own Defence, by which the People who do not ſee the Neceſſity it is under to do this, condemn, and conſider as Attempts offenſive, when they are in reality defenſive.—The Inſults of the one, and the Arts of the other therefore both encreaſe, till neither think themſelves ſecure, (which is the Misfortune, and in long run the Ruin of all mixed Governments) without new Laws, to encreaſe Power on the one Hand, and Privilege on the other.—And, for a time, it is very evident, why the Government is rather more ſucceſsful than the Popular Intereſt in theſe Attempts, becauſe the Generality of Men finding themſelves eaſy in the general Proſperity, and obſerving no material Change in the written Conſtitution, rather chuſe to ſupport the Government, though they do not approve all its Proceedings, than to abet the Popular Views,—the Peace of Society being (at leaſt for the Time) ſecured by the firſt, and always endangered by the laſt.—But, in the long run, Accidents will happen, which will either change the Perſons of thoſe in this moderate and cautious Way of Thinking, or diſtract their Principles, or confound their Judgments,—and when this happens, the Popular Spirit, having once made the Breach, blows up the Dam at once, and deſtroys, in one Hour, the Works that have been an Age erecting, to reſtrain it within its due Bounds : Thus, for want of an exact Knowledge of the different Nature of the Force, which Government employs againſt the People, and that of the Popular Intereſt againſt the Government ; and from this Circumſtance, that the *one* is *viſible* in every Step of its Encreaſe, the *other latent* and *concealed* ; and from hence, that *the one*, by

2

its

its gradual and conftantly oppofed Progrefs, is not only obferved, but magnified, while *the other* encreafes infenfibly, and without either Oppofition or Perception, it becomes, from the Nature of the Thing, extremely difficult for any, and entirely impoffible for the Generality of Men, not to be deceived in the
Condition of the Conftitution, under Circumftances fuch as
thefe. Something will arife from an impartial and judicious Reflection upon thefe Particulars, very deferving the Attention of
all reafonable Men. And the Judgment which muft refult
from it, can be defeated by nothing but a Difcovery, that the
Crown has encreafed in the fame Proportion of Power as the
Popular Intereft has fo manifeftly done; in this Cafe there is
nothing in all this Argument; but if it has not, *the Ballance undeniably preponderates on the Side of the People, more than it did at
the Revolution*, that is to fay, more than it ever did in any Period of our Government, *and confequently the Difcontents of the
People, fo far as they are founded upon a contrary Suppofition, are
moft unreafonable. unjuft, and dangerous.*

In order to determine this Point, all that is neceffary to be
done, is, to confider in what the Power of the Crown has been
encreafed fince the Æra of the Revolution, there are but three
Particulars in which it could poffibly receive Addition, in the
Encreafe of its Civil Lift; *in the Influence of additional Employments*; and laftly, *in pofitive Laws in Favour of Prerogative*;
of all thefe the firft, which is *the Property* of the *Crown*
muft be in its Operation the moft confiderable, from what we
have already obferved as to the Effect of Property. This is
therefore the Point, which we are to confider firft, and with
moft Attention:—But we muft previoufly obferve, that the Reafon why we go no higher than the Æra of the Revolution is, becaufe though no Civil Lift was fettled before, the Civil Lift Expences were enormoufly great, the Publick Charge being not
above 700,000 *l. per Annum*, and the Revenue being above
Two Millions from the Reftoration to that Time.

Now as to the Encreafe of the Power of the Crown from an
Addition to its Property, it can confift in nothing but the *Civil
Lift*; the Crown having no Ability, as it had before the Revolution, (when the publick Revenue and the *Civil Lift* were both
in the Difpofition of the Crown, and not divided,) to apply one
fingle Shilling of that publick Revenue to any Ufe, but to that
for which it is appropriated.—Let us therefore examine the
Quantum of the *Civil Lift*.

Upon the firft Face of this Examination, the Power of the
Crown appears to be encreafed, for the *Civil Lift* is now
800,000 *l.*

800,000 *l. per Ann.* whereas in the Reign of * King *William*, and the late Queen it was but 700,000 *l.* But when this Point is duely confidered it is indifputable, not only that this is no *real* Encreafe to the Power of the *Crown*, but that this Power is diminifhed, notwithftanding the *nominal* Addition to this *Revenue.*

King *William* and Queen *Anne*, as we have already obferved, had but 700,000 *l. per Annum* ; but *neither* had any Family to provide for, and *both* lived in Times, when that Income would have fupported a greater Expence, than *a Million* would now do, for the Truth of which, I appeal to the Experience of every private Family, and to the known Advance of Price in all Commodities and Articles of Expence whatfoever.——Exclufive therefore of the great Deduction, which arifes from the Expence of his Majefties numerous Progeny, there is, in fact, inftead of an Encreafe of Power to the Crown in the Proportion of 100,000 *l.* a manifeft Diminution of it in the Proportion of 200,000 *l.* which is the Sum deficient to make up a *Civil Lift* equivalent (confidering the Difference of the Times) to that of King *William*, or of the late Queen.

And indeed without a Confideration of the Difference of the Times, no fair or juft Eftimate is poffible to be made upon this Subject, every Century creates a mighty Alteration in this Refpect. In the Time of the Conqueror the King's Revenues are reckoned by all the old Hiftorians to have been enormous, and were computed at 1060 *l. per Diem*, which amounts to 386,900 *l. per Annum* ; and we might therefore with the fame Juftice reafon, that a Revenue at that Amount would be now too great, as to argue that the *Civil Lift* fhould not be greater now than it was forty or fifty Years ago ; the Objections therefore, that have been made of late upon this Head, have been fallacious to the higheft Degree, and either they, who have liftned to them, never confidered the Point as it ought to be confidered, or have *fecretly intended*, inftead of keeping the Power of the Crown to its ancient Standard, *to reduce it lower than it ever ftood in any Period of our Government.*

But when we look a little farther into this matter, however clear this Argument may be, we have no need much to infift

* At the Revolution the *Civil Lift* was fettled at 600,000 *l. per Ann.* but this being very deficient to anfwer the Charges upon that Head, the Parliament in 1695 granted the King a Sum of 500,000 *l.* to pay his Debts, and in 1699, *Anno* 9 & 10 *Gul.* III *cap.* 23 though the Queen was then dead, found it neceffary to encreafe the *Civil Lift* to 700,000 *l. per Ann*

upon

upon it ; for fince the late Alteration of the Miniftry, the Encreafe of the Appointments of the Prince of *Wales*, has wholly taken away this Objection; his Royal Highnefs now enjoying his complete Allowance of 100,000 *l. per Annum*, which is the whole of that *nominal* Encreafe of the *Civil Lift*, above what it formerly was before his Majefty's Acceffion. When this comes to be confidered, the Power of the Crown, with refpect to Property, is not at all increafed, even its firft Afpect ; but is on the other Hand, when juftly compared in all its Circumftances, greatly and undeniably *decreafed*, fince the Period I have mentioned. Yet fuch is the malignant Temper of this Age, that we have more to combat than Arguments and Facts— *Bonaque ac Mala non fva Natura, fed Vocibus Seditioforum æftimantur* [a]; Infinuations of a malicious Tendency have Weight fuperior to all the Reafon in the World, and we muft fight through thefe upon every Turn. Of this Nature is that vaunted Affertion in *The Cafe of the* Hanover *Troops* [b], of the late Queen's Generofity in a Prefent made by her out of the *Civil Lift* of 100,000 *l.* in one Year, towards carrying on the War with *France* ; and from hence an oblique Argument is attempted to be drawn of a Superabundance in the prefent *Civil Lift*, and an indirect Reflection, both upon the Mifapplication of the Surplus, and the Want of an equal Tendernefs to the Publick in his prefent Majefty ; it is further manifeft with what a wicked Intention this invidious Comparifon is made, from the officious Care of that infamous Author to remind the Reader, that that Princefs was a Daughter of King *James* II. and from the Tendency of his whole Performance, which is plainly calculated to incline the People to regret the Lofs of that Family, by a Side Wind to trumpet the Fame of his own Faction, and to recommend it to the ignorant and deluded Multitude ; the Queen being notorioufly, at that Time, in the Leading-ftrings of *Jacobites.*

It is impoffible fufficiently to admire either at their Confidence or their Impudence in this Mention of a Particular, which can be fo ftrongly retorted upon them : In fact, this pretended Generofity was one of the moft fcandalous Actions, that the Crown was ever led to commit by any Adminiftration ; it was a manifeft and grofs Cheat upon the Publick, who were extravagant Lofers by it ; for fome time after, *viz.* upon the 25th of *June*, 1713, the Queen was advifed to acquaint the Houfe of Commons by Meffage, that fhe had contracted a very large Debt upon her *Civil Lift* Revenues, which fhe was unable to

[a] *Tacitus*, Lib. Hift. 4.   [b] Page 79.

pay,

pay, and therefore defired them to make good ; and fuch was the Complaifance of a *Tory* Parliament, that notwithftanding the Deteftation, which muft have arifen in every honeft Breaft, upon the Detection of this clumfy Juggle ; and though Mr. *Smith*, one of the Tellers of the Exchequer, honeftly informed the Houfe, that the Eftimate of this Debt was aftonifhing to him, being made to amount in *Auguft* 1710 to 400,000 *l.* whereas he was able to affirm from his own Knowledge, that it amounted at that Time to little more than 100,000 *l.* and though many others undertook to prove that the Funds given for the 700,000 *l.* had, in reality, amounted to 800,000 *l.* and though thefe Gentlemen had prevailed fo far, as to procure an Addrefs to the Crown for an Account of the *Civil Lift* Debt at *Midfummer* 1713, and for a yearly Account of the Nett Produce of the *Civil Lift* Revenue, no Regard was paid to this Information, nor to this Addrefs ; none of thefe Accounts were ever permitted to be laid before the Houfe, and upon the very next Day they voted no lefs a Sum than 500,000 *l.* for this Service. This is the Truth, and the whole Truth of that generous Exploit of the *Jacobite* Adminiftration, under the Daughter of King *James* II. which was no more than a mean Trick, in which they bafely employed the Name, and abufed the Honour of that unfortunate Princefs, to gull the Nation of 400,000 *l.*

From hence refults an evident Proof, not only that the prefent *Civil Lift* is not greater than that of the late Queen, but that the *Civil Lift*, though we fhould wave the ftrong Fact of the Inequality of the fame Revenues from the Difference of the Time, could not nearly fuffice to anfwer the Expences of the Crown, even forty Years ago ; it muft follow therefore, either that a much greater Part of it was employed in *fecret Services* and to *unwarrantable Purpofes*, during that favourite Reign ; or that the Oeconomy, even of the late profufe Minifter, muft have far exceeded that of the boafted Adminiftration of a Set of Men they labour fo much to ingratiate with the People.

The *Faction* reduced to this Dilemma, may poffibly rather chufe to confefs the *latter* than the *former* ; but in doing this they muft, in the firft Inftance, acknowledge a manifeft Advantage to this Country from the Oeconomy of his prefent Majefty, who, though he has already reigned fome Years longer than the late Queen, has hitherto neither demanded or received from his People on this Account, more than one fingle Sum of 115,000 *l.* and if they give it the only Turn that can be given to it, (after what we have already proved,) viz. *that it is equal to the Publick, whether the Civil Lift be greater or not, if his Majefty can afford out of it more than his Predeceffors could afford*

*to thofe fecret Services, which are fuppofed to affect the Publick In-
dependency*, this is what I abfolutely and juftly deny. Becaufe
(allowing it to be true in its utmoft Extent) it is but a temporary Influence arifing from a peculiar Turn, Temper, and, I
may call it, a Virtue in its firft Principle, which is accidental in
the Perfon of one Man, may probably perifh with him, and
cannot be looked upon as an real, folid or permanent Encreafe
of Power in the Crown, or Change in the Spirit of the Conftitution. If this be duly confidered, it ought greatly to quiet
the Apprehenfions raifed in the Preafts of a very great Number
of well-meaning Men, by the *Report* of the late *Secret Committee*;
for however great the Sums there fpecified to have been impro-
perly applied to *Secret Service* out of the *Civil Lift*, may be, (and
very unwarrantable, in fome Particulars, undoubtedly they are,)
yet the Conclufion drawn from thence is not juft, that our Conftitution is decayed, in this refpect, or in a worfe Condition than
it has been in former Times. For this certainly cannot be the
Cafe, when the *Civil Lift* is evidently not encreafed, either in fact,
or in effect ; and the utmoft that can be drawn from this Report,
or any Difcovery that hath or can be made, muft amount to nothing more than *that a temporary Circumftance had put it in the
Power of a late Minifter to make a worfe Ufe of it, than his Predeceffors had been willing, or than, in all Probability, for any Time to
come, his Succeffors can be able to do.*—Which may indeed affect
that Minifter, but ought not juftly to affect the Conftitution,
or lead the Publick to any rafh and violent Alterations of it.

I am fenfible, that this Doctrine will not, at firft, fuit well
with the falfe Notions, which many have fo paffionately entertained of this Matter ; but I am very indifferent upon that
Head, *Magna eft Veritas & prevalebit* ; Truth may be borne
down for a while by Prepoffeffion and falfe Infinuations, but
will force its way at laft. As therefore it is my fole Intention in thefe Papers, to bring my Countrymen into a juft and
moderate Temper, to allay that dangerous Ferment, which is
now raifed, and during the Continuance of which, it is impoffible for them to make a right and impartial Judgment of
their Affairs, I fhall make no Scruple to oppofe myfelf to their
ftrongeft Prejudices without any Regard, whom I may oblige or
difoblige , I neither fear the Refentments of the Friends of the
former, nor court the Favour of the prefent Administration, I
am not to be deterred by the Malice and Scandal of a *Faction*,
nor will I humour the Paffions and Folly of a People, whom
every honeft Man muft endeavour to preferve, even againft
their Inclination, when they precipitate themfelves, through
Paffion, Credulity, or Ignorance, into Ruin and Deftruction.

To

To speak therefore farther with the same Freedom upon the
Subject of this Misapplication of the *Civil Lift*, as I have done
upon every other Topic, which has hitherto fallen under my Consideration, I must observe, that it is not easy for the Publick to
judge, whether the Sums now discovered by this Report to be
expended out of the *Civil Lift* in the way, that they have appeared to be expended, were not, upon the whole, as great in
former Reigns : the Presumption is strong that they have been
much greater, because it is evident, the *Civil Lift* could have
afforded it much better ; and as no Parliamentary Enquiry was
ever made before as to this Point, or directed to this Particular,
at least, their Information cannot extend to determine positively
against this Opinion.

But what if we should be able to discover, that in Truth
notwithstanding the Greatness of this Sum, *the Charge of the
Government upon this Head was greater formerly than it is now?*
Yet this seems in a great Measure capable of being proved by
Facts and Figures, the strongest Evidence that can support any
Proposition in the World :

For upon the great Settlement of our Constitution at the
Revolution, the Parliament having called for all the Lights they
could procure to enable them to judge of the Expence of Government in all its Branches, in order to make that *Separation* of
the *Charge* of the *Crown*, and of the *Publick*, which was one
of the great Benefits of that Change, and took away that extravagant Power, which the Crown before derived from having
the sole Management, and Distribution of the whole Revenue
at large, it appeared that the Article of the Secret Service alone
(besides the Allowance to the Secretary of State, 6006 *l.* and
the Pensions, which came to 146,703 *l. per Annum*,) amounted *communibus Annis* to 89,968 *l.* 8 *s.* 2 *d.* ¾ which, notwithstanding the Temper they were then in, was not at all censured
by Parliament as exorbitant at that Time.

Upon this Foundation I shall proceed to compare the Expence of Government under this Head before the *Revolution*,
with the Expence of Government under the same Head, in
the *present Time*.

It appears then that computing upon a Term of eleven
Years before the Revolution, the Expence of Government up-
on the Article of Secret Service amounted to 989,652 *l.* 10 *s.* 6 *d.* ¼
again it appears by the Report of the *Secret Committee* (in the
Appendix No. 10.) that in the same Term of eleven Years
from the Year 1731, to the Year 1741 inclusive, this Article
of Secret Service amounted to 786,355 *l.* 17 *s.* 4 *d.* to which
Sum, the Committee have thought fit to add two Articles, both
of

of which are (with Submiſſion to ſo great an Authority) in a great Meaſure, different in their Nature from that Article, which is properly called *Secret Service, viz.* Money iſſued for *ſpecial Service,* 272,504 *l.* 8 *d.* and Money iſſued *to re-im-burſe Expences* 205,390 *l.* 17 *s.* 10 *d.* which two Articles together amount to 477,894 *l.* 18 *s.* 6 *d.* They have likewiſe added further three other Articles, *viz.* 66,000 *l.* for the Secretaries of State, 68,800 *l.* upon Account, to the Sollicitor of the Treaſury, and 50,077 *l.* 18 *s.* to Authors and Printers, amounting together to 184,887 *l.* 18 *s.*

Theſe Totals of 786,355 *l.* 17 *s.* 4.—477,894 *l.* 18 *s.* 6 *d.* and 184,877 *l.* 18 *s.* come to 1,449,128 *l.* 13 *s.* 10 *d.* and with a few other ſmall Articles amount to the compleat Sum of 1,453,400 *l.* 6 *s.* 3 *d.* which is ſtated in the Report as ſuppoſed to be the Expence of the Civil Government in Secret Service, during the Space of the ſaid Eleven Years [a]. But if we are to compare the Expence of the former and the preſent Government, upon the Face of the two Accounts, it is viſible that we can only put the ſingle Article of *Secret Service* Money before the *Revolution,* againſt the *ſame* Article at this *Time*; which if we do, we ſhall find, that the ſame Article before the Revolution, amounted as above, in a Term of eleven Years, to 989,652 *l.* 10 *s.* 6 *d.* ¼. whereas it amounted to no more than 786,355 *l.* 17 *s.* 4 *d.* in the ſame Term, from 1731 to 1741 incluſive ; ſo that, in this Light, the Charge inſtead of being encreaſed is diminiſhed ſince that Period, by no leſs a Sum than 203,296 *l.* 13 *s.* 2 *d* ¼. And to conſider this Point in any other Light, though it may be done, with much Art, cannot, with any Degree of Certainty ; for if, as in the Report, other Articles of Expence are brought (as ſeeming to have ſome Relation to it) to ſwell the Amount of the Articles of Money lately iſſued for *Secret Service,* it would be requiſite to ſcrutinize with the ſame Induſtry, into other Branches of the Charge of the Civil Government before the Revolution, which is impoſſible to do at this remote Diſtance of Time : So that, undoubtedly (however exceptionable either the Greatneſs of the Sums, at the firſt Sight, may be. or the Nature of their Application, or the Manner of their being iſſued) there is not any one of thoſe other Articles, which in the Report, are joined to this Sum of 786,000 *l.* that can be directly charged to this Account.

For who is it that does not perceive a very wide Difference between *Secret Services,* and the other two Articles of *Special Service,* and the *Reimburſement of Expences.* It is perhaps but

[a] The Enquiry was appointed for ten Years ; but upon examining this Account of *Secret Service* in the Report, it appears to include eleven

two

too probable, that some Part of the Money under these two Heads have been really applied that way. Yet very great Sums must have been issued under these Titles, to Purposes very different from those which ought to have given so much Alarm to the Publick; and this was undoubtedly the Case under some other Heads in all former Times.—As it is for this Reason out of our Power to make an exact Comparison in this Way, I think it can be stated in no manner more correspondent with the Truth, than as it has been stated here, and if so, the Proposition is as sufficiently proved, as the Nature of the Thing can possibly admit, *that the Charge of Government upon this Head, was greater formerly than it is now.*---However, after having thrown this out for the impartial Consideration of the Publick, I will, for the sake of Argument, and to prevent all Possibility of Cavil, admit both these Articles to be added in their full Extent to the Head of *Secret Service*, by which it will be augmented, though not at all accurately, to 1,264,250 *l.* 15 *s.* 10 *d.*

But after this Concession I will venture to say, as to the other three Articles, *viz.* that to the Sollicitor of the Treasury, that of the Allowance of 3000 *l. per Ann.* to each of the Secretaries of State, and that of the Money issued to Authors and Printers, it should seem impossible, with any Candour, to bring them into the Charge of the *Secret Service*, and for the following Reasons:

Because as to the *first* Sum to the Sollicitor, it is given always upon Account, *viz.* for Crown Prosecutions, and other necessary, obvious and warrantable Occasions of Government, of which the Committee themselves were so well aware, that they have themselves deducted that Sum from the grand Total.

As to the *Second*, which regards the Secretaries of State, this is in effect the Appointment of an Office, and stands justly exceptionable in this Comparison, the rather, because it was made a distinct Article from that of Secret Service in all Times, and is particularly so in the State of the Revenue at the Revolution, by which this Parallel is made, being not included in the annual Sum of 89,968 *l.* 8 *s.* 2 *d.* ¾, to which the Secret Service then amounted. And this was likewise in some sort excepted by the Committee.

With regard to the *Third*, it is rather a Matter to be laughed at than considered seriously.—In the Nature of the thing, it is by no means a Secret Service. And in its Consequences, especially considering the Authors and their Productions, no Man will say, that it affected the Publick in the Way, which can only give the People any Right to concern themselves about the Disposition of the Civil List.—It would be extreamly hard, if the Crown might not be allowed the same Privilege of the Pen,

which

which is allowed to any private Man, and certainly no Minister can be censured, if by Permission of the Prince, and even by the Assistance of his private Purse, he makes use of the same Liberty of the Press to defend the Measures of his Government, which the Subject, with Impunity, employs whenever he thinks proper, (and of late, with outrageous Licence,) to censure and confound it.

As the Sums issued therefore upon these three Articles cannot be added by any just Pretence; after admitting all that can possibly be admitted in the utmost Latitude, against our own Argument, the Account will stand in this Manner:

	l.	s.	d.
Total of Money issued for Secret Service in eleven Years, from 1731 to 1741, inclusive	1,264,250	15	10
Total of Monies issued under the Head of Secret Service for a like Term before the Revolution	989,652	10	06 $\frac{1}{4}$
Ballance upon eleven Years	274,598	5	3 $\frac{3}{4}$
Annual Charge of Secret Service, at a Medium of Eleven Years from 1731 to 1741	114,931	16	10 $\frac{1}{2}$
Annual Charge before the Revolution	89,968	8	2 $\frac{3}{4}$
Annual Ballance	24,963	8	8

Which annual Sum of *Twenty-four thousand nine hundred and sixty-three Pounds, eight Shillings and eight Pence*, is the whole Encrease of the Expence of the Civil List upon this Head, after a Term little short of threescore Years, made up in a way of Accounting, the most partial and most favourable to those, who wish a false and dangerous Opinion to prevail, which even upon this State cannot prevail hereafter with any *reasonable Man*.

For every such Man will consider this Matter as it ought only to be considered, that is, upon the Foot of *an Influence acquired by the Crown over the Independency of the Subject, in proportion to the Sums applied in secret Gratuities to the Members of the Legislature, more now than in former Times*; and every such Man will form a Judgment to himself, and create an equitable Ballance, not only upon the Quantum of the Money applied in Secret Service, but will take into his Aid some farther Considerations, *viz. whether* that Part of Secret Service, which is necessary to all Government, (because as the Committee confess in the Report, *No Form of Government can subsist without a Power of*

employing

employing Publick Money for Services which are from their Nature secret, and ought always to remain so,) must not unavoidably be from the Circumstances of Time, greater than it was formerly; and again, *whether* the same Degree of Influence can be acquired in these Times by the same Sums.

Now these Things being thus candidly considered, it will appear, that our Engagements with Foreign Powers, the Difficulties of the Age we live in, and the Distractions of *Europe* have been infinitely greater since the Revolution than they were before, that our Secret Service in Foreign Courts must have therefore been greatly more expensive than it was at that Period; and the Prices of Intelligence undoubtedly much higher than formerly they were; for Things of this Nature go always on encreasing, and the Value of Money is become greatly less in every Part of *Europe*.

Add to this, that the late Enquiry was confined to a Time of Peace, and a Time of very intricate Negociation (the Prudence or Imprudence of which, is not under our Consideration in this Question) during which, Expences of this kind have no established Provision, as they have in time of War, they have then an extraordinary Allowance of 10,000 *l. per Annum*, besides a Deduction of Two and a half *per Cent.* out of the Pay of all the Foreign Forces in the Service of *Great Britain*, of which we have already had Occasion to make some mention in another Place: And this (as appears by the famous Report of the Commissioners for stating the public Accounts, at the latter End of the Queen's Reign, 1712) amounted in the same Term of eleven Years, to 393,366 *l.* 9 *s.* 7. over and above the current *Expences of the Civil Government under the same Head*, which could not fail in some measure to be lessened by it.

Upon the whole, leaving it to every Man of Candour to determine how far the two Articles of Money issued to Special Service, and to reimburse Expences, may be allowed to have their Place in this Account, and submitting to every Man of Sense and Candour the Difference of the Times, the Deduction of 100,000 *l.* out of the *Civil List* for the Prince of *Wales*, the Circumstances of all our Foreign Affairs, and one thing more, which is hardly decent to be touch'd upon, but by way of Supposition, that if there be Corruption at home, its Wages must be much higher than they were heretofore, it is impossible to deny, but that the Property of the Crown, or in other Words, the *Civil List*, is, not only not really increased, but that it can by no means operate upon the Constitution in any Degree equal to what it might have done formerly, and therefore that the Power of the Crown is not in this Respect augmented

T

in proportion to the Power of the People, but in fact dimi-nished greatly.

We should in the next place examine this Point, upon the Footing of *the Crown Influence from additional Employments*. But this will receive a sufficient Answer under the next Head ; with which it is so much connected, that it will be most proper to blend them both in one common Consideration.

We therefore proceed to the third and last Point, viz. the Encrease of the Power of the Crown, *by positive Laws in Favour of the Prerogative*. But here I conceive it beyond the Industry of *Faction* itself to discover any one Circumstance in which Prerogative has been extended.—On the other hand, it is most happy and most notorious, that Prerogative is within the last Century reduced to such a Point, that no rational Man can deny, but that we have gone even farther than in the Opinion of the most eminent Writers upon Government, is necessary to the Preservation of the Constitution of any Country : To this end, according to that famous Maxim laid down by *Machiavel, Government must be frequently brought back to its first Principles* ; but from the Period of the Restoration, we have not only constantly been employed in paring away those Luxuriancies of Power in the Crown, which had been insensibly growing from the Conquest, or at least from the Reign of King *John*, till they had in a manner over-shaded all the Liberties of the People ; but we have actually taken away many of the most important Branches, to which the Crown had been entitled from the very Beginning of our Constitution : Of which it cannot be improper upon this Occasion to enumerate a few.

First then, the Crown, from the Accession of *William* I. by the Establishment of the feodal Tenures was undoubtedly entitled to such a Degree of Influence, as went incomparably farther in every Respect, and in every Light, in which it can possibly be considered to create an universal Dependance in every other Branch of the Legislature, than any other Circumstance of human Invention, and much less any later Changes in the Constitution, were they as real as they are imaginary, could possibly do : The greatest Part of the whole Kingdom, (besides what was yet more immediately belonging to the Crown as its Domain,) was held *in capite* of the King ; and by Virtue of this Tenure, the Crown enjoyed the following Prerogatives ; 1. *The Profits of the wh . Estate of every Family such (as well of the Lords as of the Commons) during the Minority of every Heir.* 2. *The Right to dispose of the Profits of such Estates to whom it pleased.* 3. *The Guardianship of every such Heir, and the Power*

of

of delegating that Trust to any other Person. 4 *The Right to dispose of the Heir or Heiress of any such Family, during their Minority, in Marriage.* 5. *A Title to one Year's Profit of the Estate, in Cases where there was no Minority, before Possession could be taken by the next Heir.*—These, with many more of a like Nature, were some of the Crown Prerogatives, which existed legally in the Constitution of this Country from the Beginning of this Government, till about eighty Years ago, and if they are well weighed, it is impossible not to see what prodigious Means of Influence they afforded to the Crown What *Revenue*, what *Employments*, what *Civil List* could furnish out Matter of such Extensive Obligation? What Noble Family in the one House of Parliament, or what Man of great Estate in the other, but might be either tempted or necessitated to court its Favour? What Struggles would the Virtue even of a *Broad-bottom Patriot* undergo, contending with the Offer of the *Wardship* of a Duke of *Bedford*, or the *Custodium* of a *Pelham* Estate, during a Minority of fifteen or sixteen Years? In what Man is the *Amor Patriæ* so constant, passionate, and fond, that he could coldly look upon the Charms of a beautiful young Woman kindly tendred to his Arms by a first Minister, with the Titles and Inheritance of a Duke of *Marlborough?* Again, what would be the Consequence of an Education wholly directed by Tutors and Guardians appointed by the Crown, upon all the Men of Property in the Kingdom? what the Effect of Gratitude upon the Minds of Gentlemen, in whose behalf the Crown should wave some Parts of this Prerogative?—in favour of whom the Crown should remit its Title to the Profits of the Minor's Estate? or leave it in Trust to be improved by the nearest Relation for the Heir? or decline to take the Releif, or one's Years Profit, to which, even in Cases of no Minority, it was entitled? From hence, it may be worth considering whether that is quite a constitutional Principle, which has been laid down with so much Confidence of late, and in so vast Latitude, *that the Crown ought to have no Degree of Influence upon the Legislature;* the Fact certainly was the direct contrary.—Our Ancestors intended the Power of their Kings to be *real,* and they knew that without some Degree of Influence, that Power would be but *in Name ,*—their Idea was to ballance the *Popular* by the *Regal*; not, as it has manifestly been of late, to put all the Weights into the *Popular Scale :* To the People they gave the *sole Power of granting Money,* and a *Title to Resistance in Cases of extraordinary and violent Extremity*; a nominal Power could not ballance these great Privileges, they therefore gave the Crown a great Revenue, the *sole Management of the publick Money,* the

Disposition

Disposition of all Employments, in fine, *the Means of General Obligation to the Subject* ; again, to ballance the Title of Resistance in the People, they armed the Crown with *Powers of Confiscation, and even some degree of Influence in the Trials* of those, who should rashly or unjustly take up Arms against it ; these Prerogatives became at length abused, and have therefore been wisely and justly in many important Instances curtail'd, (while all the former Privileges of the People yet remain with very great Additions.) Among the rest this great one, arising from the feodal Tenures, was totally abolished in the Year 1661. By which one Act, the Spirit of this Constitution received so great an Alteration, that few are even yet sensible of all the Consequences, that either have happened, or will unavoidably result from it, in favour of the popular Interest in this Country.

The next great Encrease of Privilege to the People, was from the Act of *Habeas Corpus*, which was passed in 1673-4 ; a Law of inestimable security to the Liberty of the Subject.

By the Revolution in 1688, the whole Government was purged at once, of all Excrescencies of Prerogative, that had been growing from its first Institution : By the very Act of the Expulsion of King *James* II. and his Line, confirmed, as it afterwards was, by Law, the People acquired a right, which had never been allowed in the Constitution of this Country. In the famous Charter of King *John*, the Barons never went so far, it was there decreed that in Cases of the last Necessity, the Publick might distress the Crown, by all Manner of Means, *viz.* by the Seizure and Sequestration of its Castles, Lands, and Possessions till the publick Grievances should be redressed : *distringent & gravabunt nos modis omnibus quibus poterunt, scilicet per captionem castrorum, terrarum, possessionem, donec fuerit emendatum*, &c. But there was a strict Exception to the Persons of the *King*, the *Queen*, and the Issue of the Royal Family, *salvâ Personâ nostrâ, & Reginæ nostræ, & Liberorum nostrorum* ; there was an express Condition to save the Rights of the Succession ; the Crown was not to forfeit for its exorbitant Proceedings, the People were to return to their Allegiance again, so soon as these Exorbitances were redressed, *cum fuerit emendatum intendent nobis sicut prius fecerunt.* This Principle of an *indefasible Hereditary Right* (for it was no less) destroyed the Effect of all the strong Provisions of *Resistance* prescribed at the same time ; the Law was severely worded, but void of a sufficient Penalty to enforce it ; a temporary Suspension of the Regal Authority was the only Penalty : The Crown soon found how to avail itself of this Defect ; their Attempts upon the People were offensive, the Resistance of the People defensive only ; this was contending

upon

upon very unequal Terms ;—the Crown had never much to fear; but whenever Publick Liberty was invaded the People run the Rifk of lofing all ;—the Crown, if unfuccefsful, fuffered nothing but a Difappointment, and had nothing to do, but to quit the Profecution of its Views for that Time. It was then reftored again to what it was before, with the fame Means of renewing the Attempt upon the firft favourable Opportunity. The People it is true, have formerly gone further, and were under the Neceffity to do it, but when they did it, they acted not upon the Principles of the Law of *England*; they were obliged to have Recourfe to that grand Principle of the Law of Nations, [a] *Datâ facultate datur jus facultatem tuendi.* Yet this was but lamely underftood by the Bulk of a People, ever tender of their Laws, and, like the Bulk of every other People, little able to reafon upon higher Principles; from hence the Crown derived fo great an Advantage that for the greater Part of the laft Century our Liberties were brought into continual Hazard; it was the Revolution alone, and the Principles eftablifhed then, that could have poffibly preferved us. The Doctrine of *Hereditary Right* in this extravagant Extent was taken away, fome pofitive Cafes were enacted by Law where the Crown fhall forfeit. This has given a Blow to Prerogative, which it can never recover.

And fo far had we dwindled from the Virtue and Spirit of our Forefathers, that even that Provifion of *Refiftance*, which had been formerly made to ballance this Prerogative of *indefeafible Hereditary Right*, (infufficient as we have fhewn it to have been,) was actually wholly given up at the Reftoration, by the Oath prefcribed to be taken in the * *Act for well Governing and Regulating of Corporations;* which was in thefe Words: *I A. B. do declare and believe that it is not lawful, upon any Pretence whatfoever, to take Arms againft the King, and that I do abhor that traitorous Pofition, of taking Arms, by his Authority, againft his Perfon, or againft thofe that are commiffioned by him. So help me God.*—It was further difclaimed in the Preamble to the Act of Attainder, *Anno 12 Car.* II. cap. 30. in the following Words,—*And be it hereby declared, that by the Undoubted and Fundamental Laws of this Kingdom, neither the Peers of this Realm, nor the Commons, nor both together, in Parliament, or out of Parliament, nor the People collectively, nor reprefentatively, nor any other Perfons whatfoever, ever had, have, hath,*

[a] *Grotius de Jure Belli ac Pacis*, lib. II. * *Anno 13 Car.* II.
Stat. 2. Cap. 1.

or ought to have any coersive Power over the Persons of the Kings of this Realm.

It was again disclaimed, in the Preambles of different Acts relating to the Militia, about the same time, in these Words, *That both, nor either of the Houses of Parliament, can, or may, lawfully raise or levy any War, Offensive or Defensive, against his Majesty, his Heirs, or lawful Successors.*

How far this Doctrine of *Non-Resistance,* without any Reserve, struck at the Liberties of the People, is manifest enough; but how far the very Act of the Revolution has given Limitation to its Extravagance, we have already observed; and as to the Oath before mentioned, it was directly abrogated by the Act of the 1st of *William* and *Mary,* cap. 8.

Again, by two Acts, the one, *An Act for Safety and Preservation of his Majesty's Person and Government,* Anno 13 *Car.* II. cap. 1.—And another, *For preventing Abuses in Printing,* &c. Anno 13 and 14 *Car.* II. cap. 33. the Liberty of the Press was totally restrained. These Laws were suffer'd to expire.

By an Act against Tumults and Disorders, *Anno* 13 *Car.* II. cap. 5. the Subject had been, in effect, deprived of that Right of Petitioning either the Crown or Parliament; for it was enacted—*That, from and after the First of* August 1661, *no Person or Persons whatsoever, shall solicit, labour, or procure the* GETTING OF HANDS, OR OTHER CONSENT *of any Persons above the Number of* TWENTY OR MORE, *to any Petition, Complaint, Remonstrance, Declaration, or other Address to the King, or both or either Houses of Parliament, for Alterations of Matters established by Law, in Church or State, or accompanied, at any one time, with above the Number of* TEN PERSONS. *And that no Person or Persons exceeding* TEN, *as aforesaid, shall present any public or private Grievance or Complaint, to any Member or Members of Parliament after his Election,* &c. *under Penalty of* 100 l. *in Money, and Imprisonment for three Months, without Bail or Mainprize.*

This was virtually repealed by the Act, declaring the Rights and Liberties of the Subject, *Anno* 1 *William* and *Mary,* Sess. 2. cap. 2. wherein it was Enacted, *That it is the Right of the Subject to petition, and all Commitments and Prosecutions for such petitioning are illegal.*

By this Act the Constitution was farther restored in very many, and improved in other Instances as follow.

1. It was enacted, *That the pretended Power of suspending Laws, or the Execution of Laws by regal Authority without Consent of Parliament is illegal.*

2. *That*

2. That the Commiffion for erecting the late Court of Commiffioners for Ecclefiaftical Caufes, and all other Commiffioners and
Courts of the like Nature are illegal and pernicious.

3. That levying Money for, or to the Ufe of the Crown by Pretence of Prerogative, without Grant of Parliament, for longer time,
or in other Manner, than the fame is, or fhall be granted, is illegal and pernicious.

4. That the raifing or keeping a Standing Army within the Kingdom (in Time of Peace) unlefs it be with Confent of Parliament,
is againft Law.

5. That the Subjects, which are Proteftants may have Arms
for their Defence fuitable to their Conditions, and as allowed by
Law.

6. That Elections of Members of Parliament ought to be
free.

7. That the Freedom of Speech and Debates or Proceedings in
Parliament ought not to be impeached or queftioned in any Court or
Place out of Parliament.

8. That exceffive Bail ought not to be required, nor exceffive
Fines impofed, nor cruel and unufual Punifhments inflicted.

9. That Juries ought to be duly impannelled and returned, and
Juries, which pafs upon Men in Trials for High Treafon ought to
be Freeholders.

10. That all Grants and Promifes of Fines and Forfeitures of
particular Perfons before Conviction are illegal and void.

11. That for Redrefs of all Grievances, and for the amending,
ftrengthening and preferving of the Laws, Parliaments ought to be
held frequently.

12. That all Difpenfations paffed by non obftante to Acts of
Parliament, except in Cafes provided for by Law, fhall be void.

13. That every Perfon or Perfons, that is, are, or fhall be
reconciled to the Church of Rome, or fhall marry a Papift, fhall
be excluded, and be for ever incapable to inherit, poffefs, or enjoy
the Crown and Government of this Realm, and Ireland, and the
Dominions thereunto belonging, or any Part of the fame, or to have,
ufe, or exercife any legal Power, Authority or Jurifdiction within
the fame, and in all and every fuch Cafe or Cafes, the People of
of thefe Realms, fhall be, and are hereby abfolved of their Allegiance, and the Crown fhall defcend to the next Proteftant Heir.

This was followed by another Law, *cap.* 10. which took a-
way the Revenue arifing from *Hearth-Money*, with all the
Powers attendant on that Collection ; which, as it was juftly
expreffed in the Words of the Preamble, *was in itfelf not only a
great Oppreffion to the poorer Sort, but a Badge of Slavery upon*

2

*the whole People, exposing every Man's house to be entered into and
searched at Pleasure by Persons unknown to him.*

In the same Seffions of Parliament (*cap.* 27) one very great
and confiderable Part of this Kingdom was entirely redeemed
from a Jurifdiction utterly inconfiftent with the Freedom of a
Britifh Subject, the Court of the Prefident and Council of the
Marches *Wales,* which had been eftablifhed in 34 and 35 of *Henry*
VIII. and under which that Province had been governed till
this Act paffed, was totally abolifhed, and the People of that
Country allowed to enjoy the common Benefit of the *Englifh
Law and Liberty* ; *the Proceedings and Decrees of that Court,
having been* (as it is recited in the Preamble) *an intolerable Bur-
den to the Subject within the faid Principality contrary to the great
Charter, the known Laws of the Land, and the Birth-right of
the Subject* ; *and the Means to introduce an arbitrary Power
and Government.*

In the 2d of *William* and *Mary, cap.* 7. a very unconftitu-
tional Prerogative, (for fo it was in effect, though not directly
exerted under the Name of the Crown,) was repealed ; and it
was enacted, *That whereas the Election of Members to serve in
Parliament ought to be free, and whereas the Wardens of the*
Cinque Ports *pretended to, and claimed as of Right, a Power of
nominating and recommending to each of the* Cinque Ports, *the
two ancient Towns, and their respective Members, one Person
whom they ought to elect, to serve as a Baron or Member of Parliament for such Port,* &c. *all such Nomination or Recommendation shall be void.*

In the fame Year (*cap.* 8.) the Judgment of *Quo Warranto*
againft the City of *London,* was reverfed—its Liberties regrant-
ed, and made a Corporation.

By an Act in 1694, the 5th of *William* and *Mary,* cap. 7.
for Granting to their Majesties certain Rates and Duties, upon
Salt, Beer, Ale, *and other* Liquors, *for the raising of One Million
towards carrying on the War with* France. This Claufe was
obtained, *Provided always, and be it enacted,* &c. *That no Member of the House of Commons shall, at any time, be concerned directly or indirectly, or any other in Trust for him, in the* Farming,
Collecting, *or* Managing *any of the Sums of* Money, Duties, *or*
other Aids granted *to their Majesties by this Act, or* that hereafter
fhall be granted by any other Acts of Parliament ; *except the
Commiffioners of the Treafury, Cuftoms, and Excife, not exceeding
the present Number in each Office, and the Commiffioners of the
Land-Tax.*—But the Cuftoms and Excife were afterwards excluded, as we fhall prefently come to fhew, and continue fo
to be.

Again,

Again, by another Act the same Session, *cap.* 20. *for Granting several Rates and Duties upon Tonnage of Ships and Vessels, and upon Beer, Ale, and other Liquors, to raise One Million five hundred thousand Pounds,* &c. It was provided farther—*That no Officer or Person whatsoever concerned in any manner with the Collection or Management of the Excise, shall, by Word, Message, or Writing, or in any other manner, endeavour* to influence any Voter in Elections, *under Penalty of* 100 l. *and of Incapacity of holding any Office or Place of Trust under the Crown.*

In the 7th of *William* III. cap. 3. that famous Law was passed, which put the Lives, as well as Liberties of the Subject, upon so happy a Foundation, that no People upon the known Earth, can boast of such Security. I mean, the *Act for Regulating Trials in Cases of Treason and Misprision of Treason*, which contained the following Clauses.

1. *That the Persons accused should be intitled first to have a Copy of the Indictment five Days before the Trial.*

2. *To make their Defence by Council and Witnesses upon Oath, the Council to be chosen by themselves, and to have free Access to the Prisoner at all reasonable Hours.*

3. *Not to be indicted, tried, or attainted but by the Oath of two Witnesses, and one Witness to one Act of Treason, and another to another, not to be deemed two Witnesses.*

4. *Persons outlaw'd, upon their Return to stand Trial, to have the Benefit of this Act.*

5. *No Person to be indicted or prosecuted, unless within three Years of the Offence.*

6. *Persons tried, to have Copies of the* Pannel *two Days before Trial.*

7. *Such Persons to have Process of the Court where they shall be tried, to compel their Witnesses to appear for them at their Trials.*

8. *No Evidence to be admitted, or given of any Overt Act, not expressly laid in the Indictment, against any Person or Persons whatsoever.*

And whereas the Commons are to be tried by a Jury of Twelve, who must all agree in one Verdict to condemn any Man, and the Lords had till then lain under two great Disadvantages, *first* that one Major Vote was sufficient to condemn a Peer in Cases of this Nature, and *secondly*, that the Crown had the Power of nominating a select Number; appointing and excepting what Peers it pleas'd to sit in Judgment, it was then enacted, *that their Trials should be made for the future by the whole Body of the Peerage; and that every Peer should be duly summoned at least twenty Days before, to appear and vote at such Trial.*

U

In

In the fame Year, *Seff* 1. *cap.* 4. the Act was paffed *For preventing Charge and Expence in Elections of Members to ferve in Parliament*, providing *that Candidates after the Tefte of the Writ, or after any Seat in Parliament fhould become vacant for any Country, City, Borough, &c giving or promifing any Prefent or Reward for being elected, to any Perfon having Right of Vote, fhall be incapable to ferve in Parliament for any fuch Place as aforefaid.*

This was foon after followed by another Act of the fame Seffions, *For preventing falfe and double Returns, cap.* 7. containing the following Claufes, 1. *That in cafe of falfe and double Returns, the Party aggrieved may fue in any Court of* Weftminfter *againft any Officers or Perfons, and every one of them, and recover double Damages, and full Cofts of Suit.* 2. *Whofoever fhall make, or give any Contract, Security, Promife, Bond, Gift or Reward to procure a falfe or double Return fhall forfeit* 300 *l* 3. *The Clerk of the Crown to make Entry of all Returns within fix Days after their Receipt, under Penalty of* 500 *l. and Forfeiture of his Office.* 4. *All Returns contrary to the laft Determination of the Houfe of Commons, to be void, and to be deemed falfe, and this Act to continue feven Years.*

By the Act in the 11th and 12th of *William, For granting an Aid to his Majefty out of the forfeited Eftates, &c.* it was enacted, *That no Member of Parliament fhall after the* 24th *of* June, 1700, *be a* Commiffioner *or Farmer of the Excife, or a* Commiffioner *of Appeals, or Controller or Auditor of the faid Duty.*

In the fame Year, *cap.* 7. an Act was paffed *For preventing irregular Proceedings of Sheriffs and other Officers, in making Returns of Members*, provided, *That the Returns fhall be made to the Clerk of the Crown, within fourteen Days after the Election, &c. under Penalty of* 500 *l.*

In the fame Seffions, *cap.* 12 an Act paffed *to punifh the Governors of Plantations, in this Kingdom, for Crimes committed by them in the Plantations*, by which the moft remote Subjects of the *Britifh* Empire obtained the Protection of the *Englifh* Laws againft Oppreffions, which were before that time without a Remedy.

The next Addition of Privilege and Security to the People, and Diminution of Prerogative was obtained by the *Act for the farther Limitation of the Crown, &c. Anno* 12 *William* III. Sefl. 1. cap 2. which was then fettled upon the Houfe of *Hanover*; in this it was provided farther,

1. *That whofoever fhall hereafter come to the Poffeffion of this Crown fhall join in Communion with the Church of* England, *as by Law eftablifhed.* (The Act of 1 *William* and *Mary, Seff.* 2.

cap.

cap. 2. before-mentioned had provided against the Admission of any *Papist*, it was now, for the absolute Security of the Religion of this Country, provided, that no Dissenter from that Religion of any Denomination whatsoever, should be King of *England.*)

2. *That in case the Crown and imperial Dignity of this Realm shall hereafter come to any Person not being a Native of this Kingdom, this Nation be not obliged to engage in any War for the Defence of any Dominions or Territories, which do not belong to the Crown of* England, *without Consent of Parliament*

3. *That after the said Limitation shall take Effect as aforesaid, no Persons born out of the Kingdoms of* England, Scotland *or* Ireland, *or the Dominions thereunto belonging (although he be naturalized or made a Denizen, except such as are born of English Parents) shall be capable to be of the Privy Council, or a Member of either House of Parliament, or to enjoy any Office or Place of Profit or Trust either Civil or Military, or to have any Grant of Lands, Tenements, or Hereditaments from the Crown to himself or to any other or others in Trust for him.*

4. *That after the said Limitation shall take Effect as aforesaid, Judges-Commissioners shall be made* quamdiu se bene gesserint, *and their Salaries ascertained and established ; but that upon Address of both Houses of Parliament, it may be lawful to remove them*

5 *That no* Pardon *under the Great Seal of* England *be pleadable to an* Impeachment *by the* Commons *in Parliament.*

6. *That all Laws and Statutes of this Realm for securing the established Religion, and the Rights and Liberties of the People, be ratified and confirmed.*

Another Improvement of our Constitution was made immediately after in that Act, *for preventing any Inconvenience, that may happen by Privilege of Parliament. Anno* 12 Gul. III. *cap.* 2. by which it was enacted, 1 *That Actions may be commenced against either Peer or Member of Parliament in the Interval of Parliament.* 2. *That after Prorogation the Court may give Judgment.* 3 *That Persons may have Process against Peer or Member of Parliament after the Dissolution of Parliament, and may exhibit any Bill or Complaint against any Peer or Member of Parliament, and sequester the Parties Estate.* 4. *Plaintiffs, who are prevented from Prosecution by any Privilege of Parliament, not to be barred by any Statute of Limitation.*

The next Act of the same Nature was for adding a further Term to that formerly mentioned of 7 *Will.* III. *cap.* 7. *for preventing false and double Returns of Members to serve in Parlia-*

ment

ment *for feven Years,* which was then continued for eleven Years longer.

The laft that we fhall mention of this Great and Happy Reign, is of the fame Year 11 and 12 *Will.* III. *cap.* 10. *A. D.* 1700, entitled *An Act for granting an Aid to his Majefty for defraying the Expence of his Navy, Guards and Garrifons,* &c. in which it was provided, *That after the Diffolution of that Parliament, no Member of the Houfe of Commons fhould be a* Commiffioner *of the* Cuftoms, *or capable of holding* any Office *in that Branch of the* Revenue, *nor any Perfon concerned therein fhould directly or indirectly* influence any Election, *under Penalty of being incapacitated to hold any Office or Place of Truft under the Crown.*

We now come to the Reign of Queen *Anne,* during which the Prerogative ftill declined, and the Liberties of the People were augmented and farther fecured, for by *An Act for the better Support of her Majefty's Houfhould, and of the Honour and Dignity of the Crown, Anno* 1 *Annæ Stat.* 1 *cap.* 7. it was decreed that for preferving the Revenues of the Crown, *all Grants of Mannors, Lands,* &c. *made by the Crown for more than thirty-one Years or three Lives, or all Tenements for more than fifty Years, fhould be void,* by which the Crown was for ever deprived of that great Means of Influence, and of burdening the Publick Revenues by Gratifications to their Favourites.

Anno 2 and 3 *Annæ, cap.* 18. it was enacted, *that any Action or Suit fhall and may be commenced and profecuted in any of her Majefty's Courts of* Weftminfter, *againft any Officer of the Revenue, or any other Place of publick Truft, no fuch Action to be impeached or ftaid or delayed on Pretence of Privilege of Parliament either with Refpect to a Peer or Member of the Houfe of Commons,* and this was manifeftly a great additional Security to the Subject againft Power and Oppreffion.

In the Year 1704, 4 *Annæ, cap.* 8. *An Act* paffed *for the better Security of her Majefty's Perfon and Government, and of the Succeffion to the Crown of* England *in the* Proteftant *Line :* By which the Nation acquired the following Advantages.

1. *That the Parliament fhall not be diffolved by the Death of any* King *or* Queen *of* England, *but that it fhall continue fix Months after ; that it fhall immediately convene, meet, and fit, whether adjourned or prorogued, and in Cafe there fhould be no Parliament in being, then the laft preceding Parliament fhall immediately convene, and fit, and be a Parliament, to continue, as aforefaid, to all Intents and Purpofes.*—A Provifo which, if rightly confider'd, muft appear to be infinitely wife, and may, in future Times, prove of the laft Importance, to bring the Conftitution back again,

again, if it should ever be interrupted or unhinged in any Arbitrary Reign hereafter.

2. *The Privy Council, the Great Officers, and all Offices, Civil or Military, shall continue likewise for six Months.*

3. *The Privy Council, immediately after the Decease of the King or Queen, to proclaim the next* Protestant Successor, *under Penalty of High-Treason* —The Benefit of which these Clauses most manifestly appeared upon the Death of the late Queen *Anne.*

It may be expected of me to take Notice in this Place, that by this Act two Clauses in the Act of the 12th and 13th of *William* III. cap. 2. the first, *Concerning the signing of Privy Counsellors to all Acts of State* ; and the second, *Containing a general Exclusion of all Offices and Places of Profit, and all Persons holding Pensions from the Crown, from sitting in the House of Commons,* were repealed ; because upon this Repeal the Malecontents have taken their only plausible-Handle, to insinuate, that our Constitution has been impaired.—But this will admit of a very easy Answer—for, in Fact, this never was the Constitution ; these two Provisions were only made *in futuro,* had never actually taken Place, were repealed long before they were to be in Force, *viz.* in four Years after they were first made. and at a Period of Time, when that Government and Family they were intended to restrain, had no Power or Influence, in this Country, to procure their Repeal, and near ten Years before their Accession to the Throne —Nay farther, as to the second Clause concerning Pensions, it has actually been restored since that Accession, as we shall shew in its due Place.

4. *It was enacted by this Law, that from and after the Dissolution, or sooner Determination of that Parliament, no Person who shall have, in his own Name, or in the Name of any Person or Persons in Trust for him, or for his Benefit, any new Office, or* Place of Profit whatsoever *under the Crown, which, at any Time hereafter, shall be created or erected, nor any* Commissioner *or* Sub Commissioner *of* Prizes, and Secretary *or* Receiver *of the* Prizes, *any* Comptroller *of the Accounts of the* Army, *any* Commissioner *of* Transports, *any* Commissioner *of the* Sick *and* Wounded, *any* Agent *for* any Regiment, *nor any* Commissioner *for* Wine Licences, *nor any* Governor, *or* Deputy Governor *of any of the* Plantations, *nor any* Commissioners *of the* Navy *employed in any of the* Out-Ports, *nor any Person having any* Pension *from the* Crown *during* Pleasure, *shall be elected, sit, or vote, as a Member of the House of Commons.*

5. *No* Office to be split into Commission *farther than already done before the first Day of the Sessions of Parliament* 1705.

6. *All*

6. *All Members of Parliament accepting any Place of Profit under the Crown, during the Time of their being Members, their Elections to become immediately void, but capable of being re-elected, if the People should think proper to chuse them again under that Circumstance.* —This Clause was enacted in the Place of that which we have already observed to have been repealed by this Act, whereby *Persons holding any Employments were totally excluded.*—This Provision being thought much more consistent with the Liberty of the Subject, both *Elected* and *Electors.*—And, in the Opinion of that Time, as great a Security as could be desired by any People, since it put it out of the Power of the Representatives to deceive their Constituents, and left it to their own Option, whether they would confide their Interests again in the Hands of the *same* Person, after that Change of his Condition.

7. *A Penalty of 500 l. to be recovered by any Person who shall sue any Member who shall sit contrary to this Act, and the Election of such Member to be void.*

Greatly as the Prerogative and Influence of the Crown was reduced by this Law, it is much to be questioned, whether its Benefits exceeded that which I shall next mention; *Viz. The Act of the 7th of* Anne, *cap.* 21. *for Improving the Union of the two Kingdoms.*—For by this Act, 1st, *That inestimable Law of Treasons before mentioned, was extended to that Part of* Great Britain *called* Scotland 2dly, *It was enacted, That after the Death of the Person called the* Pretender, *when any Person shall be indicted for High-Treason, or Misprision of Treason, a List of the Witnesses that shall be produced on the Trial for proving the said Indictment, and of the Jury, mentioning the Names, Professions, and Places of Abode of the said Witnesses and Jurors, shall be also given at the same Time that the Copy of the Indictment is delivered to the Party indicted, and that Copies of all the Indictments for the Offences aforesaid, with such Lists, shall be delivered to the Party indicted, ten Days before the Trial, and in Presence of two or more credible Witnesses. And* 3dly, *That after the Decease of the said* Pretender, *and at the End of the Term of three Years, (after the Succession of the House of* Hanover *to the Throne) no Attainder for Treason shall extend to the disinheriting of any Heir, nor to the Prejudice of the Right or Title of any Person or Persons, other than the Right or Title of the Offender or Offenders, during his, her or their natural Lives only, and that it shall and may be lawful to every Person or Persons, to whom the Right or Interest of any Lands, Tenements or Hereditaments, after the Death of any such Offender or Offenders should or might have appertained, if no such Attainder had been, to enter into the same:* Which noble Provision for the Lives and Property of the Subject,

ject, taken in all its Confequences, is not to be found in any other Government upon Earth.

In 1710, 9 *Annæ, cap.* 5. the *Act* was paffed *for fecuring the Freedom of Parliaments, and the further qualifying the Members to fit in the Houfe of Commons, appointing a Qualification of 600 l. per Annum for Counties, and 300 l. a Year for Cities and Boroughs.* A Provifion wholly new in the Conftitution of this Country.

In the fame Seffion, *cap.* 10. it was enacted, *That no Poft-mafter or Poft-mafter-General, or his or their Deputy or Deputies, or any Perfon employed by or under him or them, in the receiving, collecting or managing the Revenue of the Poft Office, fhould in any Manner whatfoever perfuade or diffuade any Voter for Members to ferve in Parliament, under the Penalty of 100 l. and of Difqualification, Difability, and Incapacity of ever bearing, or executing any Office or Place of Truft whatfoever under the Crown.*

In the 10th *Annæ, cap.* 23. an Act was paffed *for the more effectual preventing fraudulent Conveyances, in order to multiply Votes for electing Knights of the Shire to ferve in Parliament, providing againft this Evil by an Oath, and inflicting the Penalty of Perjury upon the Perfon, either fuborning or taking that Oath falfely.*

In the 12th of the fame Reign, *cap.* 5. there was an Act of the fame Nature, *for the better regulating the Elections in* Scotland.

And in the fame Seffion, *Stat.* 1. *cap.* 15. *the Act concerning double Returns,* (firft made, *Anno* 7 and 8 *Gul.* III. *cap.* 4. for feven Years, then continued as we have obferved for eleven Years more, in the 12 *William, cap* 5.) *was made perpetual.*

In the Firft of *George* I 1714. *cap.* 4. *It was Enacted, that no Perfon fhall be hereafter naturalized, unlefs in the Bill exhibited for that Purpofe, there be a Claufe or particular Words inferted to declare, that fuch Perfon fhall not thereby be enabled to be of the Privy Council, or a Member of either Houfe of Parliament, or to take any Office or Place of Truft, either Civil or Military, or to have any Grant of Lands, Tenements or Hereditaments from the Crown to himfelf, or any other Perfon in Truft for him, and that no Bill of Naturalization fhall be hereafter received, unlefs fuch Claufe or Words be firft inferted or contained therein.*

In the firft of the fame Reign 1715. Sect. 2. *cap.* 56. a farther Act was made, *to difable any Perfon from being chofe a Member of fitting or voting in the Houfe of Commons, who has any Penfion for any Number of Years from the Crown, and the Penalty of 20 l. for every Day that fuch Member fhall prefume to fit or vote*

in

in that Houſe : By which Act, the one of the two Clauſes before mentioned in the Act of the 12th and 13th of *William,* which was repealed by the 4th of *Anne,* cap 8. was again reſtored.

In the ſecond of the preſent King 1728-9, *the Bill for the more effectual preventing Bribery and Corruption in the Election of Members to ſerve in Parliament was paſſed into a Law.*

And in the *firſt* Seſſions of this *preſent* Parliament, an Act was paſſed *for the farther Limitation of Placemen in the Houſe of Commons,* of which we have already had Occaſion to ſpeak, by which, *after the Expiration for ſecond Determination of this preſent Parliament,* among others are excluded the ſeven Commiſſioners *of the* Revenue *in* Ireland, *the ſeven* Commiſſioners *of the* Victualling Office, *the Clerk of the* Polls, *and all the* Deputies, Inferior Officers *and* Clerks *of theſe* Commiſſions, *and of the* Treaſury, Exchequer, Pells, Admiralty, Secretaries of State, *and* Paymaſter *of the* Forces, (two or three only excepted,) *together with the* major Part *of the* Eſtabliſhment of *Minorca* and *Gibraltar.*---This is that Act, for which the preſent Adminiſtration, inſtead of Thanks, have been repaid with the vileſt Reproaches of the *Faction,* and the moſt cruel Abuſe of their ungrateful Country.

In the ſame Seſſion paſſed that Clauſe in the Bill *for Mutiny and Deſertion, for taking the Power of* billetting of Soldiers *in the City and Liberty of* Weſtminſter, *out of the Hands of the* High Conſtable *of that City, and placing it with effectual Proviſions in the Hands of the petty Conſtables, by which a very great Abuſe and Means of Fraud and Influence were taken away.*

We now come in order of time to the *laſt Seſſion* of this Parliament, when the Pot-Act, *(which was, in effect, an arbitrary Tax, at the Will and under the Direction of the Exciſe,) was repealed.*

And laſtly an Act was paſſed *for the further Security of the Freedom of Election in that Part of* Great-Britain *called* Scotland.---The four laſt Acts here mentioned have been gained ſince the Removal of the late Miniſter, and in little more than the Space of one Year ; yet are the People taught to believe, that they have gained nothing.---*Quos Deus vult perdere dementat.*

The Reader will pardon this long Deduction of popular Laws, which I have here inſerted ; ſuch a Review can never be tedious to any Man, who ſincerely loves his Country ; and I am certain that the Recapitulation of thoſe extraordinary Amendments of our Conſtitution, here preſented to their View, will greatly contribute to the Peace and Quiet of many honeſt Men, who in the Paſſion and Hurry of theſe Times, have too

incon-

inconfiderately fuffered themfelves to be impofed upon by a
groundlefs Clamour; without either giving themfelves time, or
Opportunity to confider ferioufly how unjuft it is.

For whoever will take the Pains to look back upon the Condition of our former Government, and will reflect as he ought
to do upon thefe Laws, and Acquifitions (and many more
there are, all tending in fome Degree to the fame Improvement) and any Man, who will weigh what we have already
explained as to the Power of the Crown in its *Civil Lift*, in
its *Employments*, or in its *Prerogative*, if he really means nothing but to preferve this Conftitution, muft confefs that the
Liberty and Property of this Nation, never ftood in any Period
of Time, upon fo ftrong a Bafis, repaired in every Breach
that Time had made, fortified with additional Pillars of prodigious Security, and every Day encreafing in Solidity by the
Effect of Laws, which from the Courfe of Time and Nature
muft take Place in a few Years.

From thefe Reflections it does really appear, that Men betray their Ignorance in the moft grofs Manner, when they talk
in that unmeaning Cant, of the Neceffity of bringing back our
Conftitution to its firft Principles, fo much the Fafhion in thefe
Times; for I may defy the ableft Man in *England* fairly to
give the Inftance of any Period in this Government, where
the *Power* of the *Crown* ftood upon *lower*, or the *Liberty* of the
Subject upon *higher* Ground than it does at this Day.

Men cannot deny, that *Prerogative* was *reduced*, and the
Conftitution reftored by the *Revolution*; they will not venture to do this, becaufe the Falfhood would be too glaring, but
they have taught the People to think, that all thefe Amendments of the Letter of our Conftitution (if I may fo exprefs
it) are rendered ineffectual by the Increafe of Influence in the
Crown, from *additional Revenues*, and *additional Employments*, fince that Time. The Fact is totally the Reverfe,
as we have feen.—Half the Guards and Provifions for the Liberty of the Subject have been acquired long fince that Period;
every Reign, and almoft every Parliament have made Additions
to the Privileges of the People; infomuch that the People would
be manifeft Lofers, were they to exchange their Conftitution for
what it was at any one Inftant of Time, previous even to the laft
Seffion of Parliament: And this would be more or lefs the Cafe,
were they to go back from Year to Year, from this prefent
Year 1743, to 1066 the Æra of the Conqueft.

This Revenue of the Crown, which they magnify fo much,
is demonftrated to be lefs capable in all Confiderations to anfwer corrupt Purpofes, than it was formerly; and we have al-

X   ready,

ready, as it fhould feem, all the Laws, that the Wifdom of Man can invent, to leffen its Operation in that way.—If thefe Laws are not effectual, there is too much Reafon to fear that the Remedy is beyond the Power of Law, and that the Evil muft arife from the Ambition, which is incident to the Nature of all popular Governments, and to the Opulence of this Country, which Circumftances, coveted by all Nations, and defirable as they juftly are upon the whole, were never free from Inconveniencies of this kind , have conftantly debauched the Morals of every People; and introduced Corruption, in fome degiee, wherever they exifted.

Thofe Employments faid to be fo much encreafed fince the Revolution, are actually cut off fiom their Influence upon the Conftitution, as far as written Laws can do it, in innumerable Inftances.—Since the 5th of *William* and *Mary*, 1694, no new Employment in the Revenue can be held by any Member of the Houfe of Commons ; fince the 4th of *Anne*, 1705, no new Employment whatfoever, excepting in the *Navy* or the *Army*. Some with very good Intentions wifh thefe military Offices to be excluded too.---But this Opinion is full of Danger, for whofoever lives to fee them *totally* excepted likewife, can rationally expect nothing but a military Government.—We have therefore gained a Guard againft any Encreafe of this Evil in future, very near as far as it can be prudently defired.---The *Cuftoms, Excife, Poft-Office*, and a Multitude of other Civil Officers, which exifted long before the Revolution, (and not, as it is falfely conceived,) of later Inftitution, have been alfo weeded out of Parliament.

It is therefore an abominable Impofition upon Mankind to infinuate this Doctrine, neither are the Means of Influence equal, nor do the Laws permit it to be exerted, though the Means did actually exift.

If any thing more or better can be devifed to render our Conftitution yet more pure, that Man would be very difhoneft, who would not endeavour to attain it,---but every Quack Receipt is not a Remedy. The Cure muft be chiefly looked for in the Virtue of the People, and much Help it might receive from thofe, who bellow loudeft againft Corruption, if they would refufe to pay its Wages at their own Elections ; the Woman once vitiated by one Man, will become an eafy Proftitute to any other ; and the Countryman corrupted by the Bribe of a *Patriot*, will undoubtedly make no Scruple afterwards to fell his Vote to any *Minifterial Hireling*.

What I have faid upon thefe Heads, is not intended to deter any honeft and well confidered Attempts for any farther
Amend-

Amendments in our Conftitution, if they can be made; but it is intended and ought juftly to have its Effect fo far as to convince the Publick, that they are deceived, that their Condition is (whatever Imperfections ftill remain) in fact infinitely more fecure than it ever was fince we have been a Nation; and that therefore the Impatience expreffed by fuch Numbers is extravagant, and muft appear altogether unaccountable to every thinking Man.—Nor is it for this Reafon eafy for any Man, the beft intentioned to the People, to comply with the Humour of thefe Times, becaufe it is impoffible to know what they would be at, what would content them, or what would be the Limits they would prefcribe to their Demands.——Nor can *this be known*, nor can *they be trufted*, fo long as they found their Opinions upon falfe Facts, and Doctrines fo erroneous, as fo evidently thefe appear to be. I mean not to juftify any Faults, that have been, or may be committed in the Conduct of our Affairs; but I mean to moderate that Paffion, which mifguides them in their Reafonings upon it, which hurries them into fuch Expectations and Refentments, as muft deftroy the very Bleffings they enjoy, by grafping after more than it is their real Intereft to have: It muft be carried in Remembrance, *that our Conftitution is a Monarchy, and though limited, yet that the Crown muft be permitted a confiderable Share of Power, without which our Government, whatever we may afterwards think fit to call it, will become of another Species, a Species which certainly we are not fitted for, which, as in former Times, we fhould fuffer all the Evils of Confufion in attempting to procure; and which, when procured, we never fhould be able to maintain.*

Sitting down therefore with Minds grateful and fenfible of the very great Advantages we now enjoy beyond what our Forefathers ever knew, let us ftill entertain all reafonable Views or further Benefit, but without Prejudice or Paffion; let us correct the Faults, or even amend the Defects of Government, in all Cafes where they are real, and not imaginary, where the Circumftance of Time will fuffer it, when we have the Power to do it, and when no worfe Inconveniencies would follow from it.—But let us not meafure thefe Faults or Defects by the Clamours of a *Faction*; let us confider, that the Eye of Oppofition magnifies every Mite of Power, as much as the Eye of Power diminifhes every Object of popular Complaint. Let us therefore, when we enter upon this Work, engage in it with Moderation, and with a candid and wife Reflection, that nothing human can be perfect, that Men will have their Faults as long as they are Men; that we muft in Government, as well as in other Things, take the Evil with the Good; and that that Nation is happy

upon

upon the whole, where the latter far exceeds the former; this we may safely pronounce of the State in which we live, *Vitia erunt donec homines, fed neque hæc continua, & meliorum interventu penfantur* ----In this State of things, in fuch a critical Situation of Affairs abroad, in fuch a Ferment of the People, as we have lately feen at home, there can be no Wonder, that Men of Senfe fhould defire time to confider ferioufly what farther Alterations may be made with Safety ; we may certainly reft at prefent without any immediate Fear for Liberty, if not, it is difficult to comprehend how our Anceftors, who fell fo fhort of us, as we have fhewn in this refpect, preferved their own, or delivered any down to us ---From the Sketch, that has been offered of the laft *Place-Bill*, we fee that we fhall obtain in five Years, and perhaps much fooner, a great additional Security. If there be Truth in the Suggeftions of the *Faction*, that every Member of Parliament poffeffed of an Employment, is byaffed by it, and would act differently if he had it not (however falfely they have reprefented that Law,) it will make a mighty Difference in our future Parliaments   Though this fhort Period may be thought long, by the Members of a *Faction*, to wait for a Turn of Affairs, that may bring them into Office, it cannot be thought long, by any honeft and difinterefted Man, to wait for the Benefit of this Conftitutional Alteration.---Such a Man will confider, that *Excefs* in Regulations of this kind, brings equal Danger on the one hand, as *Imperfection* might in Time produce upon the other.---Such a Man would be unwilling to act precipitately in a Matter of this Moment, would proceed by Degrees, would defire to experience the Effect of every one Law of this Nature, before he ventured to promote another.---Such a Man will attach himfelf neither to the *Regal* nor to the *Popular Power*.---He will fix his Attention folely to maintain the true Ballance of this Government.---He will be neither moved by Difappointments from the Crown, nor by Abufes from the People.---He will act refolutely with *either*, when they are *right*.---He will oppofe *both* vigoroufly, in their Turns, when they are *wrong*.---His fole View in Power, or out of Power will be the Good of his Country.---His Study will be, to fupport the Crown, without flattering the Prince.---And he will confider more the *real Service* of the People, than their *giddy Approbation*.---He will neither be fettered by general Maxims, nor tied to any chimerical Syftem, but will be governed by Times and Circumftances, of which he will endeavour faithfully to make the beft Advantage for the Publick.---Such a Man is a

---

[a] *Tacit. Hift. Iib.* 4.

true

true Patriot, whose Fate it will sometimes be, to appear in the vulgar Apprehension unsteady, when he is most constant, and inconsistent when he is most consistent. This must often be the Case in those Countries, where Characters are won or lost by *Party* rather than by *Principle :* And such is undoubtedly the Case of this Country in which we live.

It is now time to think of drawing towards a Conclusion of this Paper, which has swelled to a greater Size than is common in Works of this kind, but which the Nature of the Thing, and the great Field of Matter I have been obliged to travel through, have rendered unavoidable. Many Suggestions and fallacious Reasonings have been passed upon the Publick in these confused Times, of which even yet I have taken no Notice.— But I have observed upon those of most Importance, and it would be not only endless, but absurd, to attempt an Answer to all those Points, upon which the simple Part of the People have been lately entertained.—Perhaps I have rather gone too far in this Attempt already in some Respects ; for it is very obvious, that the greater Part of the Arguments employed by the *Faction* against whom I write are of a Nature, which renders them of all others the most unanswerable,--they have the Property which a great Author ascribes to Nonsense,—*Nonsense*, says he, *stands upon its own Basis, like a Rock of Adamant,---there is no Place about it weaker than another,---the Major and the Minor are of equal Strength ---Its Questions admit of no Reply, and its Assertions are not to be invalidated ; if it affirms any Thing you cannot lay hold of it ; or if it denies, you cannot confute it :—In a word, there are greater Intricacies in an elaborate and well written Piece of Nonsense, than in the most profound Tract of School-Divinity.—* Such are the Productions of the *Faction* of this Time ; and the same Author observes, that of this Nature have always been the Productions of the same Men ; nor can we form by any more unerring Rule our first Suspicions of the Nature of any *Faction* in this Country : a *Jacobite Faction*, or a *Tory Party* (which as we have fully shewn before, is by unavoidable Fatality always led by *Jacobites*, whether they know it or not) eternally hath, doth, will, and *must* fight in Entrenchments of this kind.

The present *Faction*, from hence at first naturally suspected, has at length been fully detected, by all their Endeavours to preserve *France*, to sacrifice the House of *Austria*, and to poison the Principles of the People to the Protestant Succession, and to the Family now upon the Throne, by the Arts used to inflame the People, which have been the same that were ever used by the same *Faction*, and by the Tendency of every Point with which they goad the People on to Discontent and Dissatisfaction ; which

Points

Points incontrovertibly appear, when viewed in a true Light, to confift in thefe three Heads ; 1. *The Deftruction of the* Whigs, *and the Elevation of the* Jacobite Intereft *under the fpecious Name of* Tories ; 2. *The Expulfion of the prefent Royal Family* ; 3. *The Change of the Conftitution of this Kingdom.* As this is undeniably evinced by the *Deduction* of their *Conduct*, and the *Examination* of their *Principles,* and the *Evidence* of the *Facts* contained in the preceeding Pages, every Man of Honefty will think me warranted in this Undertaking to maintain, and every Man of Senfe will know, that I have fufficiently maintained, that Propofition, which I laid down in the Beginning of thefe Papers, as my principal Point to prove, *viz. That the Oppofition of this Time is not an* Oppofition, *but a* Faction ; *and that of the moft dangerous kind to this Nation.*

And now the Heads of the *Faction* for their laft Refource will feek to fhelter, and will throw themfelves among that general Herd, whom they for a while have led, but they will find no Protection there, they are fingled out ; the Reft will fee whom we have marked, will feparate, and retire from the Society of thofe, with whom they can affociate no longer, without the utmoft Danger.

We make no Doubt, that they will labour to revive the falfe Opinion, that the Principles of their *Faction* are not to be apprehended ; it is the conftant Publick Topic of Difcourfe with *Jacobites,* that there is not a *Jacobite* in *England.* But they have opened themfelves too far, their Views have been too glaring, they have unmafked too foon, and it avails nothing for a Man to deny *the Name,* while he purfues *the Thing* ; it will be hard to convince a rational Being, that a Party, driving at this furious Rate, as we have feen, in fuch a Road, can have any other View ; were it for Preferment and Employments only, it is a villainous Purfuit when followed by thefe means, and without enquiring who are the Men, how many, that are actuated by the *firft,* or that concur on Account of the *fecond* View, it is fully fufficient for the Publick, that the Conduct of the *Faction* manifeftly leads to this fatal End.

But at the fame time that we fay this juftly of the general Tendency of the prefent Oppofition, it would be highly unjuft to make no Diftinction, or to charge the Bulk of thofe Individuals, of which this *Faction* has been hitherto compofed, with the *fame Principles.*—We do it not ;—we are very fenfible that different Motives of Difcontent, and even of miftaken Honefty, have certainly drawn in many well-meaning Men to affociate with them. Yet I muft freely fay thus much even of thefe, and of all who are concerned with them, that though they may

efcape

escape the Depth of Censure, which is due to those by whom they are thus pitifully led, they are not wholly free from Blame, in tampering with Government, without taking any Pains to inform themselves; and some of them are undoubtedly guilty of a Crime, still much less to be excused, *viz.* that of resigning their Judgments to other Men, (as it is too much the Case of all Parties) with a View one Time or other, to promote or advance their private Interests by it. The Corruption is equal, to abandon the Will to the *Prospect* of Advantage, as to the *Possession* of it; and it is consequently as wicked to oppose for the *Expectation*, (though more popularly wicked) as to support Government for the *present Profit* of Employments.—God and themselves only know how many of the *Faction* are culpable in this.—But let them weigh it well, and whether the Danger to the Publick is not equal in both Cases.—Others there are who, from want of Courage to stand against unjust Calumny, are dragged along, against their Wills, by the Fury of their Party,—of these no better can be said, than that they are Cowards, and do not deserve the Name of Men.—There is yet another Class, whose Interest in their Countries and their Boroughs, compel them to flatter the heated Imaginations, corrupt Principles, or fluctuating Humours of those they represent; but this, if duly considered, is as great Corruption as the rest, and the Bottom of it is nothing better than unwarrantable Vanity, or a Preference of their own private Interest to that of the Commonwealth.—And there is yet a fourth Set of Men, who by their Pride and Resentments to the Crown, or to the Administration, for that want of Deference and Respect, which cannot be extended to all who deserve it, and is often expected by those who deserve it not, are driven into this Extravagance.—Though this is indeed that Evil to which generous Spirits are the most exposed, yet no considerate Man can think, that this, or any Motive in the World, can be a sufficient Excuse for any one to concur in the Destruction of his Country.

If the Bulk of those who now associate with this *Faction* reflect carefully upon these Things, and if all under these different Circumstances, edify as they ought to do by these Reflections, I may venture to affirm, that it will, in a short time, make that Figure, which it is the Wish of every honest Man to see it make. Leaving therefore these Gentlemen to their own Reflections, I shall now sum up what I have chiefly endeavoured to inculcate in the preceding Pages, in a few Considerations, which I submit to the general Mass of Men.

I Whether the Avowal of Principles, and the Pursuit of a Conduct really tending to serve, save, and aggrandize, and to divert the Attention of the People from the Danger of their Eternal and Implacable Enemy the *French*, obstructing all Means for the Support, and giving up the Balance, of Power, under Pretences either of Inability, Inutility, on any Plea whatever, labouring to destroy the Faith of our Treaties, and contending for the Desertion of our Allies, suggesting an absurd, infamous and evidently disproved Proposition, that we fight only for the Service of a Foreign Territory, endeavouring to prejudice the People against the *Whigs*, and to poison the whole Affections of the Nation to their *present Prince*, and to the *Protestant Succession*, was not the direct Conduct, in all its Parts, of a *Jacobite Faction*, under the delusive Title of a *Tory Party*, in the Reigns of King *William* and Queen *Anne* ?

2. Let them consider, to what Point they were hurried by that *Faction*. Whether it did not end in the Preservation of *France*, whom nothing else could have then saved, and in the Confusion of their own Country, which nothing less than the Providence of God could have afterwards preserved ? Whether the Fruits of the Blood of 200,000 Men, and of 70 Millions of Money spent in that late long War, were not cast away by this Conduct of that *Faction* ? Whether the Restoration of *France*, has not created 30 *Millions* of unnecessary Expence since that Time, a Rebellion which cost *a Million* in the next Reign, the Necessity of double the Army in Times of Peace, that we should otherwise have had Occasion to maintain, and the vast Expences we must now incur anew, to reduce within due Bounds the exorbitant Power of the House of *Bourbon* ?

3. Whether there be any other Way to learn the Principles of Men, than by comparing their former with their present Conduct, or to judge of the future Effects of their present, but by the past Consequences of their former Conduct ? Whether the very individual Methods are not now pursued by the present Opposition, that were pursued by the *Jacobite Faction* of that Time ? Whether therefore any Man who can reason at all, can conclude the present Opposition (whatever Pretences it may use, or whatever Title it may bear) to be any other than a direct and apparent Faction of the same kind ?

4. Whether the same Tree must not, by all the Laws of Nature, constantly produce the same Fruit; the like Causes, the like Effects; and then what must be the Fruit and the Effect of the Measures of the present Faction ?

5. Let the *Tories* in particular (I speak not to those *Jacobites* who assume the Name, but to those who are really no more than honest and well-meaning Men, and such in general they are, who have inherited that Appellation because their

Parents

Parents were such, or because of their Interests in their Corporations, or the Company they keep) let these, I say, consider, whether they ever got any Thing by joining with a *Jacobite Faction*, but Misery to their Country, and Shame to themselves? Whether they were ever led by a *Jacobite Faction*, but that they became their Dupes? Whether they were ever engaged with a *Jacobite Faction*, but they were brought to repent, and forced to recant at last? Whether they ever knew their Men, or saw their Danger, till it was almost too late to repent, and useless to recant? Whether they have not ever been carried away by *Names* instead of *Things*? And whether the Cry about *Hanover* now, is not what the Cry about the *Church* was formerly, raised and fomented with as little Reason, and for the same vile Purpose? Whether they have not too much Honesty to support an Alliance with a *Jacobite Faction*, to its End and Issue? Let them reflect, whether by acting as they now do, they put it not out of the Power of their best intentioned Friends to abolish those unhappy Party-Distinctions, which every well-meaning Man sincerely wishes to destroy? and which he will sincerely labour to destroy (whenever their Moderation can make it safe or possible) by a just and equal Advancement of Merit, where-ever it is found in *Individuals* among them? But let them consider fairly, how apt they have been on all Occasions to associate with, and to be guided by, Men of worse Principles, and for this Reason, whether they can expect it, while they continue to unite with these Men, and while they claim it *as a Party*, which is their present Case.

6. Let the few *Republicans*, and *Whigs*, whose Heat, Passions and Disappointments have *steeled* them into the Temper of *Republicans*, consider, whether a *Republican*, and such a *Whig*, when in Alliance with a *Jacobite Faction*, is any thing else, or better, than the *Jackall* to the *Lyon*, with whom he is, for a Time, allowed the Honour to hunt, but with whom he will never be permitted to divide the Prey? Let them analyse that Philter, they have taken to stimulate this unnatural Affection, and reflect that such a Copulation can engender nothing but a Monster.

> *Quale Portentum neque Militaris*
> *Daunia in latis alit Esculetis;*
> *Nec Jubæ Tellus generat.*——— Hor.

7. Let the honest *Whigs* consider, how often their Firmness and good Sense have saved their Country, and whether any thing but Union among themselves can do it now? Whether particular Points, though most undeniably suited to the *Whig Principle*, ought to be pursued, nay may not even consistently

Y

be for a time oppofed by *Whigs*, in a Conjuncture, when by a
Chain of Circumftances, that Purfuit would not be only vain
in itfelf, but tend to deftroy the *Whig Intereft ?*—Whether the
Support of *that* ought not to be the primary Confideration ?
And whether the gaining a few popular Laws (were this even
certainly the Cafe) at the Expence of *that*, would be for the
Benefit of this Country ? Whether the popular Laws we now
have, or thofe we might perhaps acquire, could be long preferved after the Ruin of that Intereft ? Whether therefore it is
not below the Underftanding of a *Whig*, to drop the *Subftance*
in this manner for the *Shadow ?* Whether for this Reafon it is
not more prudent to content ourfelves awhile with what we have
already, and to wait a fafer Opportunity to exert ourfelves for
the farther Improvement of our Conftitution ? Whether we
fhould not make a foolifh Bargain for our Country, if while we
were hunting after fome feemingly convenient, but yet (after
all) precarious Advantages at home, we fhould fuffer a Foreign
Power infenfibly to become our Mafter ? Or while we were too
paffionately engaged in pufhing for the farther Advancement of
our Liberty, we fhould rafhly throw our Government into the
Hands of a Family, who muft in all Probability deftroy it, or
gradually wreft it out of that Line, which is demonftrably moft
likely to preferve it ?—Whether therefore it is not our Bufi-
nefs, in our prefent Situation, to fettle and confolidate our Government, which has been not a little fhaken in the Tempeft
of the late Times, than (before that is done) to run any new
Rifque, in attempting to be *better* than *well ?*

8. Let the Publick confider fairly, whether every one of thofe
Points, upon which they have been of late fo furioufly inflam-
ed, are not wilfully and wickedly mifreprefented, and already
proved, by the Event, to be notorioufly falfe in every Inftance ?
—As to the Refufal of the *Heffians* to march,--the Inability of
the *Hanoverians* to act,—the Acceffion of the *Dutch*,---the Infidelity of the King of *Sardinia*,---the unjuft Reflections on the
King, as not intending to affift in his Electoral Capacity,---the
Veto of the King of *Pruffia*,---the Impoffibility of faving the
Queen of *Hungary*, and of refifting *France* ;—let them reflect,
to what we fhould have been reduced, if we had followed the
Advice of the *Faction*, and then refolve, whether they can follow
them any longer, without Ignominy to themfelves, and Deftruction to their Country ?

9. Let the Popular Intereft confider, as to all their Popular
Purfuits, what was their Original View in Oppofition ? with
what they would have been contented, and for what they would
have willingly compounded a little time ago ? And if their Expectations

pectations are to grow with their Succefs, how they can ever be contended? Whether they have not got the End? and if they have, whether it is not Folly to purfue the Means? Whether if the Power of the Crown, and of the Lords, were greatly lefs, the Commons could be long without engroffing all? Let them examine, whether it is not their Nature, and that of every People, to rife in their Demands for Power, as they encreafe in it? Whether, if they had as much more, as fome very honeftly, though very inconfiderately, contend for, they could curb this Nature in themfelves? and whether if they had fo much, and could not curb it, the whole Legiflature could prevent them having all? Whether their having all would be truly for their Advantage? Whether in any one Period of our Government they had half fo much? And finally (if they can be impartial and reafon fairly) whether it is not evident, that their prefent Views and Difcontents are not, in fome meafure, owing to what they have already? Whether thofe Gentlemen, who quitted the late Oppofition, at the Time they did it, inftead of deferting, have not faved their Country? Whether they have not acted the Part of a tender Phyfician to a fick Patient? Whether, if they have deceived the People, (as it is called,) they have not done it, becaufe there was no other way to bring them to do that which was neceffary for their Health? And whether the *People* are not as unjuft to thefe Men, after what has been done by their Means, as the *Patient* would be, who after he was cured of a dangerous Difeafe, fhould quarrel with his Phyfician, for having given him too good an Opinion of his Medicine, during the Time of his Diftemper, or abufe him for defifting afterwards to prefcribe the farther Ufe of it for his daily Food.

10. Let them then confider how they can anfwer, either to God or to their Country, that wicked and cruel Treatment they have given to thofe true Patriots, who have ftood their Ground, with equal Steadinefs, againft the late Minifter, and the prefent tempeftuous *Faction*; and how they can ever make thefe Men amends, for the Infults they have received, for the Lofs of their Interefts in their Refpective Countries, and the Foundation they have laid of the future Difficulties they muft infallibly hereafter undergo, by the Revival of a *Faction*, which, when once raifed, will never fail to perfecute and infeft all honeft Men? Or what Retaliation is it in their Power to give to thofe, who by popular Credulity, Folly, Paffion and Intemperance, have endured that Load of Infamy and Malice, which has been caft upon them with fuch unparellelled Injuftice, and which a worthy Man would have fooner fubmit-

ted

ted to Death, than have fuffered an Hour, if the Safety of his Country and every Thing, that was near, dear and valuable to it, had not depended upon this Sacrifice?

11. Let the People confider, (and they will confider it, if they have any Remorfe in the Compofition of their Souls,) how they ought to blufh at the bafe Encouragement they have given to the perfonal Abufe of his Majefty; who inftead of liftning to the infidious Offers of *France*, as fome other great Electors of the Empire have done, and inftead of projecting any Advantage to his Foreign Dominions, which he might have greatly encreafed out of the Spoil of the Houfe of *Auftria*, if he would have bafely concurred to its Deftruction; and which, (notwithftanding all the impudent Affertions of the *Faction*,) there is no Profpect of his being able to encreafe any other way, hath put himfelf to a very great Expence, from the very Commencement of the prefent Confufions of *Europe*, and expofed thofe Dominions to the utmoft Hazard with no other View, but to maintain the Caufe of Juftice, the Ballance of Power, and the Intereft of *Great Britain*. Let them inform themfelves; let them examine the Situation of his Countries, the Power, Views, Titles and Interefts of all his Neighbours; and let them point out one fingle Spot of Ground, that it is poffible for him, in the Nature of Things, to acquire in addition to his Electoral Dominions, by the Iffue of this Conteft.—And let them afterwards reflect how fcandalous beyond all Meafure, it has been to convert that very Hazard, and the Difficulties into which he and his Electorate have been lately brought, by his Attachment to the fole Intereft of this Country, into the wicked Pretence, that his Tendernefs to thofe Dominions, which he fo freely ventured, has been the Caufe of the War, and the Motive of his generous Conduct. Let them then generoufly and honeftly acknowledge, how ungratefully and wickedly they have concurred, upon Grounds fo utterly falfe, to alienate the Affection of the Nation, from the Perfon and Family of a Prince, who has facrificed every private Intereft to the Interefts of *Great Britain*,—who has fupported his Ally with that Steadinefs, Sincerity, and good Faith, which would have rendered a private Man an Ornament to the Society in which he lived,—who, in this Juft, and Neceffary Caufe, has expofed his Perfon to the Dangers of War, as much as the meaneft private Soldier in his Armies,—and is now at the Head of his Troops, in a Foreign Country, animating the Courage of the *Britifh* Nation, and reftoring the Antient Glory of the Royal Race of *Plantagenets*, from which he is defcended, the braveft Line of Princes that ever fat upon the Throne of any Nation.

12. Let them reflect upon their Ingratitude to Providence, and their more than *Jewish* Obstinacy, and Hardness of Heart, in the Insensibility shewn by so many upon the great Deliverance they have lately had, in their Escape from the imminent Dangers threatned to the Liberties of the whole World, and in the late miraculous Turn that has appeared in our Favour since the late Change of the Administration.

13 Let them consider, that if we improve these Advantages as we ought, we have now a Confederacy formed (with farther Prospects of additional Aid) consisting of above 300,000 of the best Troops in *Europe*; that we come fresh into the Quarrel; that *France*, by the entire Ruin of the Emperor, is left without Allies, reduced, by a Series of ill Success, and unfortunate Events, to the lowest Degree.—And that therefore, if we follow the Blow, we have the fairest Expectation, not only to get out of the Difficulties, which we had lately so much Reason to think would prove our Ruin, but to reduce that enormous Power within due Limits for a long Time to come, and that nothing but our own Impatience, and the delusive Practices of a *Jacobite Faction*, can hinder us now, from what they prevented once before by the same individual Arts, in a parallel Conjuncture.—In a word, let any Man lay his Hand upon his Heart, and say whether he thinks we are never to expect, or can always avoid a War with *France?* And when he has answered (for who can honestly or rationally answer otherwise) that the Growth and Ambition of that Power, her Breach of Treaties, our Rivalship in Trade, the natural Antipathy and Jealousies of the two Nations, must bring it unavoidably upon us in a short Time, though we should decline it for the present; let him then say, whether there can be any Sense left in the People of *England*, if they are not earnestly desirous to enter into it, and to push it with the utmost Vigour now? When we can do it with so manifest Advantage? When we stand in a Situation, in which we can hardly hope ever to find ourselves again? At which we could not flatter ourselves to arrive hereafter, even in three Campaigns, attended with the most miraculous Success?—And in fine, as to the Method of the War, whether any thing is more chimerical than the modern Fancy, of engaging with *France*, by our Maritime Force only? Whether the Trade of *England* would not suffer, during the Continuance of such a War, as much, if not more, than the Trade of *France?*—Whether *France* has not greater Resources without Trade, or during a Suspension of Trade, than *England?* Whether therefore any Distress that we might create to *France* by such a War, would be more than temporary, or could be sufficient to bring it to a

safe

fafe or found Conclufion ? Whether we can imagine effectually or durably to reduce her, or to fecure ourfelves for any long Continuance againft her Power, by any other means, than by difmembring fome of her ill-gotten Provinces, and preventing any farther Encreafe of her Dominions upon the Continent? Whether this *can be* done otherwife, than by joining with *her Enemies* and *our Allies* in a *Land War?* And if this *cannot be* done otherwife (whatever may be the Expence or Inconvenience of fuch an *Undertaking*) whether it is not Madnefs, or fomething worfe, to oppofe its being *undertaken.*

Should thefe Confiderations have no Effect upon the Publick we are a Nation doom'd and devoted to Deftruction : Our Government will be totally confounded by novel, falfe, captivating and deceitful Maxims; our Conftitution overwhelmed and buried in the Ruins of *Faction.* What Fabrick the Enemies of this Country may rebuild, is neither yet known to themfelves or me; nor when this happy Form of Government, the venerable Work of fo many Ages, fhall be no more ; will it be much worth the while of any Man among us to regard? Inftead therefore of fomenting every Subject of Uneafinefs, ungratefully repining at every Bleffing and Advantage, which we fo vifibly and abundantly enjoy, above all other Kingdoms of this habitable Earth, let us turn our Thoughts upon that immenfe Wealth, Power and Dominion, which is ftill in the Train of Great Augmentation ; upon that Conftitutional Security, however wickedly mifreprefented, which we ftill, in a high degree, enjoy at home, and the Terror, which upon all juft Occafions, we are able to ftrike through Foreign Nations. Inftead of dwelling upon improbable and diftant Dangers, which certainly never were fo far removed from us, as at this very Time, let us reflect upon our uncommon, and almoft unprefidented Happinefs. Inftead of alarming our Minds, and heating our Imaginations with the Stories of Evils that have attended the Lofs of Liberty in other Countries, in which, during the Courfe of the late Oppofition, we have been fufficiently inftructed, let us for a while apply ourfelves to a Study more neceffary at this Time, that of tracing the true Caufes, which have brought this Lofs of Liberty, and thofe Evils which attend it, upon Every People, who once were, and are now no longer free. If we do this, we fhall learn, that perfect Liberty and immenfe Riches, with its conftant Attendants, Licentioufnefs, Luxury, an unbounded Thirft after Wealth, a Want of Morals, and an Impatience of all Government and Difcipline, fomented by the *Factions* of private Men, for their own private Ambition, cloaked under publick Pretences, have ripened and brought to Maturity all thefe Mif-

2 chiefs

chiefs in the World. Let us therefore, confcious of our Profperity, and fenfible of the Dangers to which we naturally ftand
by that very Profperity expofed, fly the delufive Arts of factious
Men, who now endeavour to avail themfelves of thefe Circumftances, and practife upon us in the Manner they have ever
done in all former Ages : *Ut imperium evertant Libertatem præ-
ferunt, cum perverterunt ipfam aggrediuntur. Ceterum Libertas
et fpeciofa nomina prætexuntur. Nec quifquam alienum fervitium,
et dominationem fibi concupivit, ut non eadem ifta vocabula ufur-
paret.* Tacit Hift. Lib. 4.

FINIS.

9 781275 651401